Canadian Writers and Their Works

CANADIAN WRITERS
AND THEIR WORKS

POETRY SERIES • VOLUME NINE

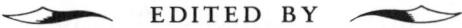 EDITED BY

ROBERT LECKER, JACK DAVID, ELLEN QUIGLEY

INTRODUCED BY GEORGE WOODCOCK

ECW PRESS, 1985

CANADIAN CATALOGUING IN PUBLICATION DATA

Main entry under title:

Canadian writers and their works : essays on form,
   context, and development : poetry

Includes bibliographies and indexes.
ISBN 0-920802-43-5 (set).–ISBN 0-920802-47-8 (v. 9).

1. Canadian poetry (English) – History and criticism –
Addresses, essays, lectures. * 2. Poets, Canadian
(English)–Biography. * I. Lecker, Robert, 1951–
II. David, Jack, 1946–   III. Quigley, Ellen, 1955–

PS8141.C37 1982   C811′.009   C82-094802-0
PR9190.2.C37 1982

Copyright © ECW PRESS, 1985

The publication of this series has been assisted by grants from the Ontario Arts Council and The Canada Council.

This volume was typeset in Sabon by Compeer Typographic Services Limited, designed by the Porcupine's Quill, and printed and bound by Hignell.

Published by ECW PRESS, 307 Coxwell Avenue,
Toronto, Ontario M4L 3B5.

The illustrations are by Isaac Bickerstaff.

CONTENTS

Introduction *George Woodcock* 1

Margaret Atwood *Jean Mallinson* 17

D. G. Jones *E. D. Blodgett* 85

Patrick Lane *George Woodcock* 133

Dennis Lee *T. G. Middlebro'* 189

Gwendolyn MacEwen *Jan Bartley* 231

Index 273

PREFACE

Canadian Writers and Their Works (CWTW) is a unique, twenty-volume collection of critical essays covering the development of Canadian fiction and poetry over the last two centuries. Ten volumes are devoted to fiction, and ten to poetry. Each volume contains a unifying Introduction by George Woodcock and discrete critical essays on specific writers. Moreover, each critical essay includes a brief biography of the author, a discussion of the tradition and milieu influencing his/her work, a critical overview section which reviews published criticism on the author, a long section analysing the author's works, and a selected bibliography listing primary and secondary material. The essays in each volume are arranged alphabetically according to the last names of the writers under study.

This is Volume Nine in the Poetry Series of *Canadian Writers and Their Works*. Other volumes in the series will be published as research is completed. The projected completion date for the entire series is 1987.

The editors wish to acknowledge the contributions of many people who have played an important part in creating this series. First, we wish to thank the critics who prepared the essays for this volume: Jan Bartley, E.D. Blodgett, Jean Mallinson, T.G. Middlebro', and George Woodcock. Our sincere thanks also go to Ken Lewis, and his assistant Scott Mitchell, for their excellent technical editing.

RL/JD/EQ

Introduction

GEORGE WOODCOCK

> ...*O mind,*
> *be nothing, be*
> *that translucent glass...*[1]

ALL THE POETS who are discussed in this volume, with various degrees of eloquence and perception, are now in their mid-forties or -fifties; the bright promises of yesterday who stayed the course, they belong to the second generation of the modern movement in Canadian writing. *The McGill Fortnightly Review*, which pioneered modern poetry in this country and which A. J. M. Smith, F. R. Scott, and Leon Edel founded in 1925, had already come to an end two years before D. G. Jones, the eldest of the five, was born in 1929. Gwendolyn MacEwen, the youngest of the group and herself a novelist as well as a poet, was born in the year Sinclair Ross published his epoch-making novel, *As for Me and My House* (1941). The other three poets, Margaret Atwood, Dennis Lee, and Patrick Lane, were all born in 1939. They grew up to enter the world of literature during the late 1950s (Jones's first book, *Frost on the Sun*, appeared in 1957) and the 1960s, at the time of what Northrop Frye has called "the great verbal explosion."

Their predecessors had worked largely in isolation, following individual visions in a society and a culture that were still conservative and puritanical; they found it impossible to live by their writing, and difficult even to get their works published, so that both Scott and Smith, despite careers of dedication to poetry beginning in the 1920s, did not see their first books in print until the 1940s and their own fifth decades. By contrast, all the poets represented in this book had published their first collections of verse before they were thirty, and did so in a receptive climate that brought them rapid recognition. They also entered a literary world which, while it remained largely regional in its loyalties and its inspirations, developed far closer means of communication between poets and other writers than had existed before, formalized eventually by organizations like the League of Canadian Poets (founded in 1966) and the Canadian Writers Union (1973), but in fact already created by the growing custom of writers, and poets especially, to wander over the country reading their work to increasingly large and appreciative audiences, composed mainly of young people; the peripatetic tradition of the troubadours seemed to be reviving.

Thus, while the five poets here discussed are greatly dissimilar in the kinds of poetry they write and would be hard to arrange in any kind of movement a literary historian might invent to tidy up the variety of contemporary Canadian writing, they are, unlike their predecessors, the heirs of an established and even ageing tradition whose basic presuppositions they instinctively accept; they are also linked by acquaintance not only with each other and their contemporaries, but also with the older surviving figures of the Canadian literary renaissance. Dennis Lee and Margaret Atwood have been friends since they were taught by Northrop Frye at Victoria College and collaborated in their contributions to *Acta Victoriana*. Atwood has written perhaps the most understanding criticism of Gwendolyn MacEwen, who later became her friend, and she selected with fine discrimination the poems for Patrick Lane's *Beware the Months of Fire* when it was published by House of Anansi (of which Dennis Lee incidentally was one of the founders) in 1974. Patrick Lane, undoubtedly, has been inclined to draw his inspiration more from experience and less from literature than the other four poets; his roots are Western whereas theirs are Eastern, which is culturally as well as politically important in Canada, but even he has never really written in isolation, for he belongs to a plebeian and unacademic subtradition that, through poets like Al Purdy and Milton Acorn and John Newlove, has long fed into the mainstream of Canadian poetry.

Of the five, D. G. Jones is undoubtedly closest to the older Canadian tradition. He was, for example, encouraged in the beginning by Louis Dudek and Raymond Souster, those poetic paladins of the 1940s, who published his poems in their magazines, *Contact* and *CIV/n*, and eventually brought out his first book, *Frost on the Sun*, with Contact Press; not accidentally, Jones did his M.A. thesis on Ezra Pound and the *Cantos*, though it is long since any vestige of Poundian influence has surfaced in his poetry. Living in Quebec as an effectively bilingual poet and scholar, he came inevitably under the personal and poetic influence of F. R. Scott, whose ironic clarity resembles his own. But also, through study and practice and empathy, he came close not only to A. J. M. Smith, that most inspired of *pasticheurs*, but also to those among the Confederation poets whose lyric sensibilities were most accessible to contemporary sympathies, Archibald Lampman and Duncan Campbell Scott.

Something of the translucency of Jones's own poetry and criticism has been osmotically transferred to E. D. Blodgett's essay on him in this volume, which is a work of notable insight. At the beginning, Blodgett counters one of my own generalizations about Jones, in which I describe him as "one of the least placeable... of contemporary Canadian poets,"[2] by making the punning counterclaim that "he cannot be 'placed,' but configurations of place seek each other everywhere in his work." They do indeed, and this—the "pastoral preoccupation" as Blodgett also calls it, with its "profound awareness of the Northern environment and its introspective pressures" — is what links him so intimately to Lampman and Scott, and makes him so articulately aware of a "distinct Canadian literary tradition, which he has absorbed thoroughly as a poet and illuminated as a critic" (most strikingly, of course, in *Butterfly on Rock*).

I have always hesitated to use the term "major poet," just as I have always avoided the use of the adjective "great" in describing any artist, since I feel that such epithets are fatally related to the idea of power, which, by inevitable association, takes one back to the conclusion Lord Acton drew from his own reflections on the effects of power, that "great men are almost always bad men."[3] Demonstrably, all unusual artists are not bad. Nevertheless, there are qualities, of lyrical clarity and philosophic intensity and sheer largeness of vision, which—among others—place a writer, perhaps not above his peers, but certainly apart from them, and I have always felt that, despite his original unfashionableness, Jones has shown such qualities and in very complex ways. His fellow poet Phyllis Webb saw his virtues as those of sound, "a distinctive voice, a poetry of lovely assonances, syllabic grace,"[4] but while this is true enough it does not take into account the acute visual sense that Jones shares with the Imagists and which leads him to what Blodgett calls "a central preoccupation with the optics of illusion," a preoccupation that emerges in the concern, reiterated in his poems, with the methods and the perceptions of painters.

It is interesting to see how far, in the later poems of *Under the Thunder the Flowers Light Up the Earth*, Jones incorporates the visual with the mythical in his poetry by transforming painters into heroes, the transmitters of myth. For Jones the myth is not merely an armature for poetry; it has also a profound social function, so that, as I once remarked, his critical work, *Butterfly on Rock*, "uses literature to discuss the myths and eventually the moral structure of a society at a critical point in its dialogue with the natural world."[5] Yet at the same time it is a statement of what —as Jones sees it in post-Frygian terms—modern Canadian writers have actually done as they

> abandon the garrison of an exclusive culture and go into the wilderness, where they experience, not a greater sense of alienation, but a greater sense of vitality and community.[6]

In *Phrases from Orpheus*, the myths essential for our present time are embodied in the hero as poet; the change to the hero as painter in the later sequences of poems inspired by the works of David Milne and Alex Colville illuminates Jones's own poetic stance, since, as I have said, he here "matches an appreciation of the lyrical qualities of these painters with a strong visual and 'painterly' element in his own verse."[7] This element, of course, has always been present in his work, reflecting an almost Taoist sense of the poet's mind as the clear transmitter of the reality of the natural world, exemplified perhaps more strikingly than anywhere else in that fine and beautiful poem from his second book, "The River: North of Guelph":

> So let my mind
>   be, like this river,
>   thin as glass
> that thunder, dark clouds, rain,
>   the violent winds, may pass
> and leave no lasting darkness in their wake:

let it be
> sheer, like crystal,
> clear, that each
tree or stone, each
> whistling bird or shrill
> face, in field or street,
may be itself, seen,
> undistorted, may be itself,
> revealed, as in the wild
brilliance of the sun. O thin stream
> if you must be the image of my mind
> let me be that glass through which the light
shines — O mind,
> be nothing, be
> that translucent glass...[8]

There are a difficulty and a tenacity about Margaret Atwood's verse which contrast sharply with the appearance of lucid ease that Jones's work always presents. "Her cast of mind," as Jean Mallinson justly remarks, "is analytical and argumentative rather than visual; cubistic and kinetic rather than two-dimensional." Nevertheless, as Atwood's work has shown over the years a personal opening out, an inclination to be less assiduous in covering traces or in finding masks behind which to speak, so she has become more inclined towards the visual, towards recording the image in its sensual fullness rather than transforming it into a metaphysical conceit.

It is, for example, as a conceit embodying a sharply felt and intended idea that one reads the terse, tense opening poem of *Power Politics*:

> you fit into me
> like a hook into an eye
>
> a fish hook
> an open eye[9]

But, in her next book of poems, *You Are Happy*, we come to a quite different use of visual imagery, in a poem where the poet presents herself unmasked, perceiving and experiencing:

> We walk through a field, it is November,
> the grass is yellow, tinged
> with grey, the apples
>
> are still on the trees,
> they are orange, astonishing, we are standing
>
> in a clump of weeds near the dead elms
> our faces upturned, the wet flakes
> falling onto our skin and melting
>
> We lick the melted snow
> from each other's mouths,
> we see birds, four of them, they are gone, and
>
> a stream, not frozen yet, in the mud
> beside it the track of a deer[10]

As Jean Mallinson comments:

> The simple declarative sentences... are descriptions, not definitions. There are no strident questions, no grim imperatives. Things are to scale with the persons who are simply there, part of a landscape which is not an emblem: it is what it is. And time is not at a standstill, nor does the poem occur in the tense space between catastrophes. There is no lyrical transcendence; the solaces of the poem are bound into time: flakes fall and melt; birds are there and gone; the stream will freeze, but not yet; the deer has been there and gone away. This poem is an expression of dailiness and ease which, because of its rarity in this poetry, is more memorable than a lyric of high intensity.

Mallinson remarks of her essay that its purpose is "to make up for a certain lack in formal criticism" in the discussion of Atwood's poetry, and indeed she does present a rather thorough prosodic examination of the texts; at times, her essay becomes quite technical, so that it would be well for the general reader to be provided with a good dictionary as a compass to lead through the occasional thickets of critical jargon. Mallinson's attitude indeed springs from the proper view that literature must first of all be read as literature:

> It is one thing to turn to poetry for one's sense of life, but to read poems as literal accounts of the progress of the soul or psyche is to neglect them as literature.

But it is hard to detach the poet's—as distinct from the reader's—"sense of life" from the actual texts she produces, and one can often find in a poem by a writer like Atwood not only the text itself—the "actual candle" which, as Mallinson says, "blazes with artifice"—but also a statement about life and often also a statement about art as well. In a considerable essay on Atwood ("Margaret Atwood: Poet as Novelist") which Mallinson has overlooked in her section on criticism, I instanced one of the poems in *Power Politics*:

> Beyond truth,
> tenacity: of those
> dwarf trees & mosses,
> hooked into straight rock
> believing the sun's lies & thus
> refuting / gravity
>
> & of this cactus, gathering
> itself together
> against the sand, yes tough
> rind & spikes but doing
> the best it can[11]

And I commented on the way in such a poem the poetic and the moral elements are mingled inextricably:

> Here is not merely an attitude to life that is evident in all Atwood's writings—an attitude appropriate to an age when survival has become the great achievement. Here is also the metaphor that expresses a personal poetic, even a personal ethic. To be (tenacity) is more certain than to know (truth); one does the best one can, shapes one's verse like one's life to the improbable realities of existence ("the sun's lies"),

and in this age and place they are the realities that impose a defensive economy, poems close to the rock, poems spiny as cactuses or caltrops.[12]

Of course, it is good to be reminded that art is dependent on the craft diligently followed and that artifice has wrongly acquired a derogatory connotation. Jean Mallinson does this admirably, and in such a way her essay fills a notable gap in Atwood criticism. But the fact that in her own criticism Atwood is inclined to be strongly thematic and even didactic should lead us to be alert to the intent as well as the artistry of her work. Atwood is, more than any other of the five poets here discussed except Dennis Lee, a politically concerned, and to a great extent a politically committed, writer. Her links with nationalism, with feminism, with the amnesty movement, are well known, and if such preoccupations affect her novels more overtly than her verse, their effect on the latter cannot be wholly neglected. We cannot forget, as Rosemary Sullivan has said in discussing the poetry rather than the fiction, that

> in a peculiarly Canadian way Atwood is a staunch moralist, essentially a writer of ideas — coldly, often brutally, insisting that modern man must reinvent himself. Her work challenges us to become human.[13]

When I read Dennis Lee, I find myself faced with the same problems as when I read a worldly-wise religious poet of the seventeenth century like John Dryden. There are no such problems with Donne or Herbert or Crashaw. In their varying ways, these poets achieve a balance of the saintly and the sinful that is comprehensible to a post-Romantic twentieth-century mind attuned to Baudelaire and Dostoevsky, to Eliot and Auden. The same post-Romantic mind has no real difficulty dealing with the combination of lyric eloquence and chiliastic politics that is represented on one level by Shelley and on another by William Morris, with Stephen Spender and Herbert Read lodging somewhere in between. But in Dryden there is a solid unspectacular faith (his apparently expedient conversion to Roman Catholicism made him unpopular, yet he stuck with it), combined with a sharply realistic eye to the political factors of his time, that accords so felicitously with the humane classicism of his style that one grants his importance as much because of his modest pretensions as because of the qualities Samuel Johnson rather exaggeratedly attributed to him: "the improvement, perhaps the completion of our metre, the refinement of our language, and much of the correctness of our sentiments."[14]

Others have perhaps better claims than Dennis Lee to credit for "the completion of our metre" (if one includes therein all of poetic utterance, even unmetrical) and for "the refinement of our language." But there is no doubt that he has laboured perhaps more than any other Canadian poet in our time to achieve "the correctness of our sentiments." He remains a difficult poet to trap and identify, and one can excuse the touch of irascibility in T. G. Middlebro's essay as he strives for a definition other critics — and even Lee's fellow poets — have struggled for in vain. Gary Geddes thought of Lee, because of his consciousness of "our discontinuity with the past, of our loss of faith in God," as a "sort of Canadian Matthew Arnold."[15] But Arnold was less sadly knowing. D.G. Jones talked of him — the words are Middlebro's — as "a modernist qualified by the ironic refusal to abandon history for myth, society for nature, or the mundane for the visionary"; a bit like a late Wyndham Lewis, in other words! Middlebro' himself declares, "He is essentially a religious poet, and as such should be evaluated." Perhaps. But comparisons with received religious poets, like Margaret Avison, arouse difficulties: "For Lee the path is willed intellectual struggle, for Avison a received intuition, and the poetic forms reflect the differences in means." Lee's form — at least in his poems for adults — is uncompromisingly didactic. He appears as the poet-evangelist, interpreting the gospel according to George Grant, and doing it with a great deal more passion and skill than Grant himself. He is a powerful threnodist, and his *Civil Elegies*, because they are uncompromising in their pessimistic realism, will probably remain as the main literary monument to the nationalist generation to which he belongs. But this — and the criticism that is pendant to *Civil Elegies* — is not all of Dennis Lee's contribution to our literature. As Middlebro' emphasizes, he does bring "a philosophic mind to the composition of poetry." But we have had — at least since Charles G.D. Roberts — other philosophic poets treating their themes as seriously, if not as skilfully, as Lee. What makes Lee so especially interesting is the combination of this serious side of him with the other self that is undoubtedly better known: the child's poet of *Wiggle to the Laundromat* and *Alligator Pie*, with his love for wordplay, for the whimsical and the grotesque, whom I often suspect Lee regards as his late-discovered real self. This other Lee deserves perhaps a little more mention than the intentions of a survey like the present series allow him.

In spite of the taste for the grotesque which they share, it would be hard to find two poets further apart than Dennis Lee and Gwendolyn MacEwen. Lee represents religious rationality and moves in history even if his hopes are less than eschatological. MacEwen lives so securely in the timeless yet ever contemporary world of myth and magic that one is tempted to see in her a mystic "Kanadian" union of the Delphic Pythoness and Madame Blavatsky. There is at times even a touch of the self-consciously exotic in her writing that seems to verge on Blavatskian mumbo jumbo, yet always, because of her well-nigh impeccable sense of poetic propriety, she pulls back into authenticity.

Because of the nature of her poetry and her fiction, with its frank antirealism and its location in times and places and states of mind on the verges of history, MacEwen's central attitude has always been a matter of disagreement among her critics. Gary Geddes presented the adverse point of view — given his own sensitivity to contemporary political issues — when he claimed that "from the beginning she has repudiated the actual world for one that is ancient and mythic...."[16] Jan Bartley, in the essay here printed, disagrees, claiming that "...MacEwen is not repudiating the actual world; rather, she is stressing her personal involvement in a complex world in which the myth is inherent, renewed, and reinterpreted in the process of day-to-day living."

MacEwen's own statement, which Bartley quotes early in her essay, seems to bear out the latter contention:

> In my poetry I am concerned with finding the relationships between what we call the "real" world and that other world which consists of dream, fantasy and myth. I've never felt that these "two worlds" are as separate as one might think, and in fact my poetry as well as my life seems to occupy a place—you might call it a kind of no-man's land—between the two.... In my attempt to describe a world which is for me both miraculous and terrible, I make abundant use of

myth, metaphor and symbol; these are as much a part of my language as the alphabet I use.[17]

And if one sees in MacEwen's poems, as I do, a working out through ancient legends and archetypes, through the myths of magic and alchemy, of the predicament of modern man, then her poetry is as contemporary and as relevant as the writings of such great modern interpreters of the human psyche, individual and collective, as James Frazer and Carl Jung.

But the felicity of mythological constructions does not alone make good poetry, and the secret of MacEwen's appeal, extending as it does to writers whose approaches are quite different from hers, lies in her extraordinary verbal virtuosity. George Bowering, for example, remarks that "Gwendolyn MacEwen gives eloquent testimony to the fact that artificial imagery can still be expressed with beautifully chosen sound patterns, and this is what makes her poetry worthwhile."[18] But it is not all that makes her poetry worthwhile. Margaret Atwood has warned of the temptation "to become preoccupied with the original and brilliant verbal surfaces she creates"[19] and in this way to neglect the profundities of thought and feeling that are to be encountered in her poems and no less in her novels, which MacEwen herself regards as equally important; indeed, she has said, as Bartley records, "I don't regard myself as a poet only, but as a writer."[20]

MacEwen, who first published verse when she was seventeen, a quarter of a century ago, developed as a poet, as Patrick Lane did, without benefit of a university education, and this means that her apprenticeship came through direct access to the writings of others and not through academic mediation, which I think often slows down a poet's development. This may be one of the reasons why she moved so uninhibitedly into her Gothic world of the imagination, and why she has understood so clearly the Manichaean patterns of history.

Yet perhaps the most striking aspect of her work in recent years has been its slow shedding of the self-consciously exotic, its movement towards oracular seriousness. It is true, indeed, as Bartley has said, that "...MacEwen's poetry is at its most golden, its most evocative and accessible, when she submits to her craft, to the sensuality and rhythm of language and form that displace dogmatic statement." But it does not follow from this that her work is lacking in statement of its own kind, and if one compares her two volumes of selected poems, *Magic Animals*, dating from 1974, and *Earth-Light*, published eight years later in 1982, the growing seriousness of intent and density of presentation are striking. The poems in the latter selection are more solid in texture, more concrete in imagery, more sharp in their visualizations, and while they are still preoccupied with the archetypal patterns that emerge and re-emerge from ancient times until now, they are concerned also with human lives lived mundanely within such patterns. Her *T. E. Lawrence Poems* — in which the voice seems so hauntingly and consistently Lawrence's own — may well be the most sustained act of successful empathy in Canadian poetry.

I wrote the essay on Patrick Lane that appears in this volume, and I have nothing to add specifically in the way of thoughts about that excellent poet's work. But seeing poets together rather than individually is always productive of insights of another kind, and when I return to Lane's work after reading the four other poets and what their critics have written about them, I am aware how much he stands apart from them, yet in what striking ways he remains their aloof poetic sibling.

Lane talks of writing a "poetry born in the bondage of experience,"[21] and his work is indeed closely related to the hard and wandering life he has led. He endures his epiphanies; they are not given as a benison. In a typical Lane poem, the poet is there physically in the episode described; he is moved emotionally by what he observes, and sometimes shares in, and out of the combination of observation, complicity, and emotion emerges a symbolic statement about existence.

It is usually a pessimistic statement, and in this group of poets, who all in their various and sometimes oblique ways are notably philosophic in their inclinations, Lane stands at the nihilist end of the spectrum, closely resembling the Céline he admires in the combination of acceptance and anger with which he regards the pain and cruelty he sees everywhere around him. Evil exists palpably in his poems, and the poet is the agonized and often participating witness to it; in offering judgement, he accepts guilt and so implies compassion, in its original sense of "feeling with." In Lane's poems, the redemption lies in the acknowledgement of complicity.

In this stance, he differs profoundly from the Taoist way of moving with nature that inspired the best poems of D. G. Jones, and unlike Dennis Lee he has no politics of the unpolitical, for he is as much without faith as Céline that such expedients can basically change man's instinct to dominate and destroy. He does not share, either, the sense of the terrible and the glorious somehow balancing out, which Gwendolyn MacEwen has derived from her magical and alchemical excursions. Perhaps, in the end, he is nearest to Margaret Atwood, for there is a deep streak of moralism in that insistence on presenting the cruel and the destructive elements of life as he has seen them, in spite of the disapproval of many squeamish critics, from Louis Dudek downward. The vision of a different world is there as a hope Lane can rarely bring himself to express, yet to which he at times urges himself, as well as his readers, when he declares,

> We must not hide
> our innocence, the distant
> singing we call love.[22]

Perhaps it is impossible to be a true poet without some vision of the light; from our stance in Purgatory, the Inferno is always balanced by the Paradiso. All the great nihilists have begun with the dream of goodness which they saw the world denying, and when they abandoned that dream they went mad, like Swift, like Nietzsche. The dream lies as surely in the dark heart of Lane's poems as it does in the gnarled roots of Atwood's vision.

NOTES

[1] D.G. Jones, "The River: North of Guelph," in *The Sun Is Axeman* (Toronto: Univ. of Toronto Press, 1961), p. 12.

[2] George Woodcock, "Poetry," in *Literary History of Canada: Canadian Literature in English*, 2nd ed., gen. ed. and introd. Carl F. Klinck (Toronto: Univ. of Toronto Press, 1976), III, 313.

[3] Lord Acton, *Historical Essays and Studies*, (1907); quoted in *The Penguin Dictionary of Quotations*, ed. J.M. Cohen and M.J. Cohen (Harmondsworth, Eng.: Penguin, 1960), p. 1.

[4] Phyllis Webb, "Guests and Natives," rev. of *The Sun Is Axeman*, by D.G. Jones, *Canadian Literature*, No. 12 (Spring 1962), p. 59.

[5] George Woodcock, "The Garrison and the Wilderness," rev. of *Butterfly on Rock: A Study of Themes and Images in Canadian Literature*, by D.G. Jones, *West Coast Review*, 5, No. 3 (Jan. 1971), 71.

⁶D. G. Jones, *Butterfly on Rock: A Study of Themes and Images in Canadian Literature* (Toronto: Oxford Univ. Press, 1970), p. 136.
⁷George Woodcock, "Jones, D.G.," *The Oxford Companion to Canadian Literature*, ed. William Toye (Toronto: Oxford Univ. Press, 1983), p. 401.
⁸Jones, *The Sun Is Axeman*, p. 12.
⁹Margaret Atwood, *Power Politics* (Toronto: House of Anansi, 1971), p. 1.
¹⁰From the "Circe / Mud Poems," in *You Are Happy* (Toronto: Oxford Univ. Press, 1974), pp. 69–70.
¹¹Atwood, *Power Politics*, p. 36.
¹²George Woodcock, "Margaret Atwood: Poet as Novelist," in *The Canadian Novel in the Twentieth Century: Essays from* Canadian Literature, ed. George Woodcock, New Canadian Library, No. 115 (Toronto: McClelland and Stewart, 1975), p. 319.
¹³Rosemary Sullivan, "Atwood, Margaret," *The Oxford Companion to Canadian Literature*, p. 31.
¹⁴Samuel Johnson, *Lives of the English Poets*, ed. George Birkbeck Hill (Oxford: Clarendon, 1905), I, 469.
¹⁵Gary Geddes, "Lee, Dennis," *Supplement to the Oxford Companion to Canadian History and Literature*, ed. William Toye (Toronto: Oxford Univ. Press, 1973), p. 187.
¹⁶Gary Geddes and Phyllis Bruce, eds., *15 Canadian Poets* (Toronto: Oxford Univ. Press, 1970), p. 280.
¹⁷*Rhymes and Reasons: Nine Canadian Poets Discuss Their Work*, ed. John Robert Colombo (Toronto: Holt, Rinehart and Winston, 1971), p. 65.
¹⁸George Bowering, "The Canadian Poetry Underground," rev. of *Than Any Star*, by Pádraig Ó Broin, *D-Day and After*, by Frank Davey, *The Drunken Clock*, by Gwendolyn MacEwen, and *Poems*, by David Donnell, *Canadian Literature*, No. 13 (Summer 1962), p. 66.
¹⁹Margaret Atwood, "MacEwen's Muse," *Canadian Literature*, No. 45 (Summer 1970), pp. 24–32; rpt. in Margaret Atwood, *Second Words: Selected Critical Prose* (Toronto: House of Anansi, 1982), p. 67.
²⁰Patricia Keeney Smith, "Interview with Gwendolyn MacEwen," *Cross-Canada Writers' Quarterly*, 5, No. 1 (1983), 14.
²¹Patrick Lane, "To the Outlaw," *New: American and Canadian Poetry*, No. 15 (April–March 1971), p. 56.
²²Patrick Lane, "I Am Tired of Your Politics," in *The Measure* (Windsor, Ont.: Black Moss, 1980), p. 46.

Margaret Atwood (1939-   )

JEAN MALLINSON

Margaret Atwood (1939–)

JEAN MALLINSON

Biography

FOR A LYRIC POET like Margaret Atwood, a close relation between the poet's life as lived and the poetry as written is, with some justification and despite the poet's disclaimers, often assumed. An interested reader could piece together a minimal life story from evidence in the poems, but it would be intermittent, largely geographical, and entirely devoid of the names of persons, even her own. But if the poems cannot be construed as evidence for events in the life, it remains true that some elements of biography are important to the poems; by her own admission and in the shared view of critics, some of the circumstances of Margaret Atwood's life are crucial to her poetry.[1] Her experience, as a child up to the age of twelve, of living for eight months of each year in the Quebec or Ontario bush, with resourceful parents and one male sibling for company; the entomologist father, the absence of doctrinal religious training, the family atmosphere of looking things up, finding out facts, how things worked, how to make things; the years at Victoria College, of the University of Toronto, including her friendship while there and after with Jay Macpherson and Dennis Lee; the early formed and lasting friendship with Charles Pachter, graphic artist and sometimes collaborator with the poet; her time with House of Anansi Press; her spell as a graduate student at Harvard; her teaching at Sir George Williams University, Montreal, and at the University of British Columbia; her marriage to and subsequent divorce from an American, Jim Polk, a fellow graduate student at Harvard; her *de facto* marriage to Graeme Gibson and the birth of their daughter; her involvement with the Writers Union of Canada and recently with Amnesty International — all these are some of the markers in her life, though not its substance.

The fact that on both her mother's and her father's side there is a family history of habitation in North America going back to the seventeenth century is probably of momentous importance in terms of her sense of the past and the land, and her sense of the legitimacy of her claims on life and literature; she does not have the uncertain stance of the newcomer, whether it be expressed as diffidence or bravado. Certainly her personal presence, combining, as it does, strength and a beauty which is both sharply contemporary and Pre-Raphaelite, has had something to do with the astonishing amount of attention paid, not only to her work, but to her life. In interviews, she is candid about what she wishes to discuss, reticent about what she prefers to keep private.

A poet, any poet, as she appears in her poems, is an invention, part of a poetic fiction; the lines of power that link the image of the self in the poem, or speaker of the poem, with the creaturely self composing the poem must be there, but they may be invisible, to be surmised but not ascertained. My essay traces the extent to which Margaret Atwood consents to be an image in her poetry, the strategies and disguises through which this self-dramatization — not self-revelation — is accomplished. The pattern that emerges is a movement from near invisibility, with a sense of high risk and vulnerability, through mask lyrics in which the poet speaks through the personae of Susanna Moodie, Circe, and others, to poems in which the poet speaks *in propria persona*, making formal arrangements of words which render her sense of being where she is. If her later poems are closer to what Wallace Stevens calls "The poem of pure reality, untouched / By trope or deviation..."[2] it remains true that in any poem, the actual candle blazes with artifice.[3]

Tradition and Milieu

Between Margaret Atwood's first book, *Double Persephone* (1961), and her second, *The Circle Game* (1967), she moved from a reliance on the conventions of traditional lyric poetry to an accomplished ease in the prosodic conventions of her contemporaries. The poems of the first small collection appear on the page with patterned stanzas and with initial capital letters in each line of verse; they use internal and end rhyme to establish formal design and are written in cadences which are based on prosodic measure or stress. Syntax is regular, and there is little enjambement: line endings, for the most part, correspond to a pause in major syntactical units. These early poems seem closer to traditional song lyric than to speech. In contrast, the poems in *The Circle Game* are marked by the absence of initial uppercase letters; by variable line length, related more to syntax and the looser rhythms of speech than to metrical feet; and by irregular stanzaic patterns, or the typographical placing of the poem on the page according to variable pauses between the units of the poem, whether word, phrase, or cluster. There are, of course, formal continuities, which will be discussed later in this essay. The question for now is: who were her models, early in her writing?

By the time Margaret Atwood began to write, Canadian poets had for some three decades been publishing poems in the whole range of modern idiom, yet it was not necessary to perceive them as an establishment with a canonical style against which one had to react. They were there; they could be read, and learned from. Atwood says,

> I was lucky enough to be living in a house when I was twenty that had a library of current Canadian poets in it. I started off in 1957 with A. J. M. Smith's *The Book of Canadian Poetry*. That had a lot of early stuff which I, at that age, wasn't very interested in. But then it also had moderns and moderns at that time were Reaney and P. K. Page and A. M. Klein, Pratt a bit before that, Frank Scott, Layton, Macpherson. Avison I was very smitten with at that time and still am.[4]

In another inverview, she varies this list a little:

> When I first started writing I was sixteen and in high school, in Toronto, in the fifties, and I knew nothing about either modern poetry or Canadian poetry. So my first influences were Poe and Shelley! When I got to university, I began discovering modern and Canadian poetry, chiefly the latter. I read my way through the library of a faculty member who, being a poet herself, had an extensive collection. I might mention such names as P. K. Page, Margaret Avison,

whose *Winter Sun* I reviewed when I was in university, James Reaney, D. G. Jones, and certain poems of Douglas Le Pan. These poets were important to me not only as poets but as examples of the fact that you *could* get a book published.[5]

In a recent interview in the United States,[6] she mentions Anne Hébert, Phyllis Webb, and Gwendolyn MacEwen as contemporary Canadian women poets who have influenced her work, and cites Robert Bly and Adrienne Rich as two American poets whom she has read with interest.

We know, of course, that there must have been others, including those who are her friends, or whom she has edited or reviewed: Dennis Lee, bill bissett, John Newlove, Al Purdy, Eli Mandel, Erica Jong. And there are, too, the modern classics in English: Yeats, Pound, Eliot, Stevens, Williams, Auden, Dylan Thomas. In the pages that follow, any pervasive presence, such as that of T. S. Eliot, or any particular influence — especially if, like the echoes of Keats and Hardy, it comes as a fine surprise — will be pointed out in context. It remains, briefly, for now, to look at some of the early poems and consider what influences seem strongest in them.

In terms of invention, formal arrangements, diction, genre, and title, *Double Persephone* shows the influence of Jay Macpherson, P. K. Page, Yeats, and, I think, Anne Wilkinson and Wilfred Watson. The turning to ballad and folk song as model or for allusive effect is a strategy which Atwood, like these poets, uses in these early poems.[7] The pervasive influence is the poetry of Macpherson.[8] In the sequence "Fall and All,"[9] the influence of James Reaney is apparent in the Gothic fictions combined with the matter-of-fact tone. The fact that Atwood's early Gothic verse can be linked with the practice of James Reaney is important, because a critic unaware of this connection might subsume Atwood's Gothic poems under the critical category of "Female Gothic."[10] "The Slideshow," with its aunts and uncles and Ontario monuments, is also like Reaney, as is the jaunty, colloquial, comic hyperbole of "The City Girl," both in the selection of poems published in *Poésie/Poetry* 64.[11] The final poem in this group, "Houses," is — except for the initial capitals and the placing of lines rigidly against the left-hand margin — in a style which the poet will develop and vary, but essentially retain, from now on. Since it will be her version—or versions—of the central, received style of her time, it is impossible to say precisely where she got it; it was all around her. But a glance at Gwendolyn MacEwen's "The House," a few pages on in the same collection (p. 116), suggests one source, an influence which Atwood has acknowledged. There is, however, in MacEwen's tone, even in her witty poems, a lustrous quality of diction and a suavity of cadence which Atwood never emulated.

Much later, when she was looking for a public voice, she turned to some of the poems of Auden and Henry Reed; when she was composing sardonic, antiromantic, argumentative love poems, she shows the influence of John Donne. The fact that poets whom she must have read, like Hopkins and Dylan Thomas, left little discernible trace in her poetry is due to sensibility, preferred genres and figures, and linguistic habit or custom. Though, as Atwood correctly averred (Struthers, p. 19), she writes consistently in the lyric mode, even when she speaks through personae like Susanna Moodie or Circe, she centres her work in a reflective, conversational style, choosing irony over lyric intensity. And, unlike Dylan Thomas, whose work is most often developed from a central image, in terms of its powers of association, following the patterns of feeling and the cadences of sound, Atwood's poems are most often organized in terms of argument or the patterns of thought.

Sylvia Plath, with whom Atwood has been linked (Hammond, p. 28), writes a dense, packed line, alliterative and strongly stressed, often seeming to reach very far back to Old English measures; her fondness for compound words adds to this impression. Atwood's syntax is less compact, closer to the speech norms of the patter of English,[12] because of her use of prepositional phrases and her preference for simile over metaphor — simile, requiring the preposition *like*, lengthens the line. Her early poems share with Sylvia Plath's an extreme discretion, so that what is most personal is used only in disguise, through fiction or allegory. Rather than being, as they have sometimes been called, confessional, both Atwood and Plath are reserved about their private lives, although, in the domestic poems in some of her recent collections, Atwood selectively allows the reader to share some of the occasions of her life, transformed into poetic fictions.

Thus, in terms of some aspects of technique — varied line

length, and conversational tone and syntax — Atwood is no doubt accurate in maintaining that she feels more affinity with Adrienne Rich (Hammond, p. 28), whose range of interests, as revealed in her poetry, is wide[13] and who tends, like Atwood, to generalize from personal predicament to other cases. There remains the question of the shared interest in Gothic fiction and personae; Ellen Moers holds that Sylvia Plath "renewed for poets — Anne Sexton, Adrienne Rich, Erica Jong, and many others — the grotesque tradition of Female Gothic."[14] I have suggested that Atwood's use of Gothic fictions in poetry goes back to her early association with James Reaney, but it is true, too, that poets like Plath and Sexton helped to create a new — and to some, shocking — voice for women poets, and that some of Atwood's poetry in the Gothic mode found an audience already schooled to listen to this voice. Of all her poems, the "Speeches for Dr. Frankenstein" in *The Animals in That Country* and some of the lyrics in *Power Politics* are most like Plath's poems, with their strident theatricality, their sinister vocatives, their clinical detail, and their use of the manic first person singular. It is certainly clear, from echoes in some poems, that Atwood read Plath, and they share, in a number of poems, a sense of the abundance and sinuosity of vegetation as threatening, but this may be a matter of sensibility rather than influence.

The question of Atwood's relation to the imagistic tradition in modern poetry will be discussed in my comments on the judgements of other critics, and in my analysis of the way in which her poems work. Once a poet understands the conventions of free verse — the abandoning of rhyme used for structural purposes, the eschewing of initial capital letters, and the irregular disposition of lines of verse on the page — there is still a choice as to how to organize poems. Atwood has, quite consistently, used implicit narrative only, but her syntax is usually complete, even if occasionally elliptical, and her poems are ordered, not through patterns of association and juxtaposition which leave the reader to surmise the links between images or clusters, but according to the patterns of coherence which follow and link lines of thought and feeling and small narrative in relation to image. She has tended to avoid the extremes of contemporary practice in poetry, never going to the lengths of some minimalists in austerity of diction and the eschewing of figures of speech, nor to the extremes of some deep imagists who elaborate, through personal association, images which may remain obscure to the reader. Her cast of mind is analytical and argumentative rather than visual; cubistic and kinetic rather than two-dimensional. She has worked, and continues to work, with an ever-widening range, in the central genre of the reflective lyric.

The question of Atwood's use of genres which can be said in some sense to be Canadian cannot be profitably discussed because the terms of reference are problematical. She, herself, has rejected the idea that the journal is a Canadian form (Struthers, p. 19), and the same can be said of other formal elements in her poetry, such as her fondness for the sketch or daybook frame, or her interest in cartography as a base for description. She has declared her concern with North American Indian myth as a new perspective and source of fictions, and the most that can be said is that she shares with contemporary Canadian writers an interest in using historical documentary sources for poetry.

Her influence on her fellow writers is difficult to assess since her practice as a poet is central, not eccentric, and what might seem to be learned from her could have been picked up in a dozen other places. The range of her work — her use of historical documentary narrative as a base for lyric poetry, her venturing, recently, into contemporary political concerns — may well be an example to other poets; the individual qualities of her style, within the conventions she shares with other poets, are not easily imitable. Certainly her public presence as a poet, her generosity in giving information about her work, and the kind of attention paid to her must encourage poets who are wondering about the wisdom of turning their sense of vocation into a life's work.

Critical Overview and Context

Criticism by contemporaries has two immediately useful functions: by drawing attention to a work, it helps ensure that the text remains available; and by perceptive commentary, it can attract and guide potential readers. There is a third contribution, of less importance to the writer and the general reader: the analysis of a work in one literary context or another, in an attempt to locate it in a tradition. In all these respects, Margaret Atwood has been well served by her contemporaries. The fact that her first collection of some length won the Governor General's Award drew critical attention to it, and a selective reading of the early reviews of *The Circle Game* reveals that critics welcomed with discernment a new and interesting poet. It is clear from a survey of the criticism devoted to her over the last decade that she has addressed herself to her contemporaries and been fairly well understood by them. No one critic sees her completely; some misread her to suit their own ideologies or critical preferences; but taken together, if one could construct a composite, monster critic, and pare away the false perceptions, the distortions, such a critic could be said not to have missed much.

Canadian critics usually discuss her work in one of the following contexts: the Canadian, with attention to the vexed question of Canadian genres and modes, and to the tradition of Canadian poetry, however that may be construed; the modern, with attention to genre and prosody in relation to modernist conventions; the feminine or feminist, with a concern to relate Atwood's work to the newly defined tradition of writing by women; and the Gothic. There are also the usual general attempts to state and elucidate her concerns and preoccupations, as these may be deduced from her poetry; there is a fair consensus about these matters — not always with approval. Criticism in Canada, perhaps more than elsewhere, tends to be entangled with ideological commitments, whether moral or political, and the poet's work must sometimes suffer the scrutiny and judgement of critics predisposed to find it wanting because it does not accord with or confirm their notions of reality. There is not space, in a brief overview of criticism, to comment on American views of her poetry, except to remark that American critics tend to read her as a North American writer or, in certain contexts, as a woman writer. Looking, as they do, through a different lens, they can see certain things which we may miss, but they can also grievously misread poems through a lack of knowledge of the cultural context in which the poems were written.[15]

A sampling of the reviews of *The Circle Game* suggests some of the directions that later, more prolonged critical discussion of Atwood's poetry will take. Hugh MacCallum observes of the poems that "an ancient world of totems, floods, and pre-historic landscapes lies just behind the familiar world...." "The vision," he says, "is one in which ritual and pattern create a world of bondage, a charmed circle of art that imprisons mind and feeling." He notices her "flair for presenting metamorphosis" and also her restraint, her "reliance on calm, dispassionate statement."[16] Peter Stevens comments, "Dangerous evolutionary menace lurks under the surface and it seems that whatever order we can impose will be only temporary." He notes the "parenthetical statements and qualifications" in the patterning of her poems. He longs for "a dogmatic statement, for the violence to break surface."[17] For Michael Ondaatje, reviewing the same book, it already has. He finds the poet pitting herself "like an arsonist, well armed with 'remnants of ancestors / fossil bones and fangs,'" against the "ordered, too-clean world." He observes that "she tends to see people as mechanical too quickly...." Almost alone among early critics, he notices her sense of humour, which he sees operating in the opening poem, "This Is a Photograph of Me" — a poem which has been subjected, over the years, to more high serious criticism than any other single poem written by Atwood. Ondaatje is acute about "the reason for the breaking of the rhythms, circles, and the order": it is "to get at the meat in others." But "the violence of exploring others results in destruction."[18] Eric Thompson, while admiring her "sureness of touch," chastises her for her failure to "investigate these 'foregrounds' of consciousness" — an unwillingness which, he avers, "mark[s] Miss Atwood as a minor poet."[19] A risky judgement to make on the basis of one book of poems; and yet, there is some truth in his response because it is precisely the foregrounds in Atwood's poetry which remained, until her most recent poems, unpeopled.

These remarks, though only a selection, are representative of a criticism which takes poetry very seriously, which is more intent on meaning than on pleasure. The vice of this kind of probing is to read poetry as a spiritual guide, the account of a quest for enlightenment, as Gary Ross does in his article on *The Circle Game* published in 1974:

> A direction is plainly emerging. The poet's perspective is changing, the voice is becoming more confident. The polarization of the inner and outer worlds is a stride toward reconciliation.[20]

In a similar vein, Jean Gibbs discusses *Procedures for Underground*:

> She has only refuse with which to build, but in the final image of the poem there is the possibility of hope. There is something redemptive about life after all, and the poems of the final third of the book leave little doubt of that.[21]

It is one thing to turn to poetry for one's sense of life, but to read poems as literal accounts of the progress of the soul or psyche is to neglect them as literature. Yet even a perceptive critic like Frank Davey allows his quest for meaning, and his dogmatic sense of the real, to skew his commentary on certain poems. He, like Robin Skelton, is one of the few critics to ground his reading of Atwood in her very early poems; he is acute about her central concerns; he attempts to place her, in terms of style, in the modernist tradition; and he understands that form is a dimension of meaning. Yet his insistence that she prefers space over time leads him incorrectly to place her poems structurally in the tradition of "modernist collage" and the "transcendence-seeking poetry of the early Imagist movement." He names poems as examples but fails to provide a textual reading to support his contention that "the very structure of many of the poems is spatial. Both sections and many stanzas in the multi-section poems... appear to be in arbitrary sequence; no temporal logic would be offended by their rearrangement."[22] He also fails to notice the subversiveness of the "Songs of the Transformed" (in *You Are Happy*), so intent is he on believing that the personae of the singers have "been, in fact, removed or 'transformed' from time by human acts of mythology and stereotype" (p. 160). And he misreads a crucial passage of the "Circe / Mud Poems" in which, he says, the persona "speaks with a self-detachment that places her consciousness outside the temporal frame in which her body exists and which presents this body as principally an object in a spatial design" (p. 162):

> We lick the melted snow
> from each other's mouths,
> we see birds, four of them, they are gone, and
>
> a stream, not frozen yet, in the mud
> beside it the track of a deer[23]

To miss the presence of time in "lick" and "melted," in the time between "we see birds" and "they are gone," in "not frozen yet," in the image of "the track of a deer," is to fail to understand this passage, which is a beautiful rendering precisely of a sense of time present, past, and future captured in tiny narratives and verb forms all the more temporal for their quality of nuance.

Gordon Johnston's views in "'The Ruthless Story and the Future Tense' in Margaret Atwood's 'Circe / Mud Poems'"[24] are a useful corrective to Davey's, in his perception of Atwood's enduring obsession with narrative, with the ruthlessness of story. Russell Brown, in "Atwood's Sacred Wells,"[25] observes that she is not, as Davey would have it, uninterested in narrative, but intent on the subversion of conventional narrative.

Robin Skelton's "Timeless Constructions: A Note on the Poetic Style of Margaret Atwood"[26] is, like Davey's "Atwood's Gorgon Touch," one of the few essays of any length to focus on style and structure. He agrees with Davey, but in different terms and with admiration rather than disapproval, that "...Margaret Atwood, in many of her poems, has used a structure I call 'modular,' as a number of twentieth-century and earlier poets have done" (p. 109). Rather more drastically, he maintains that a number of her poems can be rearranged in stanzaic sequence without affecting "the essential message of the poem," and "at small cost to the meaning of the poem" (p. 113).[27] Unfortunately for his contention, the examples he gives of such dislocations of sequence, rather than proving his case, result in serious misreadings which speak against him. His error, rather than being, like Davey's, grounded in an ideological view of reality as "process," is based on a belief that the poems are symbolic, and "...symbolism, being plurivalent, is open to manipulation" (p. 112). "In a world," he continues, "in which all the events are mental events," we can accept the following lines:

After that I could see
for a time in the green country

which we later ate.

Killed, it was a
grey tongue hanged silent in the smokehouse.

The correct version is:

Killed, it was a
grey tongue hanged silent in the smokehouse

which we later ate.

After that I could see
for a time in the green country[28]

Considering that the object described as a "grey tongue" is an eel, the poet's version seems more appropriate. Even more important, Skelton's rearrangement misses the point of the narrative: in folk tales, it is drinking the blood or eating a part of a creature from another world that confers on the eater or drinker the power to see or hear things previously closed to her senses. Skelton's misreading of the poem is a particularly ludicrous example of how, even with the best of intentions, adherence to a theory can blind a sensitive reader to the words on the page.

Any single piece of criticism exists in the context of others; criticism is a cantata for mixed voices, not a solo performance. Since the focus of my essay will be the relation of form and style to meaning in Margaret Atwood's poems, I have here paid most attention to those few critics who have concerned themselves with these matters. There are others, whose remarks on particular facets of the poet's style will be noted in the context of my argument. The strains of criticism other than the formal — the Gothic, the Canadian, and the feminine — are available in a variety of accomplished essays. Eli Mandel was one of the first critics to discuss the poet's interest in Gothic themes and fictions in her poetry,[29] a concern which Judith McCombs explores in terms of Female Gothic in "Atwood's Haunted Sequences: *The Circle Game, The Journals of Susanna Moodie* and *Power Politics.*"[30] Her inclusion of *The Circle Game* is particularly interesting because it completes the otherwise broken link with the very early Gothic poems. Sandra Djwa, in "The Where of Here: Margaret Atwood and a Canadian Tradition,"[31] places the poems in the context of a certain strain of Canadian narrative and imagery. Gloria Onley, in her 1974 essay "Power Politics in

Bluebeard's Castle,"[32] presents a brilliant feminist analysis of certain poems by Atwood, in relation to *Surfacing* and *The Edible Woman*, and in the context of the history of discourse about Western culture. Lorna Irvine, in "One Woman Leads to Another,"[33] reads *Two-Headed Poems* as a feminine text: in contrast to the "nihilism" of the earlier poems, with their apocalyptic imagery, she sees continuity, a rooted present, the animals domesticated as a child's toys. George Bowering's "Margaret Atwood's Hands" argues in similar fashion, in a different context, that "...domicile and habitude are first grudgingly accepted, then fondly celebrated, and they drive the menace away...."[34] As I suggested earlier, there is among sensitive interpreters of Atwood's poems a certain consensus, though they may start from and maintain different points of view. The purpose of my contribution is to make up for a certain lack in formal criticism, to provide a supplementary and in some cases a corrective reading of certain poems, and to trace certain continuities in the poetry which may add to, rather than gainsay, the patterns observed by other critics.

Atwood's Works

The poems in Margaret Atwood's first collection, *Double Persephone* — allegorical, dense with metaphor, and traditional in their formal organization — contain the genesis of her later style and reveal some of her enduring preoccupations. The title poem conveys a sense of the world external to the speaker as portentous, having to be deciphered, iconic rather than imagistic; and another poem is called "Iconic Landscape." The central predicament in the poems is the schism between art and life, the static and the kinetic. As stated in the fiction[35] of the central poem, "Formal Garden," the dilemma is not soluble; it constitutes a knot, an impasse:

> The girl with the gorgon touch
> Stretches a glad hand to each
> New piper peddling beds of roses
> Hoping to find within her reach

> At last, a living wrist and arm
> Petals that will crush and fade
> But always she meets a marbled flesh
> A fixing eye, a stiffened form
> Where leaves turn spears along the glade
>
> Behind, a line of statues stands
> All with the same white oval face
> And attitude of outstretched hands
> Curved in an all-too-perfect grace.[36]

The poem may be a parable about poetic form, expressing the young poet's sense that the traditional stanza and rhyme schemes she is using do not render the vitality of the world; but it can be taken, too, as a veiled statement of a larger dilemma because the later poems justify this interpretation.

Another preoccupation in the early poems, blazoned in the title of her first collection, is doubleness. The poet's concern with the double will generate many of her later poems: one recent collection is called *Two-Headed Poems*; other titles — *Procedures for Underground* and *The Animals in That Country* — suggest a diagramming of the world in terms of two parts. A wry, ironic attitude towards traditional romance modes is also present in the poems in the early collection and will be used later in *Power Politics* and the "Circe / Mud Poems" in *You Are Happy*. The early poem "Pastoral" in *Double Persephone* gestures in the direction of the conventions of the genre, and then destroys it with a fiction of seasonal life and death. The antipastoral agent in the poem is a controlling female, who "Makes the amorous shepherd dance," and who, "...never one to pine, / Smirks as he dwindles down to spine." It is perhaps not too much to discern in this resilient lady — who will use conventions but not become lost in them — an early sketch of Circe and the woman in *Power Politics*.

Another early poem which is of interest because of its subject and tone, and because of its later elaboration in the "Circe / Mud Poems," is "Pig-Girl."[37] This poem, about the squalor of being alive, is in a sense a dispraise,[38] but there is a certain bold relish in it. This voice will be used again, in a more polished manner, in the "Songs of the Transformed." The Pig-Girl, who invites "...Circe's wandering men to taste / The grassroots puddle of her cup," is

...a realist, and knows
The only thing that keeps
The mud outside her in the stye
Of land and sky, from the red mud within
Is a thumb-wide scum of skin.
. . . .
And there's scant difference between
Her wallowed fodder-lovers,
Her latest love-child, and
Her newly-swallowed farrow

It is clear, of course, that the young poet has been reading Yeats; and, typical of an early piece, the poem has packed inside it a number of motifs which will be elaborated in later work. The Pig-Girl is an early, very substantial version of the termite queen[39] and the mud woman (*You Are Happy*, p. 61); the image of the "thumb-wide scum of skin," which protects the outside from the inside and vice versa, will occur in later poems about skin as obstacle and protection.

After *Double Persephone* and before *The Circle Game*, Margaret Atwood published two selections of poems: "Fall and All: A Sequence"[40] — seven poems, one of which was reprinted in the second group, in *Poésie / Poetry 64*.[41] Formally, these poems are transitional: there is less structural use of rhyme, some irregularity of line length, and cadences closer to the rhythms of speech. The title poem of the sequence, "Fall and All," tells a story of a Circe-like figure, a witch with a "gorgon's head" who, out of anger at their "...freedom of motion, / / Resemblance to real flesh..." turns her lovers into "small jointed dolls." "The Acid Sibyl," from the same sequence, who, "Sitting in a bottle / On an antiseptic shelf / Still prophecies," will turn up quite soon in a poem in *The Circle Game*. "The Slideshow," from the *Poésie / Poetry 64* group, is the first of many poems about the fiction of the camera image, especially the family-album still: the deception, poignant and mandacious, that nothing has been lost, that reality can be carried around in a flat box. "The Mad Mother," from the same group, is an exercise in

Gothic ballad. It contains the image of the foetal child which will recur in later poems:

A yellow jack-o'-lantern face, its vine
Twisting her shrunken heart:

A bloated head, drowned
In her squeezed shrunken garden

The image in this poem of human life as vegetable in its origins, as well as the jack-o'-lantern face, the description of the pregnant woman, "...her stomach / Swelling like a pumpkin," the drowning, the image of a lost, diminished garden — all these will occur again in later poems.

It seems worthwhile to dwell at some length on these early pieces because they are not readily available to readers of Atwood's poetry, and in them we find the beginnings of almost everything which will be elaborated in later poems: the poem as statement of predicament; as allegory or extended metaphor; the rhetoric of direct address; Gothic fictions and personae; a concern with the relation between the static and the kinetic; fictions about power, especially the power to harm; a subversive stance towards traditional romantic modes; a sense of the world as portentous, signifying something which may or may not be decipherable; fictions of paranoia, which are the negative side of the longing for meaning.

And, though she moved rapidly from the conventions of traditional prosody used in most of these poems to the different formalities of contemporary verse, one can observe in the early poems the rhetorical devices which are characteristic of her later poems: enjambement, with its risks and revisionary disclosures; double similes, often oxymoronically paired; the epithet, with its impaling power; apposition, those equivalents with their promise or parody of linked significance; synecdoche, particularly as a way of apprehending the human body in fragments; apophasis, the most dissembling of figures; periphrasis or kenning, witty and oblique; and hyperbole and irony, that pair of extremes between which the poet often moves in a single poem.

The rhetoric of parenthesis, with its inclusion of often momentous information in a covert manner, a characteristic device in her later poetry, is used only scantily early on; but it is crucial in the first poem in *The Circle Game*, as is another element largely missing in the early pieces, but central to the later poetry: fictions of catastrophe, which usually occur outside the poem, either before or after, and which precipitate or account for it. It is as though the sense of predicament often present in the early poems has been rendered in an implied narrative, which begins and ends with catastrophe; the space in which the poem is spoken is the small, cleared space between catastrophes.

"This Is a Photograph of Me"[42] is a postcatastrophic poem, though this information is, characteristically, given to us in parentheses. The strategies of this piece are typical of Atwood's way of making a poem, at this point in her writing life. The title uses a demonstrative pronoun, so that the reader, by inference, is led through the flat surface of the page into the poem, and, later, through the flat surface of the snapshot into the landscape it depicts. It is the trick of breaking through the glossy surface tension of the photograph — analogous to the trick in "A Descent through the Carpet" (pp. 21–23) — which creates the excitement and movement in the poem, and which is parallel to the breaking through the surface tension of the water in the drowning, which, we are told, took place outside the fiction of the poem. The tone is flat, laconic, matter-of-fact; the speaker's stance is that of a guide, and she uses the mode of direct address; the description is diagrammatic: an anatomy, not a visual picture. The reader is led, with deliberate casualness, to the shocking disclosure in parentheses.

The rhetorical function of parenthesis is to allow words to be on the page yet apart from the links of syntax; hence, in this poem, it imitates the presence/absence of the speaker within the fiction of the poem. The poet as voice is firmly in control, having contrived the whole display, which is also a disappearing act. It is the perfect solution; hence, the poem, though it describes a plight, has a self-satisfied tone: the speaker is hidden, and yet the centre of attention — the perfect position to have manoeuvred herself into.

"After the Flood, We" (p. 12) is also a postcatastrophic poem, setting the pattern for many of the ones that follow: an "I" or "We" is introduced, speaking; a minimal setting is given; and the poem moves into an elucidation of a situation which is desperate, but not, within the fiction of the poem, solved. The compulsion to imagine catastrophe has two possible sources: to imagine disaster is a way of feeling safe because you are already confronting the worst that might happen; and it is also a way of accounting for a sense of peril which would otherwise be alarmingly mysterious. The alternative to catastrophe is boredom, and the mischief, the meddling, the restless desire for something, anything, to happen that boredom arouses, which can be turned into poems, too.

"The Circle Game" (pp. 35–44) is such a poem: attenuated, imitating in its vignettes, in the manner of *The Waste Land*, the desultory boredom with impasse which is its subject. The violence which is its concealed goal or latent subject is held off by these muted tableaux, which take place in a kind of limbo. This wraithlike couple, these vague children, with their "...thread-thin / insect voices" (p. 44), are bored: bored with fictions; interested only in their own war games, games of surviving attacks. But what menaces them is obscure: "(of course there is always / danger but where / would you locate it)" (p. 43). Even violence is only a rumour. Something has to happen, and it happens outside the fiction of the poem, expressed in the poem only in the rhetoric of longing for escape from the "...monotony of wandering / from room to room..." (p. 44). Longing takes what will generally be its form in Atwood's poems — a series of infinitives:

> I want to break
> these bones . . .
> . . . .
> erase all maps,
> crack the protecting
> eggshell of your turning
> singing children:
>
> I want the circle
> broken.
>
> (p. 44)

"Camera" (pp. 45–46), which opens, characteristically, with the squalid details of the everyday, moves, like the opening poem, to the location of the speaker—small, marginal, but very conspicuous — at the edge of a catastrophe which she has conjured to disarray the contrived deception of the framed, square still. "Spring in the Igloo" (p. 48) is about the invention of a fiction of peril ("We, who thought we were living / in the centre of vast night") in order to sustain a desired version of reality. In this poem, the catastrophe is acknowledged to be perversely courted in order to prolong an illusion.

If "Spring in the Igloo" suggests a reason for inventing catastrophe, "A Sibyl" (pp. 49–51) — a deflating, domestic version of a prestigious piece of mythology[43] — suggests a possible source for the anxiety which prompts it. Desperate and mock-jaunty, with a kind of thin bravado, the poet turns the sibyl into a version of the deformed homunculus encountered before in "The Mad Mother." Amid an array of mundane bottles,

> my sibyl crouches
> in one of them
> wrinkled as a pickled
> baby, twoheaded prodigy
> at a freakfair
>
> (p. 49)

The sibyl has to be kept bottled up because she is a reminder of mortality. Instead of uttering the traditional text, "I want to die," she threatens, "...you must die / later or sooner alas / you were born weren't you / the minutes thunder like guns / coupling won't help you / or plurality" (p. 49). The bottling of the sibyl is a way of containing catastrophe, and her warning suggests that the disaster towards which the poems move, or which they contrive to avoid, is death:

> time runs out
> in the ticking hips of the
> man whose twitching skull
> jerks on loose
> vertebrae in my kitchen
> flower
> beds predict it
>
> (p. 50)

Impaled on this knowledge, the speaker cannot move towards love — here deflatingly called "coupling" — or community — here reduced to "plurality."

Many of the poems, so far, seem to represent strategies for dealing with the problematics of risk rising out of the apprehension that living is the most dangerous thing you can do. The influence of T. S. Eliot is marked, and the atmosphere of suspended or inhibited action, covert violence, and a sense of peril for which the poet has to invent objective correlatives is quite like the temper of much of *The Waste Land*. The distaste for what the world has to offer, the premature dismissal of what is given, could be considered arrogant, were it not for the sense the poems express of plight and crisis. The place where the speaker stands, and what she sees from there, seem like constraints; they are obscurely necessary, but limiting. The subject of meaning and the rhetoric of praise are not possible, from there. The nostalgia for meaning, for something lost or hidden "that informs, holds together / this confusion..." (p. 76), is expressed in "A Place: Fragments" (pp. 73–76) in the metaphor of a hieroglyph or pictograph which cannot be deciphered.

The title of her next collection, *The Animals in That Country*, suggests a bifurcated geography which is alluded to, and used in the poems to set up contrasts, but never located or diagrammed. Many of the poems elaborate fictions of quiet desperation or dislocation. The squalor and routine riskiness of the highly selective world in which these vignettes occur are sustained by a kind of grudging wit; the poems often move towards epigrammatic endings, resentful substitutes for the kind of meanings which are either absent from the poems or present in cryptic vestigia:

these once-living
and phosphorescent meanings
fading in my hands

I try to but can't decipher[44]

At the centre of "The Shadow Voice" (p. 7) is a sense of radical deprivation, which takes the only revenge it can by slandering what the world has to offer. The poem projects a kind of hopelessness that life will even provide the sustenance the speaker longs for, and a kind of rage and resentment, a perverse pleasure, even, in sustaining herself on the meagre diet she gets. In tone these poems range from the florid irony of "A Foundling" (p. 5) to the sinister substitutions of "The Shadow Voice": "Isn't the moon warm / enough for you"; "The trees outside are bending with / children shooting guns" (p. 7).

Compared with the cryptic and oblique scenarios of the poems preceding it in this collection, often only obscurely referential, and at some distance from their implied narratives, "The Green Man" (pp. 12–13), subtitled "For the Boston Strangler," is a brusque and precise Gothic narrative, luring the reader to its lethal conclusion. A version of one of the poet's favourite fictions — the Protean or shape-changing man, both domestic and terrifying — the poem proceeds by some of her preferred devices: naming accompanied by iconic epithet or metonymic adjective, and narratives condensed into descriptions, which become attributes because they are given as customary:

> The green man, before whom
> the doors melted,
>
> the window man, the furnace man, the electric
> light man,
> the necessary man, always expected.
>
> He said the right words,
> they opened the doors
>
> (p. 12)

Since he is a sufficient fictive embodiment of a terror which is often, in the poems, unlocated, he provides a centre of energy which pulls together the poet's resources.

"A Fortification" (p. 16) is one of Atwood's poems of self-disclosure through a metaphor of concealment. The stance is not — as in "This Is a Photograph of Me" — that of a guide pointing another to the concealed self, but a statement to no one in particular, announcing strategies of defence, and providing a glimpse of "...the other creature, / the one that has real skin, real hair, / vanishing down the line of cells / back to the lost forest of being vulnerable" (p. 16). The "thumb-wide scum of skin" which, in "The Pig-Girl," kept the stye without from the red mud within has here become a "metal spacesuit":

> I have armed myself, yes I am safe: safe:
> the grass can't hurt me.
> My senses swivel like guns in their fixed sockets:
> I am barriered from leaves and blood.
>
> (p. 16)

The fact that the speaker seems overprotected for the occasion would seem comic, were it not for the sense the poem gives that her feeling of peril calls for overkill.

"The Totems" (p. 22) is a kind of tangential lament, commencing with a predicament posed, typically, in the form of a question, and proceeding to a rare lyrical evocation of the vanished paradise which was only one country — a transient solace followed almost at once by an expression of loss which barely allows itself the idioms of grief. In these early poems, the epiphanies, moments of solace or transcendence of the plight which generates the poems, are dreams, rumours, half-remembered, placed in some precatastrophic past; only later will such moments occasionally be described as present. "Elegy for the Giant Tortoises" (p. 23) is an exercise in mock liturgical cadences, sonorous and playfully lugubrious. Yet the burlesque tone conceals a grief for what has been lost, and a sense of guilt for the speaker's involvement in the loss. The poem, like "The Totems," could be a lament, but the voice does not permit itself lament.

"The Gods Avoid Revealing Themselves" (p. 24) is a kind of negative epiphany, but the first stanza describes the gods before they wheel and disappear. Like the heraldic animals in the second stanza of the "The Totems," they would still be visible if some catastrophe, like the one hinted at in the last stanza of "Elegy for the Giant Tortoises," had not occurred. "What Happened" (pp. 26–27) is a series of cryptic vignettes presented as evidence for a catastrophe which both happened in some past, obscured by amnesia, and endures as a condition of life inside which the speaker and her companion are closed. Typically, in these poems, there is a "you," a pronoun of direct address: what Helen Vendler calls "the 'thou' of remedy" in traditional lyric;[45] but the "you" addressed in these poems does not provide remedy. In "Roominghouse, Winter" (pp. 28–29), a poem about attempting to make some kind of home in a place of dereliction, where "My window is a funnel / for the shapes of chaos" (p. 29), the "you" is only thinly there, and he gives no comfort; his final words, the last ones in the poem, are "Nobody ever survives."

In the brilliant "Speeches for Dr. Frankenstein" (pp. 42–47), the gorgon touch, instead of being withdrawn because of its power to do harm, is extended to risk creation, and the catastrophe is written into the text, embodied in the creature. The rhetoric of public oratory implied in the title, and the setting of the operating theatre, allow the poet to elaborate in strident histrionics two of her characteristic modes: the aggressive declarative sentence and the bold, demanding question. In the speeches, we find flamboyant exaggeration, a distortion of the gestures of utterance which borders on the comic grotesque, like a horror film which takes the conventions of the genre too far, deliberately. This poem series, which, like the frame narrative, is in the Female Gothic tradition,[46] provides a distancing fiction which becomes a vehicle for what we can only surmise to be the poet's anxieties about creation. Its exuberance comes from the freeing and focusing of energies in an invention which is — for now — perfectly adequate to her concerns. The often brutal hyperbole, the sardonic vocatives, the strident interrogatives —

> O secret
> form of the heart, now I have you.
> . . . .
> What equation shall
> I carve and seal in your skull?
>
> What size will I make you?
> Where should I put your eyes?
> . . . .
> You arise, larval
> and shrouded in the flesh I gave you;
> . . . .
> What was my ravenous motive?
> Why did I make you?
>
> (pp. 43–45)

— are strategies reminiscent of certain of Sylvia Plath's poems.[47] The scenario of the poem moves, like the original novel, to one of the poet's favourite landscapes: a "...vacant winter / plain, the sky...a black shell." Dr. Frankenstein's creation becomes Sasquatch, Abominable Snowman; "...his arctic hackles / bristling,...his paws on the horizons, / rolling the world like a snowball" (p. 47), he is almost beautiful. The poem is half a celebration of his monstrous energy, half a lament for his fantastic inappropriateness.

In this poem series, as in "Backdrop Addresses Cowboy" (pp. 50–51) and "Progressive Insanities of a Pioneer" (pp. 36–39),[48] Atwood is beginning to find personae which allow her to invent poems that arise out of narrative or event, thus leading her to a way out of the attenuated tableaux, the half-speech gestures which coil back on themselves, the half-life of impasse which generates obscure imaginations of disaster, of many of the earlier poems. This display of personae will be central to the complex, comprehensive inventions of the Susanna Moodie series, *Power Politics*, the "Songs of the Transformed," and the "Circe / Mud Poems." These mask lyrics[49] occupy a place in her work between the earlier expressive lyrics, often concerned with the problematics of whether to appear in the poem at all, and if so, in what disguise, and the later meditative lyrics in which the poet speaks in an abstraction from her own voice, in settings which, however minimal, are drawn after a palpable and immediate world.

The Journals of Susanna Moodie,[50] rightly judged to be one of Atwood's finest accomplishments, employs, as did the Dr. Frankenstein poems, the extended figure of metalepsis[51] to create a series of linked poems. The use of a prior narrative, and an established persona, gives implicit substance, an historical context, and variety of incident and detail to the series, breaking through the solipsism of some of the early contextless lyrics. The use of a narrative from a previous text frees the poet to do what she does best: argumentative and reflective lyric that is both introspective and allusive. The figure of Susanna Moodie lends itself to a subtle rendering of the poet's preoccupations: the problem of how to exist and act without interfering and destroying; the risk of, the possible salvation through, merging with what is there before you come; the problems of frame, code, and genre — the necessity of patterns for the preservation of sanity, and the difficulty of telling any sort of truth inside available conventions.

The mask lyrics spoken by Susanna Moodie are flawless in their decorum; the poet's obsessions are rendered but do not seem to intrude on Mrs. Moodie's voice. Mrs. Moodie, benign incubus, possesses the poet; the poet, *animateur*, inhabits Mrs. Moodie and speaks through her lips. The varied pace and shapeliness of the series, the fact that it contains the first positive apotheosis in the poems so far, attest to the poet's skill in matching the poem series to her sense of the prior text. Through the range of locations — wilderness, city, underground — and the occasions of her life — emigration, settling, a fire, the death of a child, moving to the city, dying — the persona and her narrative provide the poet with a variety of rhetorical occasions and genres which she could scarcely generate out of her own life. Mrs. Moodie's death and apotheosis permit the poet to express the consummation of union with the natural world which is approached in earlier poems, but never arrived at.

If, as I surmise, this poet's central concern is with first whether, and then how, to be in the world, the Susanna Moodie poems are crucial in her writing because their essential subject is settling. The fact that in her next collection, *Procedures for Underground*, there are a number of poems dealing with family history suggests that Margaret Atwood is moving towards establishing some kind of real, circumstantial presence in the poems. The first poem, "Eden Is a Zoo" (p. 6), uses the fiction of a child's drawing of its parents to talk about the distance between the child's *imago* of the mother and father and their surmised reality. In keeping with the poet's tactile rather than flat, two-dimensional diagramming of her poems, the drawing is animated, made substantial, and the reader is led through its surface and into it. "Game after Supper" (p. 7) is half elusive childhood memory, half sinister hide-and-seek poem: she hides and the reader seeks, but the clues are so abundant that it seems clear that she is hiding in order to be discovered. "Girl and Horse, 1928" (p. 10), another family-history poem, renders through a personal fiction her abiding concern with the contrast between the static and the kinetic, using the "still" picture, its lie of permanence and safety, as a focus for the sense — expressed in the demanding yet solicitous questions in the second and third stanzas — of the scandal of this deception, its pretense that there is no death:

> Why do you smile? Can't you
> see the apple blossoms falling around
> you, snow, sun, snow, listen, the tree
> dries and is being burnt, the wind
>
> is bending your body....
>
> (p. 10)

Perennial concerns, like love and death, move a poet towards traditional images — or towards a deliberate resistance to those images. Like the images of mortality in "Girl and Horse, 1928," the image of flowers fading in "We Don't Like Reminders" (p. 22) is traditional, but the curt staccatos and reductive diction of the poem are contemporary.

Some of the poems in the collection look both forward and backward: "Interview with a Tourist" (p. 23) reads like a formal rehearsal for the dialogue patterns of the later Circe / Ulysses encounters, yet the emotional centre of the poem is located outside it, in an obscure catastrophe which precipitated the predicament which is the ostensible formal cause of the poem:

> Once, when there was history
> some obliterating fact occurred,
> No solution was found
>
> Now this country is underwater;
> we can love only the drowned
>
> (p. 23)

"The Creatures of the Zodiac" (p. 29) is a poem in the manner which will be perfected in the Circe poems: the description of a world peopled by projections of the speaker's hatreds, and her fear of their power to do harm: "They were once dust and ordinary / hatreds. I breathed on them, named them: / now they are predictions" (p. 29).

"A Soul, Geologically" (pp. 58–59) delineates one of Atwood's central fictions: person-into-landscape. It is as if the only safe way of knowing another is as landscape, a metaphor. This extended analogy is in a sense an enormous periphrasis, a huge circumlocution. She herself tends to be present in poems in synecdoche, in fragments; others tend to be massively there, as landscapes. In this poem, the transformation is happening: the other in the poem is turning into something she can relate to—or avoid relating to; finally, he disappears and becomes a containing form, a place of "white silences" which she can walk in. In "Two Versions of Sweaters" (pp. 62–63), the couple are defined by metonymy, in terms of their garments, but sweaters, unlike landscapes, at least have the shapes of bodies which will briefly occupy them; they are not so drastically surrogate. In "Delayed Message" (p. 19), the speaker makes one of her show-stopping entrances, embodied / disembodied in a wraithlike double, which walks, dripping, out of the lake after rising "... a long time through / silver, until the light broke / over my head."

"Woman Skating" (pp. 64–65) is another family-history poem, and the central figure is made graphically present in a parenthesis which contains not, as usual, a covert piece of information, but a fragment of documentary, a source. The woman in the poem is made into an emblem of precarious balance in the midst of time, change, death, and her epiphany is not viewed with irony, but tenderly kept safe:

Seeing...
. . . .
...the years
in sequence occurring
underfoot, watching
the miniature human
figure balanced on steel
needles...
...on time
sustained, above
time circling: miracle

Over all I place
a glass bell

(p. 65)

"Dancing Practice" (pp. 77–79), the final piece in this collection, is a poem series beginning with a half-comic, pedestrian, descriptive narrative, a family scene, a vignette informed by a drastic sense of time and change: "...the clock hands / whipping round, the dance / whose pattern we could not / see almost forgotten; / then it will be night, / then morning..."; but the series ends with a lyrical evocation of the dance as it "should have been" and an assertion — one of the first — of benign power: "...(because / I say it)." It is a carefully composed pastoral epiphany, using the traditional image of the dance to suggest sexual concord and community.[52]

Power Politics,[53] in contrast, is a linked argument or demonstration — in part, a series of vignettes which can be read as exempla — to prove that coupling, the basis of settling and community, will not do; intimacy is lethal. The poems are love poems in which the private is made generic and public in a flamboyant way. They are concerned with the histrionics of love, and the coercive power of paradigms. Insofar as they proceed by definition, argument, example, and hyperbole and draw their diction and figures from public theatres of war, politics, and commerce, they are in the Metaphysical tradition. Their chief quality is exuberance of invention, the pleasure taken in wit and contrivance. They are high-spirited and literary, echoing or alluding to a wide range of fictions — Proteus, Bluebeard, Frankenstein, Scheherazade, and images from pop culture like Superman — and to such poets as T. S. Eliot, Anne Sexton, and Sylvia Plath. The marginal narrative line which accompanies many of the poems is a distancing, generalizing device, and a comic one, pointing to the tension between plain speech and surreal hyperbole which sustains the poems.

The poet's perennial concerns, the predicaments which release her energy, are present, of course, in this series. There are scenarios of catastrophe:

> The accident has occurred,
> the ship has broken, the motor
> of the car has failed, we have been
> separated from the others,
> we are alone in the sand, the ocean,
> the frozen snow
>
> (p. 23)

There is the motif of postcreation anxiety: "How can I stop you / / Why did I create you" (p. 47). There is the transformation of the other into a condition which is so amorphous in space and time that it is beyond landscape, even:

...you rise above me
smooth, chill, stone-

white / you smell of tunnels
you smell of too much time
. . . .
you descend on me like age
you descend on me like earth

(p. 53)

Her characteristic tropes are effectively present, too: the coupling of disparate elements — "the proliferation of sewers and fears" (p. 37); the stating of equivalence through apposition — "the gifts we bring / ... warp in our hands to / implements, to manoeuvres" (p. 37); epigram, notoriously in the opening aphorism, which also, characteristically, uses simile and revisionary apposition: "you fit into me / like a hook into an eye / / a fish hook / an open eye" (p. 1). The surprises of enjambement are also here in such phrases as "...drowned / stomach..." (p. 4), "Next time we commit / love..." (p. 35), and "...you refuse / houses, you smell of / catastrophe..." (p. 47). In these poems, hyperbole is the norm, and irony often takes the form of the double take or wisecrack:

You rose from a snowbank
with three heads, all
your hands were in your pockets

I said, haven't
I seen you somewhere before

(p. 2)

The decorum of these poems is the decorum of burlesque, which allows for blatant extremes of travesty, hyperbole, and even, in "After the agony in the guest / bedroom" (p. 6), blasphemy. The stances are theatrical, but the technique is closer to cinematic cutting and juxtaposition. One of the literary models parodied is *The Waste Land*,[54] and the pervasive sense of sexual encounter as impasse or disaster is a quality which *Power Politics* shares with Eliot's poem.[55]

The poems are as much about story telling, the irresistible urge to invent, as they are about the ludicrousness of what passes for love. Talk, the talk that turns into poems, can be a way of putting off whatever it is that cannot be faced: in some instances, death; in this instance, whatever truth is left over after fictions have been exhausted:

> If we make stories for each other
> about what is in the room
> we will never have to go in.
>
> (p. 50)

The second-to-last poem is a kind of palinode, a confession of artifice and responsibility:

> They were all inaccurate:
>
> the hinged bronze man, the fragile man
> built of glass pebbles,
> the fanged man with his opulent capes and boots
>
> peeling away from you in scales.
>
> It was my fault but you helped,
> you enjoyed it.
>
> (p. 55)

The first poems in her collection, *You Are Happy*, read like leftovers from *Power Politics*. "Gothic Letter on a Hot Night" (pp. 15–16) is a kind of settling of accounts, an apologia for her addiction to invention, to

> Stories that could be told
> on nights like these to account for the losses,
> litanies of escapes, bad novels, thrillers
> deficient in villains
>
> (p. 15)

There is an aesthetic of a kind implied in this account: stories made up lead to losses, and further stories have to be made up to account for the sense of loss: "Who knows what stories / would ever satisfy her" (p. 16).

"Digging" (pp. 19–20) and "Spring Poem" (pp. 22–23) move into new territory, bucolic, but not pastoral; yet not entirely new, because it is reminiscent of the territory of the Pig-Girl and her truth about slops. They are ruthlessly, relentlessly itemizing, in a vocabulary deliberately brutal: a kind of mordant exaggeration of the opening of *The Waste Land*, with its lyrical angst turned to an intentional harshness. After an inventory of fecundity which is not a celebration, which displays fertility without beauty, she questions herself:

> ...from beneath
> this decaying board a snake
> sidewinds, chained hide
> smelling of reptile sex / the hens
> roll in the dust, squinting with bliss, frogbodies
> bloat like bladders, contract, string
> the pond with living jelly
> eyes, can I be this
> ruthless?
>
> (p. 22)

The "Songs of the Transformed" (pp. 29–44) in a way exhaust for now this mood of disgruntlement — "I dig because I hold grudges / I dig with anger" (p. 19) — through the arias sung by the creatures into which Circe, in the terms of the framing fiction, has changed Ulysses' men. In these songs, the usually inarticulate — victims of man's fear or disgust or brutality or need to exert power — have their say. They are songs of the worm's turning, or dreaming and plotting of turning; the downtrodden give voice to their point of view, which consists, in the main, of self-love, anger, and dreams of revenge. "Pig Song" (p. 30) is like the early "The Pig-Girl" in its sense of the squalor of being alive, but the tone is different. The later pig has a pragmatic sense of her own merit; she does not overestimate her importance, or think of herself in inflated literary terms: she is self-congratulatory, content, and sturdily impudent:

> I have the sky, which is only half
> caged, I have my weed corners,
> I keep myself busy, singing
> my song of roots and noses,
>
> my song of dung. Madame,
> this song offends you, these grunts
> which you find oppressively sexual,
> mistaking simple greed for lust.
>
> I am yours. If you feed me garbage,
> I will sing a song of garbage.
> This is a hymn.
>
> (p. 30)

The songs are high-spirited exercises in various literary genres; the object of their satire is our own squeamishness, the narrowness of our range of sympathies, the meagreness of our tolerance for norms other than our own: in a word, our lack of imagination. "Rat Song" (p. 32) is a dramatic monologue, resentful, narcissistic, ending with a fantasy of possession; "Crow Song" (pp. 33–34) is a failed political speech; "Song of the Worms" (p. 35) is a lyrical, sinister manifesto, ending, as manifestos will, in a vision of apocalypse and destruction. "Owl Song" (pp. 36–37) is the elaboration of an emblem out of a terse narrative; "Siren Song" (pp. 38–39) is a parable about myth: what seems to be an escape from, a subversion of, the rigours of mythological fiction turns out to be only another version of it. "Song of the Fox" (p. 40) is a complaint; "Song of the Hen's Head" (pp. 41–42) is a mordant commentary on the Orphic tradition in poetry, a contempt for the transcendental mode; "Corpse Song" (pp. 43–44), the last, is a warning, a prophecy, and a prayer about the desolate choices of the dead.

In contrast to the varied genres warbled by the transformed, the pieces in the next series, the "Circe/Mud Poems" (pp. 45–70), are reflective, argumentative mask and dramatic lyrics, interspersed with passages in prose. They use the Circe/Ulysses episode from the *Odyssey* as a frame narrative within which the poet can explore, through the fictions of poetry, the relation between a woman and a man—the subject of *Power*

Politics. Another concern is the power of the paradigms of narrative — life stories — over our actions. The range of tone in the poems suggests, not war, but chess war, manoeuvres; the presence of the antagonist / lover is more firmly established than in *Power Politics*. The poems move through definitions, imperatives, questions, and analogies to a kind of clarity, in which what is there can become visible. Various fictions are called up and dispelled: the hero, augmented by his varied accoutrements; the desert island, as backdrop for an idyll; the mud woman, passively promiscuous, comfortable, and renewable; the dead, with their monotonous genre of complaint or warning, who whisper, "Die, Die" (p. 62); and the "queen of the two dimensions" (p. 63), Circe's other aspect, intent on power, suffering, and refusal.

The final prose piece in the series expresses misgivings about the implacability of story, the ruthless narrative base which generates the songs, the arguments, the lyric cries. But the poem / epigraph which closes the "Circe / Mud Poems," a kind of coda, posits another place, another island, where the predetermined narrative is not imposed, where novelty can occur. The poem describes a landscape not tormented by the disgust at the squalor of living expressed in "Here are the holy birds" (p. 66), not defaced by anxieties about Circe's own destructiveness and the possibilities of catastrophic futures, but a place which belongs in another tradition. On the first, known island, "...I am right, / the events run themselves through / almost without us / / we are open, we are closed, / / we express joy, we proceed / as usual, we watch for / omens, we are sad / / / and so forth, it is over, / I am right, it starts again, jerkier this time and faster" (p. 69). In contrast to this brusque, staccato recitation, predictable and boring, the second island is not yet known, "because it has never happened; / / this land is not finished, / this body is not reversible" (p. 69). The simple declarative sentences which compose this poem are descriptions, not definitions. There are no strident questions, no grim imperatives. Things are to scale with the persons who are simply there, part of a landscape which is not an emblem: it is what it is. And time is not at a standstill, nor does the poem occur in the tense space between catastrophes. There is no lyrical transcendence; the solaces of the poem are bound into time: flakes fall and melt; birds are there and gone; the stream will freeze, but not yet; the deer has been there and gone away. This poem is an expression of dailiness and ease which, because of its rarity in this poetry, is more memorable than a lyric of high intensity.

It is not that she breaks completely from her old manner, but that she now has another range of expressiveness available. "Four Evasions" (pp. 77–78) is a reflective lyric of address, but it is different from the many poems in that mode already written by the poet: the linguistic model is not argument or definition, but talk — seemingly desultory, uncomposed, not bent on climax, or on the epigram which will stop conversation. It is tentative in tone, spare in diction. She has renounced augury, with its imperatives; she is no longer, even, mistress of words:

> unable to say how much I want you
> unable even to say
> I am unable
> . . . .
> thinking of my reluctance, way I withdrew
> when you came towards me, why did I.
>
> Easier to invent, remember you
> than to confront you, fact
>
> of you, admit
> you, let you in.

(pp. 77–78)

Syntax is looser, more elliptical: some pronoun subjects and some articles are left out. The small series is carefully designed, visually, but is not ostentatiously well made, does not move towards a predetermined climax; it is low-key, fugitive, candidly expressive rather than emblematic or argumentative, its prosody a matter of cadence and tone.

In "Four Auguries" (pp. 84–86), the body of the one addressed is still present mainly through synecdoche, but it can be touched and holds promise: "I gather you, ear, collar, tuft of damp hair, / creases in your suddenly unfolding face / / You are more than I wanted, / this is new, this greed for the real" (p. 86). "Head against White" (pp. 87–91) uses the rhetoric of phrases, latent syntax, rather than setting up patterns of beginning and end. Analogy is restrained; imperatives are not orders, but vocatives of insistent longing: "*Be alive*, my hands plead / with you, *Be alive*" (p. 87). The argument which links the poems is couched, not in the rhetoric of example and proof, but in the urgent phrases of caring persuasion: "*Break* it, I tell you, *Break* / it" (p. 90). The series ends with the infinitives of longing: "To move beyond the mirror's edge,... / ...to pronounce / / your own flesh. Now / / to be this / man on fire... / ...From these hardened / hours... / / to rise up living" (p. 91).

This tentative rhetoric, with its nuances of expression, its transformation of definition, argument, and imperative into rendering, suggestion, and longing, is perfected in the last three poems in the book. "There Is Only One of Everything" (p. 92) is a statement of revelation: an imagining of the aliveness, the being there, of everything, in time. Time as real time — not the speeded-up time of the deathwatch, or the knife-edge between catastrophes — can be allowed into the poems:

Not a tree but the tree
we saw, it will never exist, split by the wind
               and bending down
like that again. What will push out of the earth

later, making it summer, will not be
grass, leaves, repetition, there will
have to be other words.
                                       (p. 92)

The tense aesthetic of the earlier poems moved the poet towards tropes of evasion, fragmentation, or disguise — periphrasis, synecdoche, kenning; of containment or power — the impaling epithet, the simile in oxymoronic pairs; of risk and the cancelling of risk in enjambement balanced on revisionary disclosure; of the high theatrics of hyperbole and the accumulation of elements in apposition. But "There Is Only One of Everything" is a poetry of the immanent, which does not require fixing through epithet, or enlarging through simile.

It is preferable not to read the poems as a progression, since genre and intention determine prosodic arrangements; but certain images recur throughout the poet's work, and the continuity of the work can be established through relating them. In "There Is Only One of Everything," a realization of the particular aliveness of things and people in the world, there is an image of a man dancing:

> I look out at you and you occur
> in this winter kitchen, random as trees or sentences,
> entering me, fading like them, in time you will disappear
>
> but the way you dance by yourself
> on the tile floor to a worn song, flat and mournful,
> so delighted, spoon waved in one hand, wisps of
>   roughened hair
>
> sticking up from your head, it's your surprised
> body, pleasure I like.
>
>   (p. 92)

The man is addressed in the second person, as "you"; his transience is not denied; it is part of his presence; but the delight he radiates makes of his acknowledged mortality an undertone. The poetic line is long, reaching out, at ease and in leisure. Contrast this passage from "A Sibyl" in *The Circle Game*:

> and a man dances
> in my kitchen, moving
> like a metronome
> with hopes of staying
> for breakfast in the half-empty
> bottle in his pocket
> . . . .
> time runs out
> in the ticking hips of the
> man whose twitching skull
> jerks on loose
> vertebrae in my kitchen
>
>   (*The Circle Game*, p. 50)

The lines are short and staccato; the man is not addressed, but referred to in the third person; he is skeletal, described in terms of skull and vertebrae: his twitching, jerking movement is an image of the Dance of Death; he means death and nothing else; he is a hieroglyph of warning. The distance between these two solo dances is as great, and as significant, as the distance between the "prisoning rhythms" of the circle in "The Circle Game" and the transfigured dancers in "Dancing Practice" (*Procedures for Underground*, pp. 77-79).

"Late August" (p. 93) is less tentative than "There Is Only One of Everything"; it is a celebration of consummation in time, in a modified pastoral tradition: the setting is not an idyll, but a real harvest, and the mood is sensuous and erotic. As its imagery implies, this poem exists within the encompassing presence of Keats's "Ode to Autumn"[56] and Marvell's "The Garden" and "The Bermudas":

This is the plum season, the nights
blue and distended, the moon
hazed, this is the season of peaches

with their lush lobed bulbs
that glow in the dusk, apples
that drop and rot
sweetly, their brown skins veined as glands

No more the shrill voices
that cried *Need Need*
from the cold pond, bladed
and urgent as new grass

Now it is the crickets
who say *Ripe Ripe*
slurred in the darkness, while the plums

dripping on the lawn outside
our window, burst
with a sound like thick syrup
muffled and slow

The air is still
warm, flesh moves over
flesh, there is no

hurry

(p. 93)

The demonstrative "This" is one of her characteristic ways of beginning a poem, but it is used here with a difference: not to define, or to point to, but to commence an incantatory description through listing — the trope of plenitude. The pattern of the predicament or crisis poem is present, but concealed: the third stanza describes a predicament which is referred to as past and, in effect, outside the milieu of the poem; it is surrounded on each side by stanzas which announce the "Now," in contrast to the "No more."[57] The time in the poem is present, the mood quietly declarative; there are no imperatives, no questions, only affirmations. "Book of Ancestors" (pp. 94–95) is a palinode: Part I is a catalogue of the icons which peopled her earlier poetry, the fictions which kept her going; Part II is a farewell to these presences, with their "static demands . our demands, former / demands, death patterns" (p. 95).

These three poems at the end of *You Are Happy* mark a difference in the poet's work. Her poems from now on tend to be spoken from the midst of things, not from their edges; she is no longer fleeing towards some horizon, or disappearing off the right-hand corner of the page, or invisible under water; she is where we all are, and admitting it. Her old obsessions are still present; how could they disappear? Yet, in "A Paper Bag" from *Two-Headed Poems*,[58] the image of the double seems less sinister because the bearer of it is childlike and domestic: the face cut in a paper bag. The "Five Poems for Dolls," from the same collection (pp. 16–19), are emblem poems: poems formally organized by an object or objects, which become a focus for meditation.[59] The intent of the emblem poem, both traditionally and now, is moral, not aesthetic; it is tracking meaning, not beauty. For this poet, the genre provides a concentration of her tendency, from the very earliest poems, to see things and landscapes as iconic and portentous.

The poems in *Two-Headed Poems* tend to move towards — though they cannot always be subsumed under — either this genre, or another, more difficult to name in one word: the occasional, reflective lyric or lyric series, adapted from the model of the Romantic poets, especially Wordsworth and Coleridge; weaving together thought and feeling; moving, usually, from setting, to predicament, to elaboration, to some sort of resolution or catharsis. This variable model allows for sense impression, probing question, memory, analysis, speculation; and it usually moves through space—first the immediate setting, then the larger context—and in time—through the naming of season, ceremonial occasion in time, or the tracing of some small narrative pattern, not for its own sake, but for the thought it evokes. Such poems are formally organized, not, like emblem poems, by a movement to and from or around a focusing image, but in a linear fashion, following the movement of thought, changes in nuances of feeling, or narrative. The speaker—rather than, as in the emblem poem, the object—is at the centre of the poem. Some of the poems in this collection, like "A Red Shirt" (pp. 102–06), combine both modes, as the shirt itself becomes an emblem, part of, yet apart from, the occasion which the poem celebrates.

This second genre can be adapted to a series, as in the Daybook poems, or to an epistle, as in "Letters" (p. 30). The openings are usually references to place and time as a setting for musing: "Midnight: my house rests" (p. 27); "Eleven and no moon..." (p. 29); "Almost winter, and in the gravel drive-/way under the stripped trees" (p. 30); "Snow packs the roadsides, sends dunes/onto pavement..." (p. 76); "A tree hulks in the living-/room, prickly monster..." (p. 81). This last piece, "Solstice Poem" (pp. 81–85), is, as the opening suggests, a blending of the two modes. One title, "April, Radio, Planting, Easter" (pp. 96–97), suggests the time/place nexus which organizes, in part, these poems. The scenarios—unlike those in *Power Politics*—are not cryptic, but explicit: "My sister and I are sewing/a red shirt for my daughter. / She pins, I hem, we pass the scissors/back & forth across the table" (p. 102).

The degree to which the poet has consented to enter her poems —to use the available conventions for being present in them— can be measured by comparing "This Is a Photograph of Me" in *The Circle Game* with "Today" (pp. 22–23) in *Two-Headed Poems*. In the early poem, the fiction or contrivance which organized the poem is a strategem of disappearance, which bears a relationship of ironic reversal to the opening announcement. The settings of the two poems are similar: in the first, a tree, a slope, a house, a lake. The speaker of the poem is, we are give to understand in parenthesis, under water, drowned. In the second poem, the speaker is watching her small daughter walk through a landscape which also includes grass, a slope, a pond. There is potential danger in the poem: "...the lawn holds / my daughter like a hostage" (p. 22). But the admonition in parenthesis is a gesture towards saving from drowning:

(Watch the slope, hard clay with bladed
stones, posing
innocuous as daisies:
it leads down to the pond,
where the ducks beckon, eleven
of them....

(p. 22)

The poet is present in the poem as both the recorder and the speaker of the warning in parenthesis.

One of the patterns which can be traced through Margaret Atwood's poetry is the movement from absence (often conspicuous), to a theatrical presence through personae, to wary, tentative presence, to a reluctant consent to what it seems appropriate to call settlement, to be "half of a pair, / half of a custom, / ...part of this ancient habit" ("Two Miles Away," in *Two-Headed Poems*, p. 21). The temporal dimension of settling is established in terms of personal past in "Five Poems for Grandmothers" (pp. 33-40) and in terms of regional history in "Four Small Elegies" (pp. 52-55), both in *Two-Headed Poems*. Her sense of history and community in time is, of course, involved with language; as she says in one of the "Four Small Elegies," "A language is not words only, / it is the stories / that are told in it, / the stories that are never told" (p. 54).

Settling has its celebrations, present in *Two-Headed Poems* in the emblem poems: "Apple Jelly" (p. 93), a meditation on "...these tiny / glass pots of clear jelly" as safekeepers of "...the sun / on that noon, your awkward leap / down from the tree, / licked fingers, sweet pink juice, / what we keep / the taste of the act, taste / of this day"; and "All Bread" (pp. 108-09), the final emblem poem in the book, which records a kind of reconciliation with the muck of the world, the ooze and dung and dirt of it, which is part of the poet's dispraise of life in other poems. This poem is a small epiphany of community, her acceptance of settlement, and the small deaths it requires if we are to live together:

to know what you devour
is to consecrate it,
almost. All bread must be broken
so it can be shared. Together
we eat this earth.

(p. 109)

Such epiphanies are interspersed in a poetry of dailiness and plight, its solaces meagre and sparse, its diction reductive, recording a life rooted, but half-improvised; it is frugal, resisting comfort, insisting that all the negative evidence be brought in. Scrupulous, candid, resisting hyperbole, its rhetoric is musing, conversational. These poems are scarcely complaints, scarcely prayers, but half inventories, half minimal gestures towards meaning. There is the given; there is the longed for; there is the space in between. It is a rigorous poetry, selective in its details; her lists are always, still, evidence; the patterns of argument have given way to the broken cadences of musing, but the habit of argument is still there.

Nor are all the emblem poems positive epiphanies; "After Jaynes" (p. 31) presents an emblem of poetry stunning in its archaic brutality; "The Man with a Hole in His Throat" (pp. 41–42) is a linked conceit, a series of brilliant kennings, approaching in its sardonic tone the gallows grimness of "Marrying the Hangman" (pp. 48–51), which can be read as an exemplum, a narrative emblem representing marriage. Some of the old fictions of division are present, too: "The Right Hand Fights the Left" (pp. 56–57) is in part a fable of internecine warfare, drawn from Julian Jaynes,[60] whose account of human history in terms of the bicameral mind gave the poet a powerful new metaphor for her old sense of dichotomies, and a new version of the initial catastrophe which lay outside of, and presided over, the texts of many of her early poems.

"Marsh, Hawk" (pp. 88–89), beginning with a scene of desolation rendered through selective listing and reductive epithet, moves to a conclusion of longing (expressed, characteristically, in the infinitives of desire) for her old dream of the disappearance of the skin barrier: merging — not intrusion, that fracturing of surface — but immersion, which is a blending. The drowning in "This Is a Photograph of Me" and other poems is a cheat, a false version of this longed-for consummation:

> intrusion is not what we want,
>
> we want it to open, . . .
> . . . the water
> to accept us, . . .
> . . . .
> to immerse, to have it slide
> through us, disappearance
> of the skin, this is what we are looking for,
> the way in.
>
> (p. 89)

The poem uses "we"; the speaker's longing is shared by a companion addressed in the poem. Certainly a dominant impression that this collection gives is of a domestication of fear, which is diminished by the presence of a companion and a child, and the responsibility which they entail. "The Puppet of the Wolf" (pp. 100–01) takes the risk of enclosing momentous considerations — death and rebirth, murder, punishment, the conflict between the left hand and the right — in a daily domestic frame; the seriousness is not lessened, but it is somehow tamed by the perspective. The imbedded narrative of the three pigs and the wolf, a tale of destruction and death, is framed by a benign or saving narrative — the sequences of bathing a child. "A Red Shirt" (pp. 102–06), a reflective, emblematic poem enclosed in a narrative frame of the utmost dailiness, includes an imbedded attributive narrative about Old Woman, a reflective passage on red as a symbol of continuity among women, and an admonition about the power of fictions to determine our lives. But the poet pulls us back at intervals to the everyday — "It is January, it's raining, this grey / ordinary day" (p. 105) — and throughout the poem, enjambement is used, not, as usual, for revisionary disclosure or ironic reversal, but for continuity, which is in one sense the poem's subject.

The sense of peril is strong, still, even or especially in the final poem, "You Begin" (pp. 110–11), a poem in the tradition of instructing in, or passing on of, lore, parent to child. But warning is part of the genre, and it is brief: "This is the world, which is fuller / and more difficult to learn than I have said. / You are right to smudge it that way / with the red and then / the orange: the world burns" (pp. 110–11).

The gesture beyond settling is to turn one's attention to the world; and to some extent, the world, or one aspect of it, is the subject of the next collection, *True Stories*. "Footnote to the Amnesty Report on Torture," in *Two-Headed Poems* (pp. 45–47), was a suggestion of the poet's new preoccupation; and yet, it is not so new: it is as though her sense of peril and her obsession with the vulnerability and fragmentation of the human body have finally been located, not in Gothic fantasy, but in the real world. Of course, the history of writing poems is a history of the transformation of the obsessions one begins with, which spell out nothing more nor less than one's initial sense of reality.

There are many continuities in *True Stories*, along with some novelties. "One More Garden"[61] illustrates both. It is a version of a genre with which her previous work has made us familiar: a contempt for gardens, with their vegetable sexuality, their distasteful proliferation. Her old image of the female as telluric icon of fertility rounds out the poem, with a caustic reference to another familiar image — the circle dance. What is new is the brutality of diction, which is pervasive in these poems, and makes one realize just how chaste, for a late twentieth-century poet, her diction has been:

I'd stand more chance
here as a gourd, making
more gourds, as a belly
making more. Kiss your
thin icon goodbye, sink memory
& hope. Join the round
round dance. Fuck the future.

(p. 17)

"Late Night" (p. 20) ends: "Screw poetry, it's you I want, / your taste, rain / on you, mouth on your skin." It may be germane to consider that all the poems in the first half of the collection are, in their perverse way, love poems from abroad; Helen Vendler associates brutality of diction in poetry with "...desire without an object of desire, / All mind and violence and nothing felt."[62] "Postcard" (pp. 18–19) concludes: "Wish your were / here. Love comes / in waves like the ocean, a sickness which goes on / & on, a hollow cave / in the head, filling & pounding, a kicked ear" (p. 19). "Hotel" (p. 23) is a story told to a listener impaled, constrained to hear it, in brutal terms: "Upstairs there's a woman / / with no face and an unknown / animal shuddering in her. / / She bares her teeth and whimpers." The sound she makes "...tests the air here and finds / space. It enters / / me and becomes mine." "Dinner" (pp. 24–25) begins as a Swiftian contempt for human beings not seen as whole creatures — souls — but in distasteful synecdoche:

Engorged buttocks and
thighs jiggle by,
surly soft paunches.
Sugar etches the teeth.

(p. 24)

But it ends in a reversal, a candid inclusion of herself in the scene in all its banality: "*I love you*, whines the soprano. / / It's the same song, and mine is / also" (p. 25). The "...ancient / rhythms, constant and constantly / broken, our cut feet move to" (p. 25), which the speaker declines to sneer at, are a harsh, diminished, but still acknowledged version of the idyllic conclusion to "Dancing Practice" (*Procedures for Underground*, pp. 77–79), where the dancers move, "their faces turning, their changed hands / meeting and letting go, the circle / forming, breaking...."

"Small Poems for the Winter Solstice" (pp. 27–39) is a series of love poems, desultory and bleak vignettes, little scenarios to keep fear — and perhaps hope — alive, resolutely imagining the brutality of the world: "How can I justify / this gentle poem then in the face of sheer / horror?" (p. 34). The final poem in the series is a meditation on the power of the poet, and a clear rejection of the tradition of love poetry in which the apotheosis of the beloved is to exist in a poem, in blazon or contempt or praise. As she does at the end of "Dinner," the poet, here, opts for life, with its clutter, its mess, its real time; and she incorporates herself and the other in a contemporary genre, demotic and domestic, relinquishing by choice the hyperboles of the tradition of which *Power Politics* is a distorted echo.

The last piece in the prose series "True Romances" (pp. 40–44) can be read as a companion piece to this poem. It is a love poem in prose, but its general subject is one of the poet's old preoccupations: the difficulty of changing an aesthetic to which one is deeply committed; to move from inventing fictions — horrors, portents, transformations — about the world and others, to a task which is, for her, much more difficult: imagining the real. Most of her early poems are based on an aesthetic of invention; *Power Politics* is a burlesque of this aesthetic; the later poems are mixed. But nowhere in the poems is her dilemma, its reasons, and her present preference stated more clearly than in this passage:

> When I do think about you it's not what you'd expect.... I like to consider you going about your routine.... I find it soothing to think about you eating these mundane and in fact somewhat austere breakfasts. It makes me feel safe.
>
> But why should you go on eating breakfast at the same time, in the same way, day after day, just so I will be able to feel safe?... One of these mornings, when you reach the bottom of your cup,... you will look and there will be a severed finger, bloodless, anonymous, a little signal of death sent to you from the foreign country where they grow such things. Or you will glance down at your egg, four minutes, sitting in its dish white and as yet uncracked and serene as ever, and sunlight will be coming out of it. But on second thought your coffee cup will be vacant and the egg, when you finally close your eyes and slice it open blindly with the edge of your spoon, will have nothing in it that is not ordinarily there. Then you will know that at last I have imagined you perfectly. (p. 44)

This passage goes some way towards justifying my earlier contention that a sense of peril — variously rendered in fictions of catastrophe and loss — informs much of the earlier poetry. Even the desire to "feel safe" is risky because it involves making oneself vulnerable by turning one's back on possible danger. Here, the speaker's safety is entrusted to an other, who becomes, through this charge, a soul-keeper, a safekeeper. But her involvement with fictions of harm is so habitual that she is tempted to contaminate even her refuge — the other's imagined reliability, expressed in gestures of custom and habit — with warnings, dismemberments, transformations. Only at the end — and only in this piece — does the speaker give up her relentless embellishing, her addiction to danger, what she calls near the end of *Power Politics* "my candles, my dead uncles / my restrictions" (p. 51). And the tone of the words in which she relinquishes this paraphernalia suggests that she does it, not in order to be safe, but out of love for the reality of the other.

The middle section of this collection, as well as a poem series within it, is called "Notes toward a Poem That Can Never Be Written" (pp. 45–70). The title poem (pp. 65–70) deals, through the trope of extended apophasis, with the problem in aesthetics at the centre of the prose poem just quoted: the difficulty of imagining the real; and the related, larger problem: how can an art based on formal invention tell truth? Some of the poems before the title sequence are warning exempla, mock-objective, using the banal rhetoric of headline and slogan to express through understatement the horror of the events described. The brutality of "A Women's Issue" (pp. 54–55) is deliberate and stunning. These poems are evidence, bitter, grim, and direct; they have designs on the reader; they say, "I accuse." And yet "Trainride, Vienna-Bonn" (pp. 58–62) returns to an old motif: her own possible complicity in wrongdoing. The component poems here are in the linked reflective lyric mode of the Daybook poems in the previous collection: the "I" carefully placed in space and time, the movement linear, following the progress of the train and the musing patterns of thought, and also focused, expanding from a central motif: the hunter in the snow, an old and resonant image in her poetry. The scene from the outset is composed to convey meaning, "what the eye puts there" (p. 60). Poem iv makes explicit the central fear, the "... old fear: / not what can be done to you / but what you might do / yourself, or fail to. / / This is the old torture" (p. 61). And the series concludes with an even more succinct disclosure of the speaker's sense of involvement in the infliction of suffering (in a phrase that echoes lines from a very early poem, "The Revenant" — "I raise my hand / ... and trace / The growing outline of an / / Alien vein and bone: / That other hand, lying / Too close within my own"):[63]

This forest is alien
to me, closer than skin,
unknown, something early
as caves and buried, hard,

a chipped stone knife, the
long bone lying in darkness
inside my right arm: not
innocent but latent.

(p. 62)

The poem series "Notes toward a Poem That Can Never Be Written" (pp. 65-70) is an extention of the traditional trope of apophasis, a rhetorical admission that the project will fail. The poems perform a lament, through naming, for the terrible things that have been done to people and for the limitations of language. The real, the extremes of the real, are intractable; they will not enter into discourse, into "poems like this one" (p. 66), and remain real. These poems are a brave attempt to speak the unspeakable, to cut through poetics and slice into life, framed in a poignant acknowledgement that the attempt will fail, but that it must be made.

"Vultures" (pp. 72-73), which follows, is a contempt for poetry, in style like the "Songs of the Transformed," in matter like "After Jaynes." In "Last Poem" (pp. 74-75), Atwood returns to one of her central genres: the utterance just before catastrophe; it is also a love poem. Its authenticity comes from the circumstances, surmised from many earlier poems, that for her this imagined moment is the one time she feels most real, because she is facing the worst, and most composed, because now fear can stop, now the catastrophe has arrived. As she says at the end, "Each poem is my last and so is this one" (p. 75); and this statement has imaginative truth because the time in which she feels most at home, through habitute, is the day before disaster. The composed setting is revealed only towards the end: the interior contains icons of communion — a table, two glasses, and a candle; the persons, the couple, are present only through synecdoche — "two hands." Outside, there is "a charred landscape with the buildings and trees still smouldering" (p. 75). This poem comes out of a long tradition, including, of course, "Dover

Beach," and this poet's contribution to the genre is spare, minimal in a contemporary way, but very moving. "Earth" (pp. 76–77) is a mixed poem, combining the poet's old genre, a contempt for gardens, with a love poem in a very old mode: an imagination of the death of the beloved, premature mourning, a kind of preventive magic to protect oneself from a possibly real "...future / / in which you're a white picture / with a name I forgot to write / underneath..." (p. 76). The fiction of the poem, an imagination of death in the context of proliferating life, suits what the speaker calls "my cowardice" — the self-preparation for the worst, which is her characteristic stance towards the future. As is often the case, in a convention she established in the first poem in *The Circle Game*, the heart of this poem is in parentheses, existing in the space apart from syntax — a safe place, if the syntax is a narrative of imagined disaster:

(I'll want to make a hole in the earth
the size of an implosion, a leaf, a dwarf
star, a cave
in time that opens back & back into
absolute darkness and at last
into a small pale moon of light
the size of a hand,
I'll want to call you out of the grave
in the form of anything at all)

(p. 77)

"Use" (pp. 78–79) is also a love poem, as close as Atwood gets to the lyrical in the sense of a small cry of allowed feeling. After the brusque questions at the start, the speaker's emotional engagement is expressed in characteristic infinitives of longing: "...I want / also to use you, I want you / to be used & to glisten / with it..." (p. 78). "Variations on the Word *Love*" (pp. 82–83) is a contemporary version of a traditional poem: the definition of love. The reductive nature of the poem's claims for love, and the fragility of its claims for lovers — "...a finger- / grip on a cliffside" — mark it as modern. "Variations on the Word *Sleep*" (pp. 86–87)[64] is a love poem, too, one of the poet's intermittent series which imagines a union of lover and beloved and an element — usually water, often in sleep. She forgoes tonelessness for the moment and takes the other risk — for her, a far greater one — the risk of tenderness: the rhetoric is that of longing; the verbs are in the infinitive. The poem is a beautiful articulation of the poet's old dream of love as osmosis, at its most diffuse, at its least threatening to the beloved; the air in the hollows of bones, between nerve filaments, corpuscles, does not trespass, is not territorially ambitious. The poem is arranged around a metaphor of identity so invisible and complete that it can dispel entirely the old nightmare of the harm that love might do. The safety of this figure of speech allows the speaker to indulge the tone of rare tenderness, as it permits her to listen to and use nuances of syntax and punctuation:

I would like to watch you sleeping,
. . . .
I would like to watch you,
sleeping. I would like to sleep
with you, to enter
your sleep....

(p. 86)

The last poems in this collection are the work of a poet for whom poetry has become habitual rather than occasional — another dimension of living. "Mushrooms" (pp. 90–93), for example, is an emblem poem series, but it is not only emblematic. Though the final poem in the series makes it clear that the mushrooms are precisely emblematic in the old sense that they are part of an equation, an analogy — "Here is the handful / of shadow I have brought back to you: / this decay, this hope, this mouth- / ful of dirt, this poetry" (p. 93) — they exist, in the poem, in both dimensions: as emblem and as image of the real.

"Last Day" (p. 103), the final poem in the book, can be read as a companion to "Last Poem" (pp. 74–75), but though both are arranged in terms of Atwood's habitual sense of an ending, the earlier piece is a love poem in a context of imagined disaster, and this poem is a ceremony of farewell. In contrast to her more usual genre, the contempt for gardens,[65] "Last Day" is a lavishly orchestrated praise of nature and its proliferations, a bucolic pastoral:

It's June, the evenings touching
our skins like plush, milkweed sweetening
the sticky air which pulses
with moths, their powdery wings and velvet
tongues. In the dusk, nighthawks and the fluting
voices from the pond, its edges
webbed with spawn. Everything
leans into the pulpy moon.

(p. 103)

For the third time in her poetry, she echoes Sylvia Plath's "Flute Notes from a Reedy Pond,"[66] its allusion to death by drowning safely enclosed in images of sensuous aliveness. But the presiding poem in this first stanza is Thomas Hardy's "Afterwards,"[67] a poem written, like "This Is a Photograph of Me," from the point of view of the day after death, but with a very different focus. The pretext of "Afterwards" is a definition of the speaking self as a lover of the created world, but the centre of interest is the world, in all its particularity. Hardy's poem is a kind of long farewell, long for the same reason an *aubade* is: he is reluctant to leave what he loves so well. Similarly, "Last Day" is a praise, in a mood of lingering love: a tarrying poem. If some kind of link were to be made between this, the last poem so far, and "This Is a Photograph of Me," the first poem in her first acknowledged collection of poems,[68] it could be said that a shift has occurred: Margaret Atwood now occupies, habitually, in her poems, not the post-ultimate position in time — the day after — but the penultimate one — the last day, which is the day before; no poems are spoken from the day itself.

The momentum of the final stanza, the repetition of "and" and "again," brings the poem to a close on a rising cadence, not a dying fall. Statements joined by "and" have cumulative feeling; they could go on and on. This syntactical openness, together with the hope in the oxymoronic coupling of "last day" and "again," suggests an expectation of a tomorrow.

One difference between the early poems and these recent ones is the difference between a voice which speaks from "all the edges there are" ("Evening Trainstation before Departure," in *The Circle Game*, p. 16) and one which speaks in "...a pause / between one future & another, / a day after a day, / a breathing space before death" ("Rain," in *True Stories*, p. 89). What is visible from the edge has a certain intensity: "in fear everything / lives, impermanence / makes the edges of things burn / / brighter" ("Highest Altitude," in *Procedures for Underground*, p. 56). But the view is limited; a sense of immanent catastrophe induces a certain myopia. The "breathing space," the "...pause / between one future & another," allows more time to look around; more of the world is pulled into the poems, less and less with a sense of its numinous portentousness for the self, more and more with a sense of things being what they are, in a space which is not hermetically sealed, but shared. Imaginations of disaster are still pervasive, confirmed by evidence of catastrophe in the world, which burns, but the terrors are framed by fictions of caring, even of saving: "Mouth to mouth / I'm bringing you back to life" ("Small Poems for the Winter Solstice," in *True Stories*, p. 29); "That's your hand sticking out of the rubble. / I touch it, you're still living; / to have this happen I would give anything, / to keep you alive with me despite the wreckage" ("Last Poem," in *True Stories*, p. 75). And there is someone in the poems, the "thou" of lyric poetry, who seems to accept her offerings: "As it is, I can offer you / only this poor weather: / my chilled hands, the fragments / of a noon in early spring, / an east wind which includes / both of us, and the stained river, / a prayer, a sewer, a prayer" ("Damside," in *True Stories*, p. 99). This candidly meagre catalogue of treasures ends in one of the poet's favourite tropes, oxymoronic apposition, an implicit statement of meaning through analogy which includes, if it does not reconcile, opposites. The final poem in the poem series "Mushrooms" (*True Stories*, pp. 90–93) ends with the same trope. In the first stanza, "hunt" and "death" and "born" are parallel in terms of syntax and stress; in the series "flesh into earth into flesh," it is "flesh," not "earth," which begins and ends the phrase. And, in the last stanza, the elements are so arranged that hope, and poetry, are given a slight edge:

> It isn't only
> for food I hunt them
> but for the hunt and because
> they smell of death and the waxy
> skins of the newborn,
> flesh into earth into flesh.

Here is the handful
of shadow I have brought back to you:

this decay, this hope, this mouth-
ful of dirt, this poetry.

NOTES

[1] Margaret Eleanor Atwood was born on 18 November 1939, in Ottawa, Ontario, to Carl Edmund Atwood, a professional entomologist, and Margaret (Killam) Atwood. Besides Margaret, there is a brother and a younger sister. She attended Leaside High School, Toronto, and later, Victoria College, University of Toronto, where she received her B.A. in 1961. She met Charles Pachter, now a well-known graphic artist, at Camp White Pine, Ontario, and what began as, and remained, a friendship also developed into an artistic collaboration. In 1961 her first collection of poems, *Double Persephone*, was published and was awarded the E.J. Pratt Medal. She studied at Radcliffe College, Harvard, receiving her M.A. in 1962. During 1964–65 she lectured in English at the University of British Columbia, where she began writing *The Edible Woman*, her first novel, published in 1969. In the mid-1960s she married Jim Polk, an American, whom she subsequently divorced. During 1967–68 she was an instructor in English at Sir George Williams University, Montreal. In 1967 her first full-length book of poems, *The Circle Game*, won a Governor General's Award. In 1967 she also received a Centennial Commission Prize, and in 1969, the Union League Civic and Arts Foundation Prize from *Poetry* [Chicago]. She received a D.Litt. from Trent University in 1973, and an LL.D. from Queen's University in 1974. From 1971 to 1973, she was an editor and a member of the board of directors at House of Anansi Press, Toronto. She was awarded the Bess Hopkins Prize by *Poetry* [Chicago] in 1974, the City of Toronto Book Award in 1977, and the Radcliffe Medal in 1980. She lived for a number of years on her farm near Alliston, Ontario, with the novelist Graeme Gibson. A daughter, Jess, was born to them in 1976. They new reside in Toronto, Ontario. She is an active member of the Writers Union of Canada, of Amnesty International, and of the Canadian Civil Liberties Association, of which she was a member of the board of directors during 1973–75. She is a contributing editor of *This Magazine*.

[2] Wallace Stevens, "An Ordinary Evening in New Haven," in *The Collected Poems of Wallace Stevens* (New York: Alfred A. Knopf, 1954), p. 471.
[3] Stevens, p. 523. I have adapted the line "But his actual candle blazed with artifice" from Stevens' poem "A Quiet Normal Life."
[4] J. R. (Tim) Struthers, "An Interview with Margaret Atwood," *Essays on Canadian Writing*, No. 6 (Spring 1977), p. 21. All further references to this work (Struthers) appear in the text.
[5] Joyce Carol Oates, "A Conversation with Margaret Atwood," *The Ontario Review*, No. 9 (Fall–Winter 1978–79), p. 5.
[6] Karla Hammond, "An Interview with Margaret Atwood," *The American Poetry Review*, 8, No. 5 (Sept.–Oct. 1979), 28. All further references to this work (Hammond) appear in the text.
[7] This influence could be documented, but there is not space in this brief overview.
[8] The influence of Macpherson is apparent in later work, too; notably, in "Songs of the Transformed" in *You Are Happy*. For a discussion of this influence, see Jean Mallinson, "Versions and Subversions: Formal Strategies in the Poetry of Contemporary Canadian Women," Diss. Simon Fraser 1981, pp. 60–61.
[9] *The Fiddlehead*, No. 59 (Winter 1964), pp. 58–63.
[10] See Ellen Moers, "Female Gothic," in *Literary Women* (Garden City, N.Y.: Doubleday, 1976), pp. 90–110.
[11] *Poésie / Poetry 64*, ed. Jacques Godbout and John Robert Colombo (Montréal: Les Editions du Jour; Toronto: Ryerson, 1963), pp. 106–13.
[12] For this term, I am indebted to Virgil Thomson, "Music Does Not Flow," *The New York Review of Books*, 17 Dec. 1981, p. 49.
[13] Like Adrienne Rich, Margaret Atwood has widened the scope of her recent poetry to include political and historical subjects, and has associated herself with certain public issues; but, whereas Rich has become an ardent feminist, Atwood's concerns are focused on Amnesty International.
[14] Moers, pp. 109–10.
[15] Gayle Wood, in her review "On Margaret Atwood's *Selected Poems*," *The American Poetry Review*, 8, No. 5 (Sept.–Oct. 1979), 30–32, after praising "Death of a Young Son by Drowning" and "Later in Belleville: Career" from *The Journals of Susanna Moodie*, calls these poems "'non-love' poems" and fails to judge them sensitively, in part, I think, because she does not understand the source. Linda Wagner, in her essay "The Making of *Selected Poems*, the Process of Surfacing," in

The Art of Margaret Atwood: Essays in Criticism, ed. Arnold E. Davidson and Cathy N. Davidson (Toronto: House of Anansi, 1981), pp. 81–94, states that "... Atwood's *Procedures for Underground* has as a central persona a pioneer woman, whose memories seem to be given voice as she looks at old photographs" (p. 88). This misinterpretation of the poems may arise from the author's failure, as an American, to imagine that the details of the poems she cites could be part of the sense of life of a contemporary Canadian.

[16] Hugh MacCallum, rev. of *The Circle Game*, in "Letters in Canada 1966: Poetry," *University of Toronto Quarterly*, 36 (July 1967), 357, 359.

[17] Peter Stevens, "On the Edge, on the Surface," rev. of *The Circle Game*, by Margaret Atwood, and *Silverthorn Bush and Other Poems*, by Robert Finch, *Canadian Literature*, No. 32 (Spring 1967), pp. 71, 72.

[18] Michael Ondaatje, rev. of *The Circle Game*, *The Canadian Forum*, April 1967, pp. 22, 23.

[19] Eric Thompson, rev. of *The Circle Game*, *The Fiddlehead*, No. 75 (Spring 1968), pp. 76, 77.

[20] Gary Ross, "The Circle Game," *Canadian Literature*, No. 60 (Spring 1974), p. 57.

[21] Jean Gibbs, rev. of *Procedures for Underground*, *The Fiddlehead*, No. 87 (Nov.–Dec. 1970), p. 64.

[22] Frank Davey, "Atwood's Gorgon Touch," *Studies in Canadian Literature*, 2 (Summer 1977), 159. All further references to this work appear in the text.

[23] *You Are Happy* (Toronto: Oxford Univ. Press, 1974), p. 70. All further references to this work are indicated in parentheses. Carolyn Allen, in "Margaret Atwood: Power of Transformation, Power of Knowledge," *Essays on Canadian Writing*, No. 6 (Spring 1977), pp. 5–17, comments on this same passage as follows: "This is a world in flux which includes them both, watching the changes, noticing small signs of life..." (p. 16).

[24] *Studies in Canadian Literature*, 5 (Spring 1980), 167–76.

[25] *Essays on Canadian Writing*, No. 17 (Spring 1980), pp. 5–43.

[26] Robin Skelton, "Timeless Constructions: A Note on the Poetic Style of Margaret Atwood," *The Malahat Review*, No. 41 (Jan. 1977) [*Margaret Atwood: A Symposium*], pp. 107–20. All further references to this work appear in the text.

[27] Pat Sillers, in "Power Impinging: Hearing Atwood's Vision," *Studies in Canadian Literature*, 4 (Winter 1979), 67–68, takes exception

to Skelton's views, arguing, as I shall do, that Atwood's style is highly rhetorical.

[28] "Fishing for Eel Totems," in *Procedures for Underground* (Toronto: Oxford Univ. Press, 1970), p. 69. All further references to this work are indicated in parentheses.

[29] Eli Mandel, "Atwood Gothic," in *Another Time* (Erin, Ont.: Porcépic, 1977), pp. 137–45.

[30] In Davidson and Davidson, eds., *The Art of Margaret Atwood*, pp. 35–54.

[31] In Davidson and Davidson, eds., *The Art of Margaret Atwood*, pp. 15–34.

[32] *Canadian Literature*, No. 60 (Spring 1974), pp. 21–42.

[33] In Davidson and Davidson, eds., *The Art of Margaret Atwood*, pp. 95–106.

[34] *Studies in Canadian Literature*, 6 (1981), 48.

[35] I use the term *fiction* to mean invention: the fabrication or artifice on which a poem is based.

[36] *Double Persephone* (Toronto: Hawkshead, 1961), n. pag.

[37] *Delta*, No. 22 (Oct. 1963), p. 28.

[38] A *dispraise* or a *contempt*—the two terms are interchangeable—is, in the catalogue of poetic kinds, the opposite of a *praise*.

[39] The "... woman image left / in cave rubble, the drowned / stomach bulbed with fertility, / face a tiny bead, a / lump, queen of the termites" appears in "She Considers Evading Him," in *Power Politics* (Toronto: House of Anansi, 1971), p. 4. All further references to this work are indicated by page numbers in parentheses.

[40] See above, note 9.

[41] See above, note 11.

[42] *The Circle Game* (Toronto: House of Anansi, 1967), p. 1. All further references to this work appear in the text.

[43] For a discussion of "A Sibyl" in the context of an analysis of the subversive re-telling, by women poets, of classical myths, see Mallinson, "Versions and Subversions," pp. 56–58.

[44] "Notes from Various Pasts," in *The Animals in That Country* (Toronto: Oxford Univ. Press, 1968), p. 11. All further references to this work appear in the text.

[45] Helen Vendler, *Part of Nature, Part of Us: Modern American Poets* (Cambridge: Harvard Univ. Press, 1980), p. 305.

[46] Moers, pp. 90–99. Moers defines Female Gothic in terms of Mary Shelley's *Frankenstein*.

[47] A number of texts could be cited, but one of the closest in cadence, tone, and some imagery is "Lady Lazarus":

> Peel off the napkin
> O my enemy,
> Do I terrify? —
> . . . .
> So, So, Herr Doktor.
> So, Herr Enemy.
>
> I am your opus,
> I am your valuable,
> The pure gold baby
>
> That melts to a shriek.
> . . . .
> Out of the ash
> I rise with my red hair
>
>   (*Ariel* [London: Faber and Faber, 1965], pp. 16–19)

The dramatic situation in this poem — the revelation of a terrible creation or re-creation — is similar to the situation in "Speeches for Dr. Frankenstein." The words in Plath's poem are spoken by the creature, not the Doctor. Both poems are formally strict: Plath uses triplets, Atwood couplets, as a norm, with some variations. Plath's "Medusa" could also be cited:

> I didn't call you.
> I didn't call you at all.
> Nevertheless, nevertheless
> You steamed to me over the sea,
> Fat and red, a placenta
> . . . .
> Overexposed, like an X-ray.
> Who do you think you are?
> A Communion wafer? Blubbery Mary?
> I shall take no bite of your body,
> . . . .
> Off, off, eely tentacle!
>
> There is nothing between us.
>
>   (*Ariel*, pp. 45–46)

⁴⁸ Although "Progressive Insanities of a Pioneer" and "Backdrop Addresses Cowboy" are significant, in other contexts, for the discussion of Atwood's work, they have received so much attention elsewhere that I have decided not to comment further on them here.

⁴⁹ See Ralph Rader, "The Dramatic Monologue and Related Lyric Forms," *Critical Inquiry*, 3 (Autumn 1976), 131–52. Rader distinguishes expressive lyric, dramatic lyric, mask lyric, and dramatic monologue. I cannot define here in detail the differences among these modes, but I am satisfied that the Susanna Moodie poems are linked mask lyrics rather that dramatic monologues. Two elements essential to the latter form are missing from them: the presence in the poem of an other to whom the poem is addressed; and a detailed circumstantiality which has, in fact, been selected by the poet to create a certain effect, but which seems to have a certain existence independent of the poem's meaning — to be simply, incidentally, there.

⁵⁰ Since there exist a number of commentaries on *The Journals of Susanna Moodie*, I have decided, space being limited, to refer to this work only briefly. Among available critiques are the following: Carolyn Allen, "Margaret Atwood: Power of Transformation, Power of Knowledge" (see above, note 23); Lorraine Weir, "Meridians of Perception: A Reading of *The Journals of Susanna Moodie*," in Davidson and Davidson, eds., *The Art of Margaret Atwood*, pp. 69–80; and Judith McCombs, "Atwood's Haunted Sequences: *The Circle Game*, *The Journals of Susanna Moodie*, and *Power Politics*" (see above, note 30).

⁵¹ Harold Bloom, *A Map of Misreading* (New York: Oxford Univ. Press, 1975), p. 74.

⁵² It is interesting to compare the image of the dancers in Atwood's poem with the image in T. S. Eliot's *Four Quartets*. The following are the lines from "Dancing Practice":

> where precise as
> crystals the new feet
> of the dancers move
> across a green lawn at evening
>
> the music now
> sounding from everywhere
> . . . .
> their faces turning, their changed hands
> meeting and letting go, the circle

forming, breaking, each
one of them the whole
rhythm....

(p. 79)

The following are the lines from "East Coker":

...you can hear the music
Of the weak pipe and the little drum
And see them dancing...
Th association of man and woman
In daunsinge, signifying matrimonie —
. . . .
Holding eche other by the hand or the arm
Whiche betokeneth concorde. Round and round...
. . . .
...Keeping time,
Keeping the rhythm in their dancing
As in their living in the living seasons
. . . .
...Feet rising and falling.
(T. S. Eliot, *The Complete Poems and Plays 1909–1950*
[New York: Harcourt, Brace & World, 1962], pp. 123–24)

I do not suggest that the earlier lines are a source in any strict sense, only that they are a modern classical instance of the elaboration of the image of communal dance as an evocation of harmony or concord. Given that Eliot is a pervasive influence in Atwood's earlier poems and that both passages have the air of demure, timeless pastoral, as well as certain shared words, it is plausible that there may be some connection between the two.

[53] As with the Susanna Moodie poems, I am commenting only briefly on this series, drawing attention to a neglected aspect of it. Judith McCombs, in "Atwood's Haunted Sequences" (see above, note 30), gives an interesting Gothic reading of these poems, and Gloria Onley, in "Power Politics in Bluebeard's Castle" (see above, note 32), gives a feminist reading in the context of modern culture construed as patriarchal.

[54] These echoes of *The Waste Land* are, I think, deliberate, half parody. The poem on page 40 refers obliquely to the famous opening lines:

Spring again, can I stand it
shooting its needles into
the earth, my head, both
used to darkness
. . . .
Thick lilac buds crouch for the
spurt but I
hold back

The lines "... the entrails of dead cards / are against me, foretell / it will be water..." (p. 41) and the image of the mother in the pond "upside down, lifesize, hair streaming / over the slashed throat" (p. 41) evoke *The Waste Land*, ll. 43–47, and possibly the later "Death by Water."

[55] Vendler, pp. 78, 85. Vendler cites I. A. Richards' early observation that *The Waste Land* reveals Eliot's "persistent concern with sex"; and she herself comments, "Though *The Waste Land* is obsessed with sex, it hasn't a good word to say for it...."

[56] See Stanley Plumly, "Chapter and Verse: Two — Image and Emblem," *The American Poetry Review*, 7, No. 3 (May–June 1978), 30. Plumly, commenting on a contemporary lyric, says that "... it reads like a lyric held within the longer, deeper breath of an ode...." He is interested in the tension between modern lyric and the "ghost poem of a wider, greater, classical, contemplative utterance," "the idea of the ode, the mind and music of the ode." He does not have in mind, as I do, a particular ode, and it is not to be thought that Atwood's "Late August" is an ode *manqué*, but it remains true that a certain reach and resonance is present in the poem for those readers who know Keats's ode.

[57] The third stanza of "Late August" is the second of three allusions in Atwood's poetry to Sylvia Plath's poem "Flute Notes from a Reedy Pond" (*The Colossus* [London: Faber and Faber, 1960], pp. 84–85), which begins, "Now coldness comes sifting down...." Specific echoes are "pond," "cold," and the rhyme of "*Need Need*" with "Reedy." The first allusion to this poem is the earlier "Weed Seeds near a Beaver Pond" (*Procedures for Underground*, pp. 30–31). Besides the obvious echo in "Pond" and the rhyme of "Weed Seeds" with "Reedy," the title precisely repeats the rhythm of Plath's title. There is one more echo in this poem: Atwood's "... too many / layers of things, too much / time, too heavy" (p. 30) suggests Plath's "Now coldness comes sifting down, layer after layer." The third allusion to the poem occurs in "Last Day," the final poem in Atwood's most recent collection, *True Stories*, in the lines "... the fluting / voices from the pond...."

My suggestion is that Plath's poem, in which the dead or dying girl / speaker is lying or crouched, the victim of suicide, at the bottom of the pond, represents in some sense for Margaret Atwood a dangerous elaboration of the image which is glimpsed at intervals in her poetry: the girl, drowned, obscurely visible under water, in "This Is a Photograph of Me"; the drowned mother, hair streaming, throat slashed, in *Power Politics* (p. 41). The allusions occur in poems which resist or negate the alluring death described in Plath's poem: "Weed Seeds" is desolate but not hopeless; the speaker is regretful but resolute, and what she has left at the pond, under the water, it not life, but "...the waiting / / lives I threw away." In "Late August" and "Last Day," the allusions are carefully placed in a context of celebration, and in "Late August" actually referred to as past, in the phrase "No more."

[58] *Two-Headed Poems* (Toronto: Oxford Univ. Press, 1978), pp. 12–13. All further references to this work appear in the text.

[59] For some of my thoughts on the emblem poem as adapted by modern poets, I am indebted to Plumly, "Chapter and Verse: Two — Image and Emblem," pp. 21–22.

[60] Julian Jaynes, *The Origin of Consciousness in the Breakdown of the Bicameral Mind* (Toronto: Univ. of Toronto Press, 1976).

[61] *True Stories* (Toronto: Oxford Univ. Press, 1981), pp. 16–17. All further references to this work appear in the text.

[62] Vendler, p. 42. The lines quoted, of course, are by Wallace Stevens, and Vendler develops her idea about the sources of brutality of style in poetry in relation to Stevens' poems (see pp. 42–45).

[63] *The Fiddlehead*, No. 59 (Winter 1964), p. 59.

[64] I thought that there was no indication, in Atwood's poems, of her ever having read Dylan Thomas; but I now think that "Variations on the Word *Sleep*" — different as it is in its formal arrangements — owes something to Dylan Thomas' "The Conversation of Prayer" (*Collected Poems* [New York: New Directions, 1957], p. 111). The sense of caring, of the perils of sleep, the longing for "sleep in a safe land" ("Conversation"), are present in both poems; and they have in common certain words: "grief," "dark," "green"; in Thomas, "stairs," in Atwood, "stairway"; in Thomas, "dark eyed wave," in Atwood, "smooth dark wave."

[65] Contrast these lines from "Spring Poem":

...frogbodies
bloat like bladders, contract, string

the pond with living jelly
eyes, can I be this
ruthless?

(*You Are Happy*, p. 22)

[66] See above, note 57.

[67] The pertinent lines from Hardy's poem are the following: "And the May month flaps its glad green leaves like wings, / Delicate-filmed as new-spun silk..."; "If it be in the dusk when, like an eyelid's soundless blink, / The dewfall-hawk comes crossing the shades to alight"; and "If I pass during some nocturnal blackness, mothy and warm" (*The Collected Poems of Thomas Hardy* [London: Macmillan, 1952], p. 521).

[68] Margaret Atwood did not include in her *Selected Poems* (1976) any poems earlier than *The Circle Game*.

SELECTED BIBLIOGRAPHY

Primary Sources

Books

Atwood, Margaret. *Double Persephone*. Toronto: Hawkshead, 1961.
———. *The Circle Game*. Toronto: House of Anansi, 1967.
———. *The Animals in That Country*. Toronto: Oxford Univ. Press, 1968.
———. *The Journals of Susanna Moodie*. Toronto: Oxford Univ. Press, 1970.
———. *Procedures for Underground*. Toronto: Oxford Univ. Press, 1970.
———. *Power Politics*. Toronto: House of Anansi, 1971.
———. *You Are Happy*. Toronto: Oxford Univ. Press, 1974.
———. *Selected Poems*. Toronto: Oxford Univ. Press, 1976.
———. *Two-Headed Poems*. Toronto: Oxford Univ. Press, 1978.
———. *True Stories*. Toronto: Oxford Univ. Press, 1981.

Contributions to Periodicals and Books

Atwood, Margaret. "The Interior Decorator"; "The Revenant"; "The City Girl"; "The Mad Mother"; "Woman on the Subway"; "The Lifeless Wife"; "The Somnambulist"; "The Slideshow"; "The Dwarf"; and "Houses." In *Poésie/Poetry 64*. Ed. Jacques Godbout and John Robert Colombo. Montréal: Editions du Jour; Toronto: Ryerson, 1963, pp. 106–13.
———. "The Pig-Girl." *Delta*, No. 22 (Oct. 1963), p. 28.
———. "Fall and All: A Sequence." *The Fiddlehead*, No. 59 (Winter 1964), pp. 58–63.

Secondary Sources

Allen, Carolyn. "Margaret Atwood: Power of Transformation, Power of Knowledge." *Essays on Canadian Writing*, No. 6 (Spring 1977), pp. 5–17.
Bowering, George. "Margaret Atwood's Hands." *Studies in Canadian Literature*, 6 (1981), 39–52.
Brown, Russell. "Atwood's Sacred Wells." *Essays on Canadian Writing*, No. 17 (Spring 1980), pp. 5–43.
Davey, Frank. "Atwood's Gorgon Touch." *Studies in Canadian Literature*, 2 (Summer 1977), 146–63.
Djwa, Sandra. "The Where of Here: Margaret Atwood and a Canadian Tradition." In *The Art of Margaret Atwood: Essays in Criticism*. Ed. Arnold E. Davidson and Cathy N. Davidson. Toronto: House of Anansi, 1981, pp. 15–34.
Foster, John Wilson. "The Poetry of Margaret Atwood." *Canadian Literature*, No. 74 (Autumn 1977), pp. 5–20.
Gibbs, Jean. Rev. of *Procedures for Underground*. *The Fiddlehead*, No. 87 (Nov.–Dec. 1970), pp. 61–65.
Hammond, Karla. "An Interview with Margaret Atwood." *The American Poetry Review*, 8, No. 5 (Sept.–Oct. 1979), 27–29.
Horne, Alan J. "Margaret Atwood: An Annotated Bibliography (Poetry)." In *The Annotated Bibliography of Canada's Major Authors*. Ed. Robert Lecker and Jack David. Vol. II. Downsview, Ont.: ECW, 1980, 13–53.
Irvine, Lorna. "One Woman Leads to Another." In *The Art of Margaret Atwood: Essays in Criticism*. Ed. Arnold E. Davidson and Cathy N. Davidson. Toronto: House of Anansi, 1981, pp. 95–106.
Jaynes, Julian. *The Origin of Consciousness in the Breakdown of the Bicameral Mind*. Toronto: Univ. of Toronto Press, 1976.
Johnston, Gordon. "'The Ruthless Story and the Future Tense' in Margaret Atwood's 'Circe / Mud Poems.'" *Studies in Canadian Literature*, 5 (Spring 1980), 167–76.
MacCallum, Hugh. Rev. of *The Circle Game*. In "Letters in Canada 1966: Poetry." *University of Toronto Quarterly*, 36 (July 1967), 357–59.
Mallinson, Jean. "Versions and Subversions: Formal Strategies in the Poetry of Contemporary Canadian Women." Diss. Simon Fraser 1981.

Mandel, Eli. "Atwood Gothic." In *Another Time*. Erin, Ont.: Porcépic, 1977, pp. 137–45.
McCombs, Judith. "Atwood's Haunted Sequences: *The Circle Game*, *The Journals of Susanna Moodie*, and *Power Politics*." In *The Art of Margaret Atwood: Essays in Criticism*. Ed. Arnold E. Davidson and Cathy N. Davidson. Toronto: House of Anansi, 1981, pp. 35–54.
Moers, Ellen. *Literary Women*. Garden City, N.Y.: Doubleday, 1976, pp. 90–110.
Oates, Joyce Carol. "A Conversation with Margaret Atwood." *The Ontario Review*, No. 9 (Fall–Winter 1978–79), pp. 5–18.
Ondaatje, Michael. Rev. of *The Circle Game*. *The Canadian Forum*, April 1967, pp. 22–23.
Onley, Gloria. "Power Politics in Bluebeard's Castle." *Canadian Literature*, No. 60 (Spring 1974), pp. 21–42.
Plumly, Stanley. "Chapter and Verse: One — Rhetoric and Emotion." *The American Poetry Review*, 7, No. 1 (Jan.–Feb. 1978), 21–32.
———. "Chapter and Verse: Two — Image and Emblem." *The American Poetry Review*, 7, No. 3 (May–June 1978), 21–32.
Rader, Ralph. "The Dramatic Monologue and Related Lyric Forms." *Critical Inquiry*, 3 (Autumn 1976), 131–52.
Ross, Gary. "The Circle Game." *Canadian Literature*, No. 60 (Spring 1974), pp. 51–63.
Sillers, Pat. "Power Impinging: Hearing Atwood's Vision." *Studies in Canadian Literature*, 4 (Winter 1979), 59–70.
Skelton, Robin. "Timeless Constructions: A Note on the Poetic Style of Margaret Atwood." *The Malahat Review*, No. 41 (Jan. 1977) [*Margaret Atwood: A Symposium*], pp. 107–20.
Stevens, Peter. "On the Edge, on the Surface." Rev. of *The Circle Game*, by Margaret Atwood, and *Silverthorn Bush and Other Poems*, by Robert Finch. *Canadian Literature*, No. 32 (Spring 1967), pp. 71–72.
Struthers, J. R. (Tim). "An Interview with Margaret Atwood." *Essays on Canadian Writing*, No. 6 (Spring 1977), pp. 18–27.
Thompson, Eric. Rev. of *The Circle Game*. *The Fiddlehead*, No. 75 (Spring 1968), pp. 76–77.
Thomson, Virgil. "Music Does Not Flow." *The New York Review of Books*, 17 Dec. 1981, pp. 47–51.
Vendler, Helen. *Part of Nature, Part of Us: Modern American Poets*. Cambridge: Harvard Univ. Press, 1980.
Wagner, Linda. "The Making of *Selected Poems*, the Process of Surfacing." In *The Art of Margaret Atwood: Essays in Criticism*.

Ed. Arnold E. Davidson and Cathy N. Davidson. Toronto: House of Anansi, 1981, pp. 81–94.

Weir, Lorraine. "Meridians of Perception: A Reading of *The Journals of Susanna Moodie*." In *The Art of Margaret Atwood: Essays in Criticism.* Ed. Arnold E. Davidson and Cathy N. Davidson. Toronto: House of Anansi, 1981, pp. 69–80.

Wood, Gayle. "On Margaret Atwood's *Selected Poems*." Rev. of *Selected Poems. The American Poetry Review*, 8, No. 5 (Sept.–Oct. 1979), 30–32.

D. G. Jones (1929–   )

E. D. BLODGETT

D. G. Jones (1929–)

E. D. BLODGETT

Biography

DOUGLAS GORDON JONES was born on New Year's Day, 1929, in Bancroft, Ontario, where his father ran a lumber and pulpwood business. After his early education in Bancroft, Jones enrolled in the Grove (now Lakefield) Preparatory College. After a period of a few years during which he considered careers as either an architect or an engineer, he graduated in honours English from McGill University in 1952. Subsequently, he went to Queen's University, where he completed a M.A. thesis on Ezra Pound's *Cantos* under the direction of George Whalley in 1954. No matter how propitious a choice Pound was for the development of Jones's poetic, his father remarked simply: "Pound. I heard that bastard from Italy during the Second World War."[1]

During the year 1954–55, Jones held a temporary position at the Royal Military College in Kingston; he then moved to the Ontario Agricultural College in Guelph, where he taught English literature until 1961. Although not a primary cause, one of the catalysts of Jones's departure from the college was a talk to the women's literary society, highlighted by a reading of Irving Layton's poem "Beauty." Jones next assumed a new position at Bishop's University in Lennoxville, Quebec. His appointment at Bishop's was of rather short duration, and its termination may be attributed to another unhappy speech, this time to a group of nurses in neighbouring Sherbrooke, after which he was accused by doctors as being a hippy and communist masquerading in a Sunday suit. In 1963 he took a position as professor of English at the Université de Sherbrooke, where he continues to teach and direct a number of dissertations in comparative Canadian literature. This final change was significant for it marked the beginning of his serious study of the francophone poets of Quebec, which issued in an important translation of Paul-

Marie Lapointe,[2] as well as the founding of the literary review *ellipse* (1969–), devoted to the mutual translation and elucidation of francophone and anglophone poets.

His marriage in 1950 to Betty Jane "Kim" Kimbark, a dedicatee of *The Sun Is Axeman* and mother of his four children (Stephen, Skyler, Tory Joanne, North), dissolved sometime after the move to Sherbrooke. In 1969 he married the translator of Québécois fiction Sheila Fischman. This marriage was of short duration, and Jones subsequently married Monique Grandmangin in December 1976, the year that saw the completion of "The Lampman Poems" and the poems set in Saint Lucia, all of which appeared in *Under the Thunder the Flowers Light Up the Earth*.

Jones first gained recognition as a poet while an undergraduate at McGill, where he won a number of prizes in creative writing. This early verse won the approval of Louis Dudek and Raymond Souster, who began publishing his poetry in *Contact*, *CIV/n*, and *Poets '56*. Somewhat predictably, his first book, *Frost on the Sun*, was published by Contact Press in 1957, edited by both Dudek and Souster. This was followed by *The Sun Is Axeman* (1961), *Phrases from Orpheus* (1967), and *Under the Thunder the Flowers Light Up the Earth* (1977), which was awarded both the Governor General's Award and the President's Medal of the University of Western Ontario (for "The Lampman Poems").

Because of their effect on his poetry, it cannot be overlooked that Jones's hobbies are painting and gardening. He is also one of Canada's most astute critics of Canadian literature. Besides a number of papers and articles, he published *Butterfly on Rock: A Study of Themes and Images in Canadian Literature* in 1970, a fundamental examination of the mythopoeic dimensions of Canadian literature. While its mythopoeic stance and the themes it identifies — particularly that of the "garrison mentality" — immediately suggest Northrop Frye as one of Jones's mentors, one may also detect attitudes more consonant with the thinking of John Sutherland and Frank Davey.[3]

In 1978, the year in which he was awarded the President's Medal, he was elected Fellow of the Royal Society of Canada. With some small measure of irony, perhaps, he was awarded a doctorate (*honoris causa*) in 1982 from the University of Guelph, formerly the Ontario Agricultural College.

Tradition and Milieu

George Woodcock asserts that "D.G. Jones is one of the least placeable and also one of the best of contemporary Canadian poets."[4] True to the degree that such a generalization can be, it contains, nevertheless, a paradox fitting for any understanding of Jones. He cannot be "placed," but configurations of place seek each other everywhere in his work. As one early reviewer observed, "Mr. Jones' world is the normal Ontario with the potential sharks and strange wasps uncovered," but he adds that "even a rake and a tub in a backyard are potentially Mars and Venus."[5] What place, one wants to ask, is Jones's image of Canada always in the process of becoming?

Jones's first encouragement came from Raymond Souster and Louis Dudek, and such encouragement has obvious connotations. Part of the significance of both Souster and Dudek for Canadian letters in the early 1950s may be seen, for example, in the editorial practice of *Contact*, a little magazine that served as an international crossroad for American, Canadian, and European poetry. Its American dimensions were perhaps the most fruitful, for not only did it evince the presence of such modernists as Ezra Pound, Wallace Stevens, and William Carlos Williams, it also published the work of Robert Creeley and Charles Olson before the Black Mountain group had assembled. It was in this milieu, along with Irving Layton, Eli Mandel, and Phyllis Webb, that some of Jones's earliest poems appeared.[6] Although commentators have suggested that traces of all these poets, with the exception of Charles Olson, may be noted in Jones, they have all, for the most part, been carefully assimilated. One may sense an early imitation of T. S. Eliot in "Faculty Party,"[7] but few poets in the 1950s failed to succumb to Eliot. When Phyllis Webb observes Williams and Pound in *The Sun Is Axeman*, she speaks of them as "influences which have been absorbed and used towards a personal utterance."[8] Douglas Barbour, reviewing *Phrases from Orpheus*, with a kind of critical sleight of hand, deftly summed up the problem of literary influence on Jones by remarking: "Although his poetry is not at all like Pound's, the debt is there."[9]

The distinctive quality of Jones's poetry — which anyone who has heard him read knows — is what Phyllis Webb calls its peculiar "syllabic grace" (p. 59). It is a grace that is, perhaps, more indigenous than possible American influences would suggest. George Bowering touches a central truth of Jones's sensibility when he aligns him with Margaret Avison, as well as such venerable masters as D.C. Scott, Charles G.D. Roberts, F.R. Scott, A.J.M. Smith, and E.J. Pratt.[10] This, combined with Robert Frost's tempered pessimism and W.H. Auden's dry voice, would seem to exhaust efforts to find a place for Jones in a strictly literary horizon.[11] The great majority of these poets, both American and Canadian, are "modern." Were it not for Jones's M.A. thesis on Pound, one would tend to speak of his modernism as filtered through Canadian versions. Despite the work on Pound, the proof of Bowering's argument that Jones has steeped himself in a Canadian tradition of which he is a continuation may be found in his most recent collection, *Under the Thunder*. As one reviewer surmised, "... in this volume... we see for the first time just how close the spirit of [Archibald] Lampman is to the imaginative centre of Jones' work."[12] Although the same reviewer asserts that both Jones and Lampman are "under the influence of the Imagists,"[13] this is somewhat anachronistic inasmuch as Lampman died in 1899. The pastoral preoccupation, particularly the sharp awareness of the transience of human life, not to speak of a profound awareness of the Northern environment and its introspective pressures, intimately relate both poets. Thus to situate Jones among the poets who were having a fresh impact on most young poets in the early 1950s means that one must, as any problem of influence requires, never forget the filter, no matter how much in process it might be, through which everything is sifted. One may speak, therefore, of a convergent imaginative stance shared by Lampman and Jones.

One should also consider the role of "place" in Jones's work and how it is perceived, if the distinction is permitted. Place is perception, the manner by which it is articulated, as well as a certain sensibility; and Jones's "place" is, as he once recalled, "the Moodie-Traill-Lampman and — now — Laurence country stretching from Rice Lake (say Port Hope) through Peterboro and the Kawarthas to get lost in the true Laurentian country of Haliburton & Hastings, the hills ringing the Ottawa valley where I still walked (or swam) every summer until my first divorce."[14] It is, to a certain extent, a country of nostalgia, but, more importantly, a country carefully translated through the eyes of several of the painters Jones admires. The artists fall into three groups: modern European (Paul Cézanne, Henri Matisse, Marc Chagall, Pablo Picasso), ancient Chinese (Hokusai, Ni Tsan), and Canadian (David Milne and Alex Colville). There is more than one reference in Jones's poems to the great Swiss artist Paul Klee, and one to the *Très riches heures* of Jean, Duc de Berry. His first book begins with an invocation to John Marin and concludes by summoning Hokusai as mentor; while *Under the Thunder* contains long meditations on both Milne and Colville, not to speak of other painters lesser known. It could be argued that Jones's life as a poet has been governed by one intention: to transpose the visual world into word. Thus he prays in an early poem, "A Problem of Space":

If I could write: Five starlings
Splashing in a muddy pool, and
All around them write a haze of sun,
That is a sort of feeling space, a thing
The Chinese once knew how to do,
I would eliminate this bombast, this
Detail of type, and leave an image,
And a space — in which the birds or trees
Find all their palpable relations with the earth.
                              (*Frost on the Sun*, p. 18)

Poetry, however, is not painting, and the discursive infiltration of painting as language within the poem gives rise to not only distancing but also an effect of doubling. Perception becomes subject, and, as Jones once observed in the course of an interview with Mary Hamilton,

> One thing about paintings generally: they are other landscapes. One can go outside oneself and into another world in terms of painting, rather than in terms of real life.... I, in a sense, inhabit landscapes in paintings as we all real ones [sic]. A painter like Ni Tsan, a Chinese painter, is very much a landscape poet — I mean, painter. He comes into a rather sad poem ["Ni Tsan," in *Under the Thunder*, p. 23] — a kind of death-wish poem, in its essence, although

> it begins by saying I'm waiting for the spring and waiting for desire. As I was looking out my window in North Hatley in the middle of winter, I was looking at the real landscape and, also, in a sense, looking at Ni Tsan's landscape simultaneously. The two became one, in a measure. This was a way to organize *my* landscape and, as well, to make a rather heavy poem, I suppose, rather witty and light.[15]

Painting, then, serves as a vehicle for irony. It permits a kind of double discourse that at once diminishes the presence of the speaking "I" and enhances the sense of polished craft that all readers of Jones note as distinctive among contemporary Canadian poets.

Are his concerns, however, shared? This is difficult to answer, if only because Jones's particular diction and cadence have proved to be inimitable. Any fair assessment, then, of Jones's significance in Canadian letters should take cognizance of his work as critic. His fundamental importance lies in his recognition of a distinct Canadian literary tradition which he has absorbed thoroughly as a poet and illuminated as a critic. It is Canadian in the best cultural sense, for it is deeply aware of the American presence which it draws upon only to refashion, just as it is also aware of European history. What distinguishes Jones even further from his contemporaries is that he is, as *Under the Thunder* evinces, one of our few bilingual poets. What makes this tradition and Jones's position in it vital is the constant reappraisal it undergoes. Speaking of a recurrent thematic complex in his work, Bowering sums up Jones's position as follows:

> Jones makes use of Frye's picture of the garrison of culture *vs.* the hostile land, and gives the sense that he has learnt to identify with the savages who were seen not as inhabitants but as representatives of that unwelcoming surround. One must, he says, learn to let the wilderness in—that is the only way that the mind-forged prison can be escaped. Such is the pre-occupation of Eastern Canadian writers and critics in this age, and Jones is still writing within the tradition, though at its vanguard. (p. 22)

Critical Overview and Context

Jones's poetry has only slowly attracted an audience, and with the exception of two articles it has been the object only of reviews and commentaries. Most reviewers have been favourable. Although James Reaney's review of Jones's first book is somewhat cursory, its recognition of "some very intricate thinking done with some pretty advanced juxtapositions" identifies what will be seen is characteristic of his later poetry.[16] Phyllis Webb's review of *The Sun Is Axeman* was quick to note its "clarity, control, and music" (p. 58). Unlike later commentators, Webb observes that "...Jones appears remarkably at home in [his] longer poems" and attributes this to the lucidity of both his poetic aims and his poetic line (p. 59). Her one demurral — and it is a significant one — is his fear of casting a wake of darkness, a fear which "results in a dodge into coyness" (p. 59). The book's major achievement is summed up as "a distinctive voice, a poetry of lovely assonances, syllabic grace" (p. 59).

The darkness that Jones seemed fearful of casting in his first two volumes enters indeed as a wake in *Phrases from Orpheus*. The book appeared, according to most reviewers, to mark a significant change in Jones's poetic. An exception to this view may be found in a review by Dorothy Livesay, who generally dismisses Jones's poems, because of their detached qualities, as "not to be quarreled with, or quarreled over. They lack the vigour and robustness that we, as Canadians, have become accustomed to in the work of Layton, Souster or Purdy."[17] This detachment may be recognized as a tendency from the earliest book, but it becomes more pronounced by the second. The gain in technique and control is marked by a loss of "concern for the exterior world of reality" (p. 41). "No clamour here," she remarks, "against the injustices of men against men, men against women" (p. 41). Peter Stevens' review is more balanced, and he, striking a position that is generally followed, finds the poet to be more at home in the shorter poems, where his "Orphic vision of the world seems genuine as poetry."[18] The most fervid review of *Phrases* was written by Douglas Barbour, who judged it *ex aequo* with Michael Ondaatje's *The Dainty Monsters* as the major collection of verse published in 1967, and he particularly praises it for its Poundian qualities, as well as its felicitous harmony of sound and meaning.[19]

Reviews of Jones's most recent book, *Under the Thunder the Flowers Light Up the Earth*, have made it apparent that not only has his discourse moved into an essential cadence, but also, in finding himself, he has found himself among some of the most enduring motifs of Canadian literature. John Cook has, as I have already mentioned, emphasized his "special relationship" with the Confederation poet Archibald Lampman, and Bruce Whiteman has observed that the pastoral motifs have become the centre of Jones's discourse. Flowers, he asserts, are "a kind of language of the land" and, as such, "...they are not unlike poems."[20] He suggests William Carlos Williams as a possible instigator of this use of language, but one might also point to "John Marin," the initial poem of *Frost on the Sun*, to find points of departure and return where the poet inquires: "Do poems too have backbones: / stalks of syntax...?" My own review of *Under the Thunder* emphasized both the increasing suppleness of Jones's technique as well as the profundity with which he has come to terms with his wakes of darkness. As I remarked, "...the world of the earlier poems was an object of terrible dissolutions and heroic restitution, but it was never affirmed that the numen of destruction belonged to the same pattern as creation, that their dance was Shiva's, intimately relating both movements into one."[21] Playing upon a recognizable dialectic in his work between garrison and wilderness, I suggested that what was new in this collection was that "...to be disarmed, to be naked, a situation that Jones frequently gives voice to, is to be in the dark and predisposed to name the new landscape" (p. 101). One result of accepting this new dwelling — outside the garrison of the spectator — is that "...*Under the Thunder* brings to fruition and closes the brief reign of nature as terror in Canadian letters" (p. 101).

In a brief critical note on Jones's poetry, Eli Mandel raises an issue implicit in any discussion of his work as part of a tradition. He asks whether originality is, "like sincerity, a doubtful notion of poetic value."[22] The other question he poses, equally worthy of consideration, is whether "'distancing' removes you from the poem or moves you into it."[23] These are central concerns for any examination of Jones's poetic that are usually, with rare exceptions, discussed without being examined in themselves. Frank Davey, for example, simply assumes that "distance" is an attitude not worthy of praise. Commenting on *The Sun Is Axeman*, he notes "an insistent iambic rhythm which works against any sense of authentic, spontaneous emotion."[24] Almost echoing Livesay, Davey suggests that Jones has lost the power of his early poems where the concentration on particularity — as opposed to "personal meditations on people and events in his private life" (p. 146) — is "the offspring of a vital, beautiful, and eternal cosmos which transcends individual mortality and gives meaning to all our petty destinies" (p. 145). Gary Geddes and Phyllis Bruce, by contrast, observe continuous growth in Jones's skill from the early poetry that was "too general, too abstract" and in which the "sense of logic, or intellect, was oppressive."[25] His second collection evinces organic metaphors, and his later poetry is praised for its "sculptural quality" and "sharpness of outline."[26]

The two longer analyses of Jones's poetic differ in one fundamental respect: while I argue in "Masks of D.G. Jones" that Jones's work is marked by a central preoccupation with the optics of illusion, George Bowering, in his article "Coming Home to the World," "narrates" the changes that have occurred in the poet's continual understanding of himself in relation to his craft and his Central Canadian tradition. My argument is based on Jones's powerful attraction to painting, the "other landscape" that serves as another dwelling. What appears to be a kind of didacticism in the early poems I take to be a function of his interest in visual proportioning, which corresponds to the ease with which he adopts various personae or masks (p. 166). This may be a reflex of his interest in Pound, a possibility that I left out of account. Giving no specific preference to either the longer or shorter poems, I tried, nevertheless, to indicate the originality of the title poem from *Phrases from Orpheus* in its relation to the European use of the myth, stressing the transformation of the theme of loss into a problem of visual deception which is effectively played out in Jones's use of language. Bowering's emphasis may be seen in the title of his paper, suggesting that Jones's development as a poet was a problem of appropriation and of learning how to abandon the perfections of idealism (p. 35). Jones's poetic is examined as a "progress from intelligence noetic to intelligence heuristic" in which the dialectic between reality and myth is resolved in favour of the actual (p. 7). The context of the dialectic is elaborated as a particularly Eastern Canadian, "Anglo" problem (and for this Bowering relies on *Butterfly on Rock* as a commentary on Jones's own poetics) whose resolution requires a "replacement of the ego" that once "peered over the battlements of the stockade [and] now...is looking for an explorer's way across the uncharted continent" (p. 22). The new position "is a placement of himself, his love, his poem, *in* nature, *as* nature" (p. 24).

Because of the usefulness of *Butterfly on Rock* as an exposition of Jones's poetic thought, some attention must also be paid to its reception. D. O. Spettigue finds its thesis "original," if not "new."[27] He criticizes its Frygian bias, its emphasis on English-Canadian as Canadian, and its willingness to adopt Turner's "frontier hypothesis" as the route to survival. Its originality is a function of its one-sided view. George Woodcock finds the study at once original and important, but not literary criticism. Rather, "it uses literature to discuss the myths and eventually the moral structure of a society at a critical point in its dialogue with the natural world."[28] For W. H. New, the energy and the limitation of the book reside in the paradoxes it affirms: "In death is life; in sacrifice is discovery; in the reality is the shadow and in the shadow is reality."[29] Part of the book's problem and strength is the variety of positions woven into it: "Jung makes it into the book, Freud is inferentially acknowledged, and Darwin is left out in the cold, yet it is Darwinian theory...that has furnished the imagery and the outlook of so much Canadian poetry."[30] It is ironic (perhaps) that Louis Dudek, Jones's sometime mentor, exuberantly turns upon *Butterfly on Rock* as the unhappy work of a "simon-pure disciple" of Northrop Frye.[31] His "main objection to Jones's book is that it overlays the literature with a formulaic myth derived from Frye"; and, moreover, Jones "flagrantly misinterprets his authors to fit his general theory" (pp. 58–59). So far from being merely one-sided or perceiving hope in a paradox, Jones is castigated for being "behindhand" in his rush to embrace the dark rather than the light; already "Hitler and Stalin were long before him in embracing 'the so-called forces of darkness'" (p. 58). Although Dudek recognizes himself as the author of the anonymous statement in the book's Introduction that "one can never be sure...the result [of such literary analysis] is not simply another poem,"[32] he fails to elaborate on the metapoetic value of such criticism. It is simply wrong because of its "godlike" didacticism that apparently predicts the future and, therefore, "breaks the First Commandment" (p. 59). The thesis of the book, however, has been readily grasped by all its readers, and its fundamental value, as for most literary criticism written by poets and novelists, is with regard to its author's own poetry. As George Woodcock accurately declares, Jones's "poetic achievement finds a mirror image in *Butterfly on Rock*."[33]

Jones's Works

Because of the implicit importance of *Butterfly on Rock* for an understanding of the themes privileged in Jones's critical thinking, it would be tempting to begin an exposition of his poetic by an analysis of those themes. But the book's virtues as a mythopoeic guide make it fundamentally deceptive as a way into his poetry for it uses Canadian fiction to tell a story. Thus his criticism is allegorical metafiction, and, if that is forgotten, the central activity of his poetic text will be lost. Hence to concentrate on the themes at the expense of the method is not to be recommended. What I shall do, rather, is begin by offering a reading of *Butterfly* by inquiring into its play as a metafiction.

By "metafiction" I follow Linda Hutcheon's definition, namely, a "fiction that includes within itself a commentary on its own narrative and/or linguistic identity."[34] It is precisely this posture — to so order a body of fiction as to produce through narration and commentary on that narration a new fiction — that marks *Butterfly* and that subordinates the criticism to a grander design. This, it must be assumed, is what Jones means when he states in the Introduction that

> ...the persistent concern of widely different authors with similar themes and images certainly suggests that the individual writers share a common cultural predicament. It may also suggest that they participate in and help to articulate a larger imaginative world, a supreme fiction of the kind that embodies the dreams and nightmares of a people, shapes their imaginative vision of the world, and defines, as it evolves, their cultural identity. (p. 4)

The new fiction, then, is a revelation of what was tentatively being sought in its several manifestations in poetry and prose, and it is "supreme" because it is drawn into one, overarching, self-articulating statement. That statement is the sum of the narration of *Butterfly*, a narrative whose story and discourse may be seen as a rearticulation in biblical and Jungian terms of Adam, Eve, Job, Moses, Noah, Abraham, David, Christ seeking new, archetypal form in Canadian fiction. "If the world of Canadian literature," it is hypothesized, "is an Old Testament world, it is a world of Adam separated from his Creator and cast out of Eden to wander in the wilderness" (p. 15). If this is true, it may be further asserted that "... the poets and novelists who produced this literature are not simply the advanced victims of a national neurosis, but also the prophets of the Old Testament who can raise the smoke from our haunted chimneys" (p. 15).

The pivotal figure in this transposed world is Job, about whom it is asked in the central chapter of the book ("The Problem of Job"): "What shall we make of Leviathan?" (p. 88). The answer is: "However terrifying Behemoth and Leviathan, we must neither cower before them nor try to annihilate them. We must somehow learn to delight in them" (p. 110). To enact this essential enterprise of Canadian literature, its writers — who are our prophets — have all learned to

> abandon the garrison of an exclusive culture and go into the wilderness, where they experience, not a greater sense of alienation, but a greater sense of vitality and community. Implicitly or explicitly, each may be said to accept the fellowship of death, to lie down with the grass snake among all the other skeletons of badgers and raccoons and men, only to discover that the one great serpent has crept out upon the sky and coiled about his head like a crown of power. The night is transfigured, and a menacing world takes on the beauty of strength broken by strength and still strong. (p. 136)

The world of Canadian literature participates, then, in a profound drama of Jungian proportions, of existential risks, and Romantic ecstasy. That a movement must take place is implicit in the basic situation that constitutes the hub of the drama, for the price of civilization's hostility towards an equally hostile nature is a sense of alienation, the point of departure of Canada's supreme fiction. It is the alienation of Adam, the "sleeping giant," parted from God, of "Eve in dejection" parted from Adam, of "the dictatorship of the mind" that drives both Adam and Eve farther from each other and their shared nature. Into this zone of alienation enters Job, speaking through both the Confederation poets and those who follow (E.J. Pratt, A.J.M. Smith, Earle Birney, and Irving Layton), who is prepared to embrace the enemy. Thus the "courage to be" translates itself into a "sacrificial embrace" in which opposition is at once overcome and reconciled, and through death one is born anew.

Although Bowering suggests that this was Jones's thinking by the end of the 1960s (p. 22), hints of such attitudes are apparent already a decade earlier. In "A Letter on Poetry and Belief," Jones remarks that "...as Conrad suggests, values must be born of experience, by abandoning oneself to the deep, deep sea and moving the arms and legs so that it bears you up."[35] Furthermore, one of his recommendations for finding significance in one's life is to

> grasp what seems significant in one's own experience; accept what others have expressed as significant, if it rings true in terms of one's own; try to make these significances explicit, and to translate those couched in older symbolism and in what appear to be outmoded theories, into acceptable language. (p. 19)

Already in this letter, Jones appeals to Jung, preparing the process of integration and individuation that will become the operative narrative shifter of *Butterfly*. The key *actant* in the story is either the artist-prophet who envisions the process as one "going beyond death" (p. 18) or a fictional character who embodies the division that civilization's hostility brings about. These figures are outcasts, Indians, half-breeds, and Eve figures, who urge upon us the necessity to "realize one's own nature and the nature of the rest of the universe (man being not opposed to nature but part of the whole)" (p. 20).

As metafiction, *Butterfly on Rock* is a self-illustration of a process that is more general than the opposition of civilization and nature. Of course, the foreground of Jones's argument is dominated by such terms, not to speak of archetypes and mythopoeia, but the operation itself, as a matrix for the story, is the opposition of division and reunion. This opposition is transposed as story, and transposed again in the final chapter into a discussion on the problem of syntax and articulation itself, which is the same problem of the story discussed as discourse conscious of itself. The story ends in discourse finding its true speech, its true "place." The process of both the story and the discourse is governed by an emphasis on transition, translation, and (inasmuch as on a certain level it means the same thing) metaphor. The process by which the Old Testament is translated into Canadian literature is metaphorical, and it is always conducted with the awareness that articulation implies allegory and that allegory implies reality. The allegory is at once in the story and its discourse; for it is the role of speech, finally, "to reveal to nature's divided things their uniqueness and their oneness, their cause for rejoicing" (p. 183). Speech names the world as allegorical by implying a noumenal order unrevealed to the phenomenal and then proceeds to unite the two by uncovering and articulating the relationship. Discourse itself is the problem and the cure, the instrument that reveals division and then translates division into identity.

Allegory, finally, is suggestively didactic, parainetic in tone, exhorting the reader to abandon the stance of the sleeping giant, urging us to "possess that much lamented sense of *patria*, or, more radically, our own souls" (p. 34). To do this, the war that we wage as part of the European heritage "on the wilderness, woman, or the world of spontaneous impulse and irrational desire" (p. 57) must not only cease, but the Apollonian lucidity and masculine arrogance that conduct the war must be transformed. That this is a Canadian challenge marks Jones's thinking as nationalistic, but of the "higher nationalism" that suggests Dennis Lee, and it is in this context that Jones considers Lee's meditations on literature, politics, and technology of such significance. What Jones celebrates in Lee is "an ironic vision that is characteristically Canadian."[36] In this he insists upon Lee's committed openness, a process that seeks identity, but never reaches it, a movement that always stops short of metaphorical fulfilment. Moreover, just as our existential situation is ironic, so is our perception of it "because the irony, for him, enters into the very structure of the moment of vision itself."[37] Thus no matter how important the goal may be, it is the interplay of more than one level of discourse, allegorical in thought and ironic in expression, that provides the functional relation between Jones's prose and his poetry.

The great power of discourse is that it does not merely speak, it gives, in fact, life, and this is the central argument of his paper on translation. "Why do we translate..?" he asks. "Because, in a sense, we have been asked to. It is an immediate response to the cry to be heard, to be recognized, to be given existence in the eyes of others."[38] Jones's sense of translation is profoundly phenomenological, and it suggests the old sense of theological translation. It is an act that not only overcomes the cleavage between "I" and "Other," but does it through the instrumentality of discourse. If one were to transpose the terms, one might readily see how "Other" is a kind of wilderness, an unknown that awaits revelation in an act that lets the wilderness as "Other" in. In a sense, the artist-prophet realizes his/her true function in the act that translates. The artist's centre of operation is fundamentally within the discourse of allegory that permits that continual uncovering of the noumenal world, the reappropriation of a world not necessarily accessible to reason, but, rather, revealed by the "optic heart."[39] That story finally comes to rest in discourse is clear in the declaration that "...the poets of the new world have at last arrived at a clear understanding of the central business of poetry, the creation of a supreme fiction in which the world is the word incarnate."[40] This, of course, is the opening note of *Butterfly*, the reminder from Wallace Stevens that permits the critic to speak almost eschatologically, articulating the supreme, perhaps anagogical, disposition of fiction. It asserts, finally, that had there been no Logos there would be no world. But his Logos is one that has itself been translated, either to its unknown origin in the "Other" or through the story of wilderness into a new revelation.

George Bowering has neatly asserted that of Jones's first two texts, the first is the work of a student and the second the work of a teacher (p.11). From the point of view of style and its development, the remark possesses a certain validity. It does not, however, address itself to what I have argued is the creative centre of Jones's text, the preoccupation with division and the search for a disclosure appropriate to the problem and its resolution. It is a discourse that both seeks the integration of metaphor and displays the problem that prompts the search for completion. Thus, in the initial poem of *Frost on the Sun*, announcing a text extending into several volumes, he asks whether poems have backbones and replies:

> so words, like lovers, their unequal spines
>   wound to frame the one
>   essential backbone
>   bend and sway
> within the rhythm of their physical joy.
>   ("John Marin," p. 5)

The only jarring element in the clause is the uncertainty of the phrase "spines / wound" which makes "wound" either a verb or a past participle, and its function as verb is unprepared. In that sense it may be considered a student's poem, but the poem as a structure insists in every line upon articulation, conjunction, and relation through metaphor. The structure is thickened by the other level of the poem that invokes the American painter John Marin, thereby suggesting the double landscape, the real and painted scene referred to in his interview with Mary Hamilton. The problem for the poet, perceiving the world as a division, sensing that perception itself is governed by an inevitable ambiguity, is knowing what kind of significance might become the most suitable closure. Thus one always senses the presence of the other landscape, ghosting the text, a landscape at once mythological and Christian, as well as the mind of the poet sometimes accepting, sometimes refusing, the closure of any code of other texts, even that of the poem. "I would," he remarks,

> ...eliminate this bombast, this
> Detail of type, and leave an image,
> And a space — in which the birds or trees
> Find all their palpable relations with the earth.
>   ("A Problem of Space," p. 18)

Thus, in the following poem, he illustrates:

> Chink
>   Chunk
> in a foggy tree:
> a muted sun
> on a grey day.
>
> ("Robin," p. 19)

But such sops to Imagism have never proved quite sufficient to Jones: he wants the metaphor, especially the myth of the garden, through which move Eve, Persephone, Christ, himself and his family, a metaphor continuously elaborated and argued with.

If the world is a kind of book, articulated by, as he writes in "John Marin," "stalks of syntax" (p. 5), the poet's problem is a reader's problem. His role is to decipher, suggesting, by doing so, that significance is everywhere. And yet, as he writes in "Birches at RMC,"

> ...these birches are inscrutable,
> A Candida who grows within the mind,
> The ribs of Adam, or the white
> Heart, the text of the November sun.
>
> (p. 15)

If they are inscrutable, one wants to ask, how are they, then, Candida, Adam, heart, and sun? To avoid the problem that such a poem poses, Jones not only plays with the structures and juxtapositions of Imagism, but also directs the reader through the values of the image in such a poem as "On the 24th of May," commenting on cows:

> They look out
> from unnecessarily
> large eyes
> at the bright
> automobiles
> driving northward,
> and are profoundly
> unmoved.
>
> (p. 26)

But the presence of the poet in the adverbs "unnecessarily" and "profoundly" is almost didactic in its insistence, and they are characteristic of one of the difficulties that inhere in a poetics of differences that seeks completion. Having once declared that the November sun has a text, the poet is obliged to read it.

To persuade us that such texts are capable of deciphering, Jones allows the mind to move beyond a free indirect discourse to become the poetic act itself, entering the apparent division between the observer and the observed to find all the "palpable relations with the earth." Thus it is possible to declare that "Birds are thoughts, alive / In the fantastic foliation of the brain" (p. 25). Thus it is the power of thaw to "release the tender shoots of sense and send / each tendril of the brain / into the air" (p. 37). A phoebe who appears to move through the verbs and marginal play of a Williams poem is finally understood through the prism of Stevens: it becomes "the configuration of the mind / performing with ease / an habitual act of thought" (p. 23). The habitual stance, then, of the poet in *Frost on the Sun* is, as one of the titles suggests, "At the Window: Late November," and it is such a stance that dramatizes distance, a space between eye and landscape, of modern world and ancient story, of mind and body, and dramatizes the movements that would suggest that such distance is either illusion or the occasion for play (from Lat. *ludere*, "to play," and *illudere*, "to make game of"). The persistent tone, in consonance with the mode of perception and the habit of thought, is ironic, but the irony is conspicuous for its lack of centre. Dissolution and recombination is a frequent isotopy, but one wonders who the speaker is whose mind is at play among the various codes that produce the scene.

Perhaps we are not to be surprised by the title of one of the poems, "The Time of the Fictitious 'I'": it could stand, in fact, as a description for the learning that the poems acquire in the book. It is an "I" at play, but the play in this collection, unlike the later volumes, has nothing at stake but the problems of observing

> a pristine world, the old
>   calligraphy of living things
>   having been destroyed.
>   ("Northern Water Thrush," p. 32)

To read "the hard crust of wintry grammar" (p. 11), to observe that concealment "...like an art intensifies, / Reveals" (p. 30) is the poet's task. But the universe implied by the text is one that does not allow the mind sufficient play to believe that beyond the limited gesture, significance of any profundity may be uncovered. Like birds, the schoolgirls that "art intensifies" "are profoundly gay" (p. 30). Beyond their gaiety there is nothing to be found there but

> a nonchalant excess of energy,
> itself
> swallowed
> in the unfathomed
> blue.
>
> ("Fire-Crackers," p. 41)

Our dilemma is that

> ... we are shipwrecked on a narrow strand
> between sea and sea:
>   beyond, such flowers and fishes foam
>   as we shall never smell nor see;
>   beyond, such abstract constellations whirl
>   as we may never
>   comprehend.
>
> ("Faculty Party," p. 36)

How much more this book is than a student's first verses: it is heavy with a certain actuality of the 1950s in Canada, "between sea and sea." It is a text whose classicism is ironic, whose sense of the garden is inscribed with wastelands, a book which can be witty ("John Donne"), resigned ("'Stars over Evil Houses'"), enamoured of self-loss ("Keynote"), but its recurrent belief, anticipating the later volumes, is that the fundamental significance of division as a structure always implies that opposition is itself a kind of completion. Thus the death of war and winter's "... wintry grammar / Lies like an eggshell on the lawn" (p. 11). It may be that "lies" is a pun, but I doubt it. The strength of the image resides in a memory of eggshells, their promise of cyclic continuity. Continuity is a myth that contains and announces others: the Christian myth, the Orphic myth, the myth of Persephone, all of which are assiduously explored in the first three books. It is also the myth (or fiction) that underlies *Butterfly on Rock*, always implying that thought and act, body and mind, nature and civilization are tragic, but unnecessary, divisions that can only be overcome by their mergence.[41] As some of Jones's readers have already hinted, such Romanticism makes the classical references appear superfluous, a violation of the organic elaboration of the poem. Such suggestions, I would argue, limit excessively the Romantic gesture, particularly its tendency to universalize the particular in the archetypal. As I have already indicated, however, the problem is not myth, but, rather, the structure by which one chooses to integrate the code.

The fundamental limitation, then, of *Frost on the Sun* is the failure of the speaker himself to enact what he calls for. Only his mind has an eye, and the suffering of the world, the division he would heal, is outside it. Rather than enter that world where, ironically, "The universe spins in a golden eye / And summer shrinks in four black claws" (p. 24), the poet's "Request" is that

> Now may my days prepare,
>   as they like trees and roofs
>   grow more precise,
>   a sky that breaks
>   like great white birds, white,
>   into the full summer of my life.
>   (p. 40)

The full measure of Jones's enterprise may be seen in the fact that summer came with more precision and unexpected pain and that he took the summer in, thus closing the distance between the observance of pain and pain itself.

Jones's second book opens with a celebration of the French-Canadian novelist and poet Anne Hébert. While it is a portrait — thus suggesting an earlier aesthetics — the subject moves, she takes her place in the room. This is a gesture that decisively marks the difference of thought and perception between the first two books. It is also important as a depiction of the writer's act:

> You define
> The morbid tissue, laying it bare
>
> Like a tatter of lace
> Dark
> On the paper.[42]

Thus the writer is no longer an observing scientist — so well implied in "Death of a Hornet" from *Frost on the Sun* — but is now an operating doctor who enters the wound so far as to lay it bare and bring it back to word "on the paper." What is brought back is "Dark," suggesting the direction the poet may now take. But the dark is not the only temptation of the book. The other temptation is the elegant play of language that not only articulates the dark, but also prevents the speaker from entering it. Thus the second poem celebrates F. R. Scott, whose game is one of contradiction and irony by which he is able "In the midst of Babel to create / A paradise from fools" (p. 4). An undertone in the poem cannot be missed, that language, the more eloquent it becomes, is its own labyrinth, creating and controlling its own oppositions.

One of the important discoveries of language and its speaker is dramatized in the poem "The River: North of Guelph," judiciously reprinted from *Frost on the Sun*. Formally, it suggests an eighteenth-century aesthetic in its design. The speaker gazes at the river, sees it as a reflection of himself, and then draws a relation between the two; but the invocation —

> Quiet river, brief
>   image of my boredom,
>   you reflect
> the flatness of my soul....
>
> (p. 12)

recalls Charles Baudelaire's famous image of the ocean as a "calme plat, grand miroir / de mon désespoir."[43] The appeal that develops from the situation is the first of several meditations that would allow the world and the mind of the poet to converge in appropriate discourse. He prays that his mind "be"

> sheer, like crystal,
>   clear, that each
> tree or stone, each
>   whistling bird or shrill
>   face, in field or street,
> may be itself, seen,
>   undistorted, may be itself,
>   revealed, as in the wild
> brilliance of the sun.
>
> (p. 12)

Thus the exchange between river and soul issues in a poetic that reveals in an allegorical gesture the otherwise hidden, thereby including a dimension that Imagism brackets out. The poem must be *dianoia*, an act of thought, but thought whose subjectivity becomes "translucent glass." It is a poem whose importance, however, is not fully realized in this volume; for, with the exception of "Soliloquy to Absent Friends," the development of a subject that speaks its mind — the world reflected through it — is subordinated to more formal problems, chiefly the design of the poem. What is the price paid by the mind for fleeing night and darkness? It is to be cut down by the sun as axeman, whose clarity and "logos" "...clear / Kindling from these rocky hills" (p. 6). But although the light is held suspect, unwittingly,

> ...moon-eyed I hailed
> My marbled flesh, my dazzling skeleton.
> I fled the night into the sun.
> ("I Fled the Night," p. 17)

The sun, however, is a necessary axeman, one that sustains mortality, sustaining life through its completion in the metamorphosis of death, and so Jones's exhorts, intimating us all as fish,

> Fall so
> and so rise
> radiant into the sun-burst spray — rooted
> in death, life flowers
>   like the golden
>   lotus on the waves.
> ("Soliloquy," p. 41)

The sun, then, symbolized through Indian thought as death, contains the death that it prevents and gives. It is the central image of Jones's poetics, the axeman that causes the division, the sun where the falcon hides (p. 60), and the sun that "...came like a sea / To flood a barren world" (p. 58).

Anne Hébert, as I have mentioned, enters space and operates with words. It is a marvellous gesture for prologues, but insufficient, as the poet discovers, for the larger act required to "deliver the dark itself."[44] Thus a number of poems in the centre of the book — "Little Night Journey," "Odysseus," "Disintegration in a Dream of Love," preceded by "I Fled the Night," and "Antibes: Variations on a Theme" — all probe the dark to a limited extent, but now it is the poet, as well as his surgical words, that begins to probe and is in turn probed. Thus, in "Little Night Journey," he awakes "like Lazarus" where "the fisherman glides, my soul in his eyes" (p. 21), learning to see the pastoral world from death's point of view. The difference between this poem and the earlier pastorals of *Frost on the Sun*, even such a poem as "Death of a Hornet," could not be more manifest: death is now gradually being incorporated.

What strikes one in this act of deliverance is the passivity of the speaker: Odysseus is entered by dark and cries, "I am struck blind!" (p. 25). Of love it is observed that it is "...as though the stars / rushed in upon a void..." (p. 26). Elsewhere Jones speaks of femininity and passivity as a necessity for the health of the world, and it is just such passivity that begins to develop in these poems as the necessary gesture of healing. Division is breached through disintegration and dissolution.[45] Thus, in "Disintegration in a Dream of Love," he appeals for "...generosity against fear — to drown, / submit, to be one / body like the dreaming god" (p. 27). Through dissolution, as he intimates in "Soliloquy to Absent Friends," one is conjoined with the key figures of *Butterfly on Rock*, the women and outcasts capable of moving through opposing zones of civilization and nature or, in this instance, light and dark. The poem begins with an epigraph that describes the sun as *"A mirror of the logos, flared / And cracked across our lives"* (p. 36), and one might infer from this that the problem of the poem is one of learning how to live with a central myth that contains its opposite. A cracked Logos would be reason gone mad, and it is just such a conjunction of reason and unreason, light and dark, that continually suggests itself as the centre of Jones's poetic. Entry into the centre is a process of dissolution, and this is the initial movement of "Soliloquy to Absent Friends." As he tells Micheline, the addressee of the poem, the towns and streets where they used to play have all dissolved, leaving only her and the speaker, who "...stare / abruptly upon tundra and the sky — / soul's frontiers where we meet" (p. 36). The situation is the inverse of pastoral, a wasteland in a time of late fall. To live with this absence is to learn, as the speaker asserts in the second section, passivity, and

>   ...to sit still
>   like a child in the yard
> while the whole bleak catastrophe of winter
> descends like a glacier into the soul.
>
> (p. 37)

It means, in the third section, "to love these hopeless things" (p. 38), such passive objects as Williams' red wheelbarrow "or a broken basket of clothespins / slowly filling with snow" (p. 37). Opposed to a notion of *homo faber* making, building, and spending, the speaker hails Quixote, whose hands are but "unproductive gestures on the air" and whose function is to "...root us in the vast / silence, the abyss where elsewise all things drift, / a rain of fragments falling into death" (p. 38). The fourth section is a magnificent *ekphrasis* designed to take the reader through winter and the death it implies by taking him through "...the winter hills / In the Duke of Berry's *Book of Hours*" (p. 39). This healing through painting is performed by transforming dissolution into an act that relates. Although the hills are dissolving,

>   No distance, no abyss,
> Between the Duke of Berry and his book,
> Between the reader and the Duke's last breath,
> No individual presentiment of death, yawns whiter
> Than the stretch of snow that patient ass
> Plods beneath the failing light....
>
> (p. 39)

From such "homely comfort" as proceeds from this modern myth of mediaeval life, the speaker admonishes, "Let us be bare, / Let us be poor," for not only will the sun's other side appear in spring, but also "...will come / ....leaves — as though our tongues / grew green with language and informed a world" (p. 40).

One cannot miss in this poem an incredible assurance, a knowledge that takes the speaker with great elegance and poise precisely where he wants to go both through the "other landscape" of painting and into a consonance of language and organic world. One cannot help but observe, furthermore, that the speaker's immediate world has become integrated with the former "nonchalant," incomprehensible universe that surrounds the poems of *Frost on the Sun*. Through the *Book of Hours*, we are bid to understand that "... so bound round is the abyss, / The winter void, by battle and by labour and by love, / By homely comfort that will warm the thighs," that now everyone "may find one bed together against cold" (pp. 39–40). This poem is the articulation of a movement of spirit that brought Jones to the apparent simplicity of such a poem as "For Françoise Adnet," where the homely act of preparing an evening meal admits of dissolutions in which "Time and space, it glows / Like the white tablecloth" (p. 53). But Jones had to wait another ten years, for the poems that formed *Under the Thunder*, to find how to allow the universe to enter this simplicity most persuasively.

The other great poem of *Axeman* is "Snow Buntings," which elaborates on the other aspect of illusion that I have mentioned, that is, play. It was written at the request of a sculptor, permitting entry again into the other landscape. The birds themselves are seen as linking figures, envisioned repeatedly in the first seven sections as "like" something else. They mark the world as allegorical, and they rhetorically invite movement between these two spaces. They are like snow, earth, "... nothing made of wood / Or stone" (p. 59), skeletons, seeds. They also recall the question raised about the discourse of poetry in "John Marin": "They are a fragile / Syntax drying in the wind" (p. 60). But while their relation with other things is through simile for the most part, they are continually "becoming something else" (p. 59). They are the synecdoche of the metamorphoses of nature, and the poet exhorts the sculptor to imitate this process by lying "... down in the dark / In the naked fields" (p. 62). His counsel, implicit in "Soliloquy to Absent Friends,"is to see art as a process of dissolution that participates in the larger dissolutions of the natural world where death is change made manifest. The birds are also a sign of the necessary passivity that is part of becoming the process of art, for they live always under the falcon hanging in the sun who "Drops like stone, like carved stone, / Explodes / / Without resentment on the timid bird" (p. 60). That the falcon also participates in the artistic process, whose assertion gives the birds' passivity its distinction, is significant, for the act of the artist is twofold: it at once invades (the sculptor cuts into stone or wood) as it is invaded. The addressee of the poem is told: "You must think of the birds / / And make them as you will" (p. 62). The sculptor recalls Anne Hébert, with whom the book opens and whose "Each decision / Cuts like a scalpel" (p. 3), but it is a role of action that is not returned to in the subsequent two volumes. The world is displayed, moreover, to the poet as a process of continual dissolution that overcomes division and difference through transformation. It is the world as seen in "Boy in the Lamont Poetry Room, Harvard" by the boy who is "Rocked by a rhetoric I cannot hear," and who might become "...Thoth, / Wild with declamation..." leaving us "like so many cows, Chagall's, in a shaken world" (p. 42). This is the adventure that may occur as a kind of synapse between the frontiers of two opposing rhetorics, codes, or landscapes through whose intersections "...as at a change of heart, / the earth renews" (p. 48).

The proleptic importance of "The River: North of Guelph" as a discovery of the mind as translucence may be seen from the first lines of "The Perishing Bird," the initial poem of *Phrases from Orpheus*: "The mind is not / Its own place / Except in Hell."[46] By means of a gesture whose significance is more profound than the thematics of death and wilderness, the poem discovers that "...the mind is not / A place at all, / But a harmony of now" (p. 8). It is a place open to articulation, receptive, always attuned to changes of configuration. Its passivity, prepared for entries, takes shape before the reader as a position in which the speaker assumes a stance of generous absence:

I have nothing to give you but a place to stand.
I will be nature and uncritical.
You may walk in me and be alone.
                    ("A Place for 'P,'" p. 51)

This book, instinct with all the assurance announced in "Soliloquy to Absent Friends," is the text that finally falls open to the dark whose deliverance is necessary to save the light. Its central myth, as the title indicates, is that of Orpheus, and its articulation is through music "...composed / Of clear chords / And silence." Filled with that music, "...we are dumb / As water / Mirroring the stars" (p. 22); and thus, as readers, we complete the opposition of music and silence, presence and absence, light and dark.

It might appear that music as a second landscape is a departure from the landscapes of painting that are so frequent in the previous two volumes. In this text, however, music and painting are linked: "I am," we are told, "Phosphor / whistling for the dawn" (p. 21). Moreover, in the title poem, just as it is intimated that Eurydice finds her analogue in Persephone, so Phoebus Apollo, the sun-god, corresponds to Orpheus. The light borne by the great singer into the underworld is music, and the darkness there is "labyrinths through which the winds / wander like a ruined cry" (p. 57). This new note that emerges from adopting the mask of Orpheus possesses one fundamental value: it frees the speaker from the lingering stasis of the earlier texts. The great quality of both *Phrases* and the subsequent volume is their admirable fluidity and modulation. What he urges upon the sculptor in "Snow Buntings" is an exhortation to which he now attends. He has learned, he has "proved upon our pulses,"[47] as Keats would say, that poetry is a response to listening well, and he is now prepared to answer his own question:

Oh, suddenly sky is a wind
And it wades through the grass, the cedars,
The water —

Who traces its passage?
                    ("Places of Memory," p. 42)

The music is passage, "a fugitive flute" (p. 43) in which "...all things / Deliquesce, arrange, and rearrange in field" (p. 15).

Part of the distinctive power of *Phrases from Orpheus* is its ambiguity: through the mask of Orpheus, Jones brings a former tendency to see event as myth to fruition and, thus, at the same time is able to abandon it. Myth no longer would come as judiciously scattered names, synecdoches that gather their stories into themselves. Its new guise would show itself as the process beneath the story — shaping, phrasing, a quality of voice. The book, then, is a celebration of "the ephemeral substantiality of things" (p. 16), dissolution as a way of losing and reclaiming. Thus, as Bowering aptly notes (p. 21), a frequent word in this text is "naked" and, one ought to add, "expose," both words sharing with "dissolution" a creative ambiguity. For exposure, as both "Beyond the Photograph" and "Development" argue, is passage into "the inexorable / emergence / / next" (p. 39). It is for this reason that, despite the incredibly assured voice, one has a sense that something in these poems has not quite reached fruition beyond the new awareness and marvellously lyrical phrasing. Where is, one wants to know, the "somewhere else" with which "Development" concludes? It is true that "All undergo / Metamorphosis," and the end of all that transformation is a silence that "... shall compose / All but the ashes in the pale dawn / And even those" (p. 22), but to what end?

The recurrent note, then, of these poems is elegiac, speaking, on one level, of the end of a marriage and, on another, of a change in poetic stance. Its beauty springs from the passivity discovered in *The Sun Is Axeman*, the almost punishing desire on the speaker's part to open himself to the invasions of dark to discover in nature that "This two-bit creek makes / / Sense at last" (p. 19). It makes sense, however, as nature, apart from man, something, as we are told in "Mr. Wilson, the World," that is there for us "to recreate" (p. 16). But while the speaker is open to process, his entry into it remains tentative, self-protective. He confesses that

> what I protect is your
> capacity for loss,
>
> your freedom to be no one, look
> so naked from that window
> you are lost in light.
> ("On a Picture of Your House," p. 34)

The elegy of which the other poems in the book are preparations and epilogues is the title poem that, by announcing itself as Orphic, must engage the problem of loss, the role of poetry, and the relation of the two landscapes which are, in this instance,

Eden and wasteland, the actual and the photographic. If the dark is to be delivered, this is the mythic context for such deliverance. The speaker is acutely aware of his particular obstacle: to enter the dark, one must, as he says by way of prologue, enter the "prison / behind the eyes" (p. 56). There is hardly a passage in the poem, furthermore, that does not reckon with eyes, sight, and photography, only to emerge with the speaker praying to be blind, as if light and sight were a curse that required expiation, as if vision and what it beheld were all illusion. This is played out contrapuntally in the following passage:

The light

winks, flames
like Cancer or the Crab
or anger

  We are fed

in the eye of God

  in solitary, albeit blind
  and intimate

(p. 62)

Only in dark does he discover what, as Orpheus, he would not have believed with the light of reason: Eurydice has become transfigured into Persephone and "her hair / is now the harp of Dis" (p. 69). Thus she is not among those who die for love, but was seduced by death itself. This is a curious conflation of myths, and this is partly why some readers have been left baffled by the poem.[48] The poem is further complicated by reminiscences of an unknown "... girl like a blonde / wolf..." (p. 59), as well as more pointed references to the speaker's father and brother. Finally, the poem does not end in insight, but exhaustion. How, then, is its significance to be derived?

   I take it that it is to be read as traditional (post-Vergilian) elegy, a purgation through music. The music is present not only as metaphor and phrasing, but also through the counterpoint of the margins that force the reader to move through seeing to hearing.

At its centre one reaches a visual dead end where the girl, the apparent object of the descent, is not "a shy / animal in grass," but "more the negative / of that / / posed photograph / and tan / girl in sunlight" (p. 68). She is not "yet exposed...but dark" (p. 68). This is either a failure of the poet's vision or, perhaps, one of the discoveries of the poem, namely, that the woman who seemed the object of the quest is only incidental to it. In every sense, Orpheus loses Eurydice, and in losing her he loses himself. This not only appears to be the argument of the book and poem, but it also suggests to the reader that this loss of myth as story was the poem's object and discovery. What could reinforce this more than the poem directly following, called laconically "Putting On the Storms"? As the speaker observes, "I clean the windows, do not see / What is inside—transparency" (p. 71). It is difficult not to read this poem as a double reflection on "Phrases" both in its tone and thematic comment. Does one return from hell to emerge in North Hatley, for what other relation is there between the "quiet lake" at the end of "Phrases" and the place in the following poem where "there are no fishermen on the lake" (p. 71)? And do these fishermen intentionally recall the fisherman (Charon) in "Little Night Journey" from *Axeman*? If they are all part of the same vision, then the moving out of "Phrases" is abrupt indeed, but it is an abruptness that nudges the reader towards a new farewell, this time "To Eve in Bitterness," in which the woman is still of legendary status, but the speaker has given up his corresponding role as Adam to be a mere anonymous angel. The following poem with its new roles of Electra and Orestes seems misplaced in the volume, but the book moves on to delicate exposures and transformations to conclude in a final retrospective elegy, "For Eve."

The book, then, is at once a giving up and a venturing forth to a new threshold, an "Aerial music" that "...transforms / / This window to a world" (p. 76). It adopts masks and myths only to acquire their secret, not their story, and their secret is that the dark does not always contain what we expect it to, that often it contains failures that conduce to no other discovery than a kind of weary disillusion. What, for example, is to be done with the dead, whose "eyes, like Argus dreaming, are / turned inward" (p. 70)? What kind of deception is this, where Eurydice is but a negative and Orpheus is rendered blind? It is a harrowing response to all the earlier poems that attempted to seize the world, the woman, and nature by simply holding each in one's gaze, suggesting from "Phrases" "those lovers withered, / crucified / / upon the beam of sight" (p. 67). Such passivity is no longer granted for it leads only to an illusion of death, mythologies of "Argus dreaming" (p. 70), and it is that death which is delivered and left exposed.

It might be said that the discovery of his most recent book, *Under the Thunder the Flowers Light Up the Earth*, is that "There is no / vanishing point / / the lens is a happy illusion,"[49] and that this is characteristic of the dissolution of the old, ocular order. For if death is in some way an optical illusion, the consequences of this insight have to be absorbed. (Di)vision is intimately dependent upon vision, especially its linearity, its trained inhibition to distinguish rather than harmonize. The lesson of death does not end in blindness, but in an openness that will look upon a northern lake and see hell's lake there. But to see it as natural and not as a touchstone to story, to see it as nature that has absorbed myth, appears inevitable after following Orpheus to a point where illusion and death meet. Yet after the pomp, the disenchantment, the bafflement of "Phrases," what could be more disconcerting than to hear Jones speak "like Lazarus saying, 'What's for breakfast?'" (p. 68). Clearly, to deliver the dark is not merely to gaze upon death and declare it good. It is to learn that death is not in the gazing, for it is not, finally, distinguishable as part of an opposition that would define life. Nor is it the false face of life, but rather a superfluous word to name a false condition. But such knowledge does not make death disappear; instead, it conducts it back to a natural order, emptied of mythologies, and into a discourse that one surmises was being sought as early as "A Problem of Space" in *Frost on the Sun*, when it was his urge to "eliminate this bombast" (p. 18). What was still to be discovered in that poem — how to be Chinese such that "... the birds or trees / Find all their palpable relations with the earth" — is at last displayed.

Yet it would be wrong to infer that Jones in *Under the Thunder* merely reaches fruition as a "nature" poet. If his discourse is one that continually engages "bird" and "tree," it does so fully conscious of itself as a discourse. George Bowering correctly notes that the mark of the new poetry is its "placement of himself, his love, his poem, *in* nature, *as* nature" (p. 24), and the manner of the finding of place is so persuasive that it has an almost religious character, a kind of Taoism that Jones has also recognized in one of his English-Canadian forerunners, F. R. Scott.[50] This, at least, would be one way of understanding the passivity that the earlier poems announce, as well as the marvellous conjunctions made between play and illusion. The poems are also, recalling the discovery of music, enactments of passage, as the high frequency of dated titles indicates.

In each of Jones's volumes, the initial poem provides serious clues to major themes and attitudes. *Frost on the Sun* invokes John Marin in order to broach the problem of nature as a certain discourse. *The Sun Is Axeman* again summons language as a surgical instrument liminally probing nature's darker discourse. *Phrases from Orpheus* begins by entering the mind as a harmony moving through time and finding its own place in hell. The discourse is music whose function is to uncover, revealing the coherence of all things. The full realization of such a possibility is announced in the opening lines of "A Garland of Milne," the first poem of *Under the Thunder*:

> He lived in the bush, the wilderness
> but he made light of it
>
> He was at home, sitting
> with the small birds around him
> gathering seeds....
>
> (p. 9)

Thus David Milne, a Canadian artist and, for Jones, a heroic figure,[51] is also invoked as the man who conjoins scenes, the real and the painted, and when he does so, he makes "light" of it, the pun serving as metaphor and allegory, and also preparing the ambiguity of "...him / gathering seeds...." This is at once play and illusion, a game-show that acquiesces in illusion, allowing wilderness to become garden. Part of the Canadian myth, which Frye has discussed at length and Bowering reminds us of, is the wilderness whose terror and chaos must be brought to order. This order, as Jones indicates elsewhere, is a metonymical order of railway and road, connecting by cutting open.[52] Far from invading, Milne *lives* in the bush. This is an essential difference with the English-Canadian myth, and the difference produces a modification in structure. Division, the opposition of wilderness and civilization, is not only an illness seeking a cure (as suggested by "Portrait of Anne Hébert"), but also a break, "...an occasion // to discover love" (p. 33). Such a pun (from a poem entitled "Dance for One Leg") is, thus, a transformational structure, demonstrating how oppositions metaphorically, not metonymically, relate. It is this new consciousness that also marks Jones, according to his own argument, as a poet who contains the cultural possibilities of both Quebec and English Canada.[53]

The other significant distinction between this collection and the previous two is the absence of a major long poem dramatizing the speaker in essential confrontation. No poem in *Under the Thunder* may be identified as in some way climactic, for all the poems are engaged in the same discourse of play. The great section is the sequence "Kate, these flowers...(The Lampman Poems)"; and if these poems are to be privileged, it is not only because of their marvellous voice, ironic shifts, and lyric ease, but also because of the subliminal imprint they all bear of names of flowers written with the first letters of the lines descending on the page. So unobtrusively does this occur that one cannot help but feel they do indeed incorporate "stalks of syntax" and thereby constitute Jones's poetic in quintessential fashion. They are the answer to so many exhortations to painters, sculptors, and musicians in the earlier poems to find and utter a discourse of nature whose former hostility is now inscribed into the design of the poem itself. The second, for example, spells "Kate my red rose," and the poet (Lampman's persona) addresses that Kate who is at once rose, beloved, and discourse; for, as the final line beautifully intimates, her mouth, kissing, makes his mouth, the synecdoche of the poet, holy, that "...would find / election in your mouth" (p. 76). It is a superb pun, reminiscent of Jones's early attraction to Donne, but displayed within a poetic wholly Jones's own, marking his own metaphor and his own allegory. The twelfth, spelling "pois de senteur" (sweet-pea), turns odour ("senteur") into "...butterflies / exhaling scent, the violet, the rose / nuances of remembered flesh," and autumn landscape in which the frost, the new wilderness of "A Garland of Milne," conspires to "restore our pristine nakedness" (p. 86). The fifth is the text of "pale snowdrops," early spring flowers, their name ambiguous, raising the initial question and movement of the poem — "Puritan or paradox?" — and answered in ambiguous assonance, "...thus apparent / paradox" (p. 79). Paradox, whether seeming or real, remains paradox, but the paradox is that syntax that admits contradiction, not becoming real "until the petalled flesh / speak as to the deaf and blind" (p. 79). That speaking is the discourse that constantly combines all objects possessed of the power to be translated into a play of language. "Thus fields," he observes in the third,

> mimic your grace, thus words
> rearticulate the trace
> of outcast energy
>
> (p. 77)

For what else are words but "petal, sepal, leaf / delicate explosions / / prestidigitations..." (p. 77)?

One might infer from these poems, if we take them as the summit of Jones's art, that they have reduced "experience" to "mere" words. I would suggest that their power resides in their longing to become epiphanies, a fundamental longing, as Paul de Man argues, of the Romantic image as structure. The mark of such an image is that it

> designates a desire for an epiphany but necessarily fails to be an epiphany, because it is pure origination. For it is the essence of language to be capable of origination, but of never achieving the absolute identity with itself that exists in the natural object.[54]

Thus poetic language is never "mere" words, nor is the discourse of these quasi-sonnets, for it is language so employed as to allow it the play that releases word from referent, thereby freeing, for the moment of the poem, nature from its own eternal self-reference to become "...Leacock's humour, the non- / sequitur / deployed against gravity" (p. 68). It is nature taught to laugh at itself, and its laughter is a quality of metamorphosis.

This aspect of nature may also be seen in the early poems, for example in "Clotheslines," the concluding poem of *Frost on the Sun*, but its presence in *Under the Thunder* is a ubiquitous energy that holds all things in the design of momentary poems. It is nature playing at I Ching, a poetics that grounds nature in a transformational grammar, a gesture attributed to Alex Colville:

> what he wished was to fix
> mass and velocity
> in the instant of change
>
> an end to division
>
> ("Pictures by Colville," p. 60)

Thus the typical poem is open-ended in space (on the page), and rarely titled except to indicate moments in time, which are, incidentally, moments that are not always consecutive. This openness relates them most readily to the longer meditations of the previous books, but without the rhetoric and the desire to reach a single meaning or focus. The direction of the poem is to "choose the centre as it moves" (p. 58).

The effect of the rapt attention that such a poetry demands is gnomic, and the process of naming, an incantation, which is displayed so finely in the first of "Three Cast with the I Ching":

> 11 / 9 / 75
> (*Chieh: Removing Obstacles*)
>
> It is not necessary to remove
> leaves from the stone path
>
> nor the orange wheelbarrow on the terrace
> until the garden is dug up
>
> let the body heal — or the heart
> autumn rain
>
> also known as deliverance, this change
> in a season of change
>
> (p. 49)

It is a quality also caught in the best of his French poems:

> J'écoute
> le temps des pommes
>
> Que tu es loin ce soir de ces pommiers
> ("11 / 9 / 75," p. 48)

It is a quality, finally, because of its didactic, reassuring tone, that unlocks the allegorical to discover it is not only "...dead crows / in the refrigerator" (p. 57), but also "exemplary / double agents, hinting / at invisible fields" (p. 64). It could be argued, of course, that the gnomic was always the most recognizable mark of Jones's style, that it had already been discovered in *Phrases* when he had written,

> No, nature regrets
> Nothing, and so words must speak
> Like tragedy, in pure Greek.
> ("Beating the Bushes: Christmas 1963," p. 23)

The persuasiveness of its use in *Under the Thunder* springs, however, from the ease with which it emerges, almost unbidden, effortlessly reminding us of "invisible fields" merely as a tone of voice, and by the manner in which the universal is brought home. Thus Leacock's humour deploys the non sequitur against gravity (both theory and tone), and yet the non sequitur is itself a norm (theory) through which "two small cups and a teapot / create their own gravitational field" (p. 68). The force of the image within the elaboration of the poem insists that the gnomic requires no special speech (e.g., Greek), but only the inevitable passage between unexpected landscapes. One is made to feel it can happen to anyone, that its truth is everywhere and not uniquely embodied in such legendary figures of passage to the other scene as Orpheus, Persephone, or Charon.

The other reason that the gnomic qualities of the recent poetry are convincing is that it "regrets nothing" and, therefore, speaks less like "Greek" and more like "nature." Its power resides in its nonelegiac informality, and in this regard it seems to have returned to those attitudes that aroused the encouragement of Raymond Souster. But if one were to consider again such a poem as "On the 24th of May" from *Frost on the Sun*, the great distance covered from the early poetics would be readily apparent. The cows ("nature") are kept indifferently apart from the automobiles ("civilization"), and the structure of the poem depends upon a neat, implicit distinction between subject and object. The mind, moreover, is not envisioned as glass through which the world is "itself." I would hesitate to say that the fundamental achievement of *Under the Thunder* is a fusion of subject and object or, if one were to speak thematically, wilderness and civilization. Rather it is the ease with which the two interchange so that the difference becomes unapparent. Were there a clear fusion, the favourite metaphor of nature as text could not be brought into play. In fact it would be the merest sentimentality on Jones's part to pretend that the subject, the observing mind of the earlier poetry, had somehow given up the game in favour of "nature." Nor would it have been possible to write in the ninth Lampman poem: "Truth, Kate, all your virtues / harrow my flesh, are flesh / etching my mind" (p. 83). The price of fusion would be the loss of metaphor and epiphany as possibility. The interplay is the source of game, the matrix of humour. As he notes with some surprise in "28 / 10 / 76":

> I wake up with your fingers discovering
> my manhood as your own
>
> I reach behind, astonished
> at my girlish bum
>
> There's a word for us: a myth
>
> (p. 45)

The possibility of myth occurring resides in the fact that object may enter subject and vice versa. In such an exchange, the meaning of subject changes, for its relation to the object, the "Other" that the eye seizes, is functional and therefore subject to modification. The impingement of nature upon the discourse that reveals it continually thickens definition, and the increase suggests a loss, an indistinguishability of subject and object:

>   the world keeps
> dismantling the syntax, escaping
> a final sentence
>   Penelope weaving
> and unweaving, night, day, to
> avoid closure
>   ("The Diamond Sutra," p. 98)

The effect of dismantling "...is not knowledge, no, but a constant / reintegration" (p. 97). How far this is from "John Marin," in which

> ...words, like lovers, their unequal spines
>   wound to frame the one
>   essential backbone
>   (*Frost on the Sun*, p. 5)

This conceit is an aggression that the former poetic of subject *versus* object requires; furthermore, since it requires aggression, this same poetic can only envision the relationship of subject and object as division.

I should not wish my last remark, itself so full of closure, to imply that the difference between the early and later texts is radical. As I have tried to indicate, Jones's poetic from the earliest poems operates by means of a fundamental structure of division and reconciliation. Its viability is demonstrated by a matrix that insists upon discovery and change. It is for this reason that I avoided labelling as dominant the position of the structure "nature" and "civilization," inasmuch as a poetic is not defined by thematic isotopy. It uses such an isotopy, but it precedes thematic exchange and also displays itself in a variety of other ways. Although it is difficult to "explain" the marvellous gnomic, nonelegiac character of the later poems, it is evident that their tone and stance emerge from the energy generated by the structure operating within Jones's poetic. Finally, an approach through story would suggest that Jones, not his persona, descended into hell, from which he returned, purged and reintegrated. Even if one were to accept this as a fiction that concealed a truth, one wonders what hell was entered, for Jones's hell is, at its centre, a hell for artists and writers. It is insufficient as an explanation for the great power of the later poems. Of course, it may be that Jones the man has known hells of various kinds, but how much the poet has revealed of this cannot be measured.

The operation of his poetic has, however, brought Jones to a threshold that marks the beginning of his maturity. He himself appears to have provided a description of where he has arrived in his description of the Québécois poet Paul-Marie Lapointe in the introduction to his translation of selected poems that appeared a year before *Under the Thunder*:

> Lapointe's whole concern in poetry has been to resist [the cynical] simplicities [of the fatalist]. He has always put the emphasis on the first draft, on the spontaneous, on improvisation. He has resisted the trap of discursive logic, linear syntax, even of his own image. Rather than pursue a conceit or extend a metaphor, he would destroy the initial image. The poem explodes like a seed and ramifies. More accurately, perhaps, it is a series of luminous tracks that betray the invisible electrons startled from their atomic sleep. Lapointe would remain faithful to the ambiguity, the indeterminacy, of the movement of experience. And with luck, the elliptical movement of the poem should retain something of its unpredictability, it mysterious coherence, its force.[55]

Evidently, Jones had to move through and gradually abandon all that Lapointe began without. But even to say "abandon" is not quite accurate enough to explain the process by which discursive logic, linear syntax, and extended metaphor, all of which abound in the earlier poetry, are gradually invaded, replaced by other logics which we may call "indeterminacy," the weak shorthand of which does not, however, quite explain the logic of interplay, the mysterious penetration of world into mind. It suggests that for Jones, a poet continually following the moving centre, there is no arrival, only, echoing his own "Letter on Poetry and Belief," "a constant reintegration."

NOTES

¹ Letter received from D. G. Jones, 13 June 1982.
² D. G. Jones, trans., *The Terror of the Snows: Selected Poems*, by Paul-Marie Lapointe (Pittsburgh: Univ. of Pittsburgh Press, 1976).
³ See Malcolm Ross, "Critical Theory: Some Trends," in *Literary History of Canada: Canadian Literature in English*, 2nd. ed., gen. ed. and introd. Carl F. Klinck (Toronto: Univ. of Toronto Press, 1976), III, 169.
⁴ George Woodcock, "Poetry," in Klinck, III, 313.
⁵ James Reaney, rev. of *Frost on the Sun*, *The Canadian Forum*, July 1958, p. 95.
⁶ See Michael Gnarowski, Contact *1952–1954: Being an Index to the Contents of* Contact, *a Little Magazine Edited by Raymond Souster, Together with Notes on the History and the Background of the Periodical* (Montreal: Delta Canada, 1966).
⁷ In *Frost on the Sun* (Toronto: Contact, 1957), pp. 35–36. All further references to this work appear in the text.
⁸ Phyllis Webb, "Guests and Natives," rev. of *The Sun Is Axeman*, *Canadian Literature*, No. 12 (Spring 1962), p. 59. All further references to this work appear in the text.
⁹ Douglas Barbour, rev. of *Phrases from Orpheus*, *The Canadian Forum*, Aug. 1968, p. 120.
¹⁰ George Bowering, "Coming Home to the World," *Canadian Literature*, No. 65 (Summer 1975), p. 8. All further references to this work appear in the text. This article was initially published in French translation as "Etre chez soi dans le monde," *ellipse*, No. 13 (1973), pp. 81–103.
¹¹ Bowering also cites *de rigueur* William Carlos Williams and William Butler Yeats.
¹² John Cook, "Special Relationship," rev. of *Under the Thunder the Flowers Light Up the Earth*, *The Canadian Forum*, June–July 1978, p. 47. Cf. my article "The Masks of D. G. Jones," *Canadian Literature*, No. 60 (Spring 1974), pp. 64–82; rpt. in *Poets and Critics: Essays from Canadian Literature 1966–1974*, ed. George Woodcock (Toronto: Oxford Univ. Press, 1974), p. 168. All further references to this work appear in the text.
¹³ Cook, p. 47.
¹⁴ Letter received from D. G. Jones, 13 June 1982. For further autobiographical reflection, see D. G. Jones, "Sequence of Night," *The Tamarack Review*, Nos. 50–51 (1969), pp. 104–26.

[15] Mary Hamilton, "D.G. Jones: An Interview, February, 1978," in *English 302: An Introduction to Canadian Literature* (Edmonton: Athabasca Univ., n.d.), p. 104.

[16] Reaney, p. 95.

[17] Dorothy Livesay, rev. of *Phrases from Orpheus*, *Quarry*, 17, No. 4 (Summer 1968), 42. All further references to this work appear in the text.

[18] Peter Stevens, "The Poetic Vocation," rev. of *Phrases from Orpheus*, *Canadian Literature*, No. 39 (Winter 1969), p. 80.

[19] Barbour, p. 120.

[20] Bruce Whiteman, "A Riot of Flowers," rev. of *Under the Thunder the Flowers Light Up the Earth*, *Brick*, No. 4 (Fall 1978), p. 59.

[21] E.D. Blodgett, "Where Land Is Love," rev. of *Under the Thunder the Flowers Light Up the Earth*, *Canadian Literature*, No. 84 (Spring 1980), p. 100. All further references to this work appear in the text.

[22] Eli Mandel, ed., *Eight More Canadian Poets* (Toronto: Holt, Rinehart and Winston, 1972), p. 74.

[23] Mandel, p. 74.

[24] Frank Davey, *From There to Here: A Guide to English-Canadian Literature since 1960* (Erin, Ont.: Porcépic, 1974), p. 146. All further references to this work appear in the text.

[25] Gary Geddes and Phyllis Bruce, eds., *15 Canadian Poets Plus 5* (Toronto: Oxford Univ. Press, 1978), p. 388.

[26] Geddes and Bruce, p. 388.

[27] D.O. Spettigue, rev. of *Butterfly on Rock*, *Queen's Quarterly*, 78 (Spring 1971), 154.

[28] George Woodcock, "The Garrison and the Wilderness," rev. of *Butterfly on Rock*, *West Coast Review*, 5, No. 3 (Jan. 1971), 71.

[29] W.H. New, "Quelques Arpents de Papillons," rev. of *Butterfly on Rock*, *Canadian Literature*, No. 47 (Winter 1971), p. 97.

[30] New, p. 97.

[31] Louis Dudek, "The Misuses of Imagination: A Rib-Roasting of Some Recent Canadian Critics," *The Tamarack Review*, No. 60 (Oct. 1973), p. 57. All further references to this work appear in the text.

[32] *Butterfly on Rock: A Study of Themes and Images in Canadian Literature* (Toronto: Univ. of Toronto Press, 1970), p. 4. All further references to this work appear in the text.

[33] Woodcock, "Poetry," p. 313.

[34] Linda Hutcheon, *Narcissistic Narrative: The Metafictional Paradox* (Waterloo: Wilfrid Laurier Univ. Press, 1980), p. 1.

[35] *Delta*, No. 3 (April 1958), p. 18. All further references to this work appear in the text.

[36] D. G. Jones, "In Search of Canada: Dennis Lee's Ironic Vision," *Arc*, No. 1 (Spring 1978), p. 27.

[37] Jones, "In Search of Canada," p. 26.

[38] D. G. Jones "Grounds for Translation," *ellipse*, No. 21 (1977), p. 78.

[39] D. G. Jones, "Cold Eye and Optic Heart: Marshall McLuhan and Some Canadian Poets," *Modern Poetry Studies*, 5 (Autumn 1974), 170–87. This is a crucial article for the understanding of the problematics of vision in Jones's poetics. It was written while the poems in *Under the Thunder* were in progress, and it takes up the divisive use of the eye that McLuhan has discussed and forces it to undergo a process of conversion to see within, to make the dark visible, and to find a corresponding language required by such a re-vision.

[40] D. G. Jones, "In Search of America," *Boundary 2*, *3*, No. 1 (Fall 1974), 244.

[41] D. G. Jones, "Myth, Frye and Canadian Writers," *Canadian Literature*, No. 53 (Winter 1973), p. 14.

[42] "Portrait of Anne Hébert," in *The Sun Is Axeman* (Toronto: Univ. of Toronto Press, 1961), p. 3. All further references to this work appear in the text.

[43] Charles Baudelaire, *Oeuvres complètes*, Bibliothèque de la Pléiade (Paris: Gallimard, 1954), p. 147.

[44] Jones, "Myth," p. 19.

[45] The psychology of this process is discussed by Kazimierz Dabrowski et al., *Mental Growth through Positive Disintegration* (London: Gryf, 1970).

[46] *Phrases from Orpheus* (Toronto: Oxford Univ. Press, 1967), p. 7. All further references to this work appear in the text.

[47] *The Letters of John Keats 1814–1821*, ed. Hyder E. Rollins (Cambridge: Harvard Univ. Press, 1958), 1, 279.

[48] See Davey, p. 146.

[49] "Pictures by Colville," in *Under the Thunder the Flowers Light Up the Earth* (Toronto: Coach House, 1977), p. 59. All further references to this work appear in the text.

[50] D. G. Jones, "Private Space and Public Space in the Poetry of F. R. Scott," in *On F. R. Scott: Essays on His Contributions to Law, Literature and Politics*, ed. Sandra Djwa and R. St. J. Macdonald (Toronto: McGill-Queen's Univ. Press, 1983), pp. 44–54. For Jones's

Taoism, especially its modernity that includes the language of science, see Fritjof Capra, *The Tao of Physics: An Exploration of the Parallels between Modern Physics and Eastern Mysticism* (Berkeley: Shambhala, 1975). See also Jones's discussion of Taoism and the union of opposites, "In Search of America," p. 243.

[51] Hamilton, p. 104.

[52] D.G. Jones, "Canadian Poetry, Roots and New Directions," *Credences: A Journal of Twentieth Century Poetry and Poetics* (in press).

[53] Jones, "Canadian Poetry."

[54] Paul de Man, "Intentional Structure of the Romantic Image," in *Romanticism and Consciousness: Essays in Criticism*, ed. Harold Bloom (New York: Norton, 1970), p. 69.

[55] Jones, trans., *The Terror of the Snows*, p. xv.

SELECTED BIBLIOGRAPHY

Primary Sources

Books

Jones, D.G. *Frost on the Sun.* Toronto: Contact, 1957.
———. *The Sun Is Axeman.* Toronto: Univ. of Toronto Press, 1961.
———. *Phrases from Orpheus.* Toronto: Oxford Univ. Press, 1967.
———. *Butterfly on Rock: A Study of Themes and Images in Canadian Literature.* Toronto: Univ. of Toronto Press, 1970.
———, trans. *The Terror of the Snows: Selected Poems.* By Paul-Marie Lapointe. Pittsburgh: Univ. of Pittsburgh Press, 1976.
———. *Under the Thunder the Flowers Light Up the Earth.* Toronto: Coach House, 1977.

Contributions to Periodicals and Books

Jones, D.G. "A Letter on Poetry and Belief." *Delta*, No. 3 (April 1958), pp. 17–20.
———. "Sequence of Night." *The Tamarack Review*, Nos. 50–51 (1969), pp. 104–26.
———. "Myth, Frye and Canadian Writers." *Canadian Literature*, No. 53 (Winter 1973), pp. 7–22.
———. "Cold Eye and Optic Heart: Marshall McLuhan and Some Canadian Poets." *Modern Poetry Studies*, 5 (Autumn 1974), 170–87.
———. "In Search of America." *Boundary 2*, 3, No. 1 (Fall 1974), 227–46.
———. "Grounds for Translation." *ellipse*, No. 21 (1977), pp. 58–91.
———. "In Search of Canada: Dennis Lee's Ironic Vision." *Arc*, No. 1 (Spring 1978), pp. 23–28.
———. "Un bricoleur parmi les technologues: la vision pastorale de Purdy." *ellipse*, Nos. 27–28 (1981), pp. 94–105.

———. "Canadian Poetry, Roots and New Directions." *Credences: A Journal of Twentieth Century Poetry and Politics* (in press).

———. "The Mythology of Identity: A Canadian Case." In *Driving Home*. Ed. Barbara Belyea and Estelle Dansereau. Waterloo, Ont.: Wilfrid Laurier Univ. Press, 1984.

———. "Private Space and Public Space in the Poetry of F. R. Scott." In *On F. R. Scott: Essays on His Contributions to Law, Literature and Politics*. Ed. Sandra Djwa and R. St. J. Macdonald. Toronto: McGill-Queen's Univ. Press, 1983, pp. 44–54.

Secondary Sources

Barbour, Douglas. Rev. of *Phrases from Orpheus*. *The Canadian Forum*, Aug. 1968, pp. 119–20.

Blodgett, E. D. "The Masks of D. G. Jones." *Canadian Literature*, No. 60 (Spring 1974), pp. 64–82. Rpt. in *Poets and Critics: Essays from Canadian Literature 1966–1974*. Ed. George Woodcock. Toronto: Oxford Univ. Press, 1974, pp. 159–78.

———. "Where Land Is Love." Rev. of *Under the Thunder the Flowers Light Up the Earth*. *Canadian Literature*, No. 84 (Spring 1980), pp. 99–101.

Bowering, George. "Etre chez soi dans le monde." *ellipse*, No. 13 (1973), pp. 81–103. Rpt. ("Coming Home to the World") in *Canadian Literature*, No. 65 (Summer 1975), pp. 7–27.

Capra, Fritjof. *The Tao of Physics: An Exploration of the Parallels between Modern Physics and Eastern Mysticism*. Berkeley: Shambhala, 1975.

Cook, John. "Special Relationship." Rev. of *Under the Thunder the Flowers Light Up the Earth*. *The Canadian Forum*, June–July 1978, pp. 47–48.

Dabrowski, Kazimierz, et. al. *Mental Growth through Positive Disintegration*. London: Gryf, 1970.

Davey, Frank. "D. G. Jones." In *From There to Here: A Guide to English-Canadian Literature since 1960*. Erin, Ont.: Porcépic, 1974, pp. 145–47.

de Man, Paul. "Intentional Structure of the Romantic Image." In *Romanticism and Consciousness: Essays in Criticism*. Ed. Harold Bloom. New York: Norton, 1970, pp. 65–77.

Dudek, Louis. "The Misuses of Imagination: A Rib-Roasting of Some Recent Canadian Critics." *The Tamarack Review*, No. 60 (Oct. 1973), pp. 51–67.

Geddes, Gary and Phyllis Bruce, eds. *15 Canadian Poets Plus 5*. Toronto: Oxford Univ. Press, 1978, pp. 387–89.

Gnarowski, Michael. *Contact 1952–1954: Being an Index to the Contents of Contact, a Little Magazine Edited by Raymond Souster, Together with Notes on the History and the Background of the Periodical*. Montreal: Delta Canada, 1966.

Hamilton, Mary. "D.G. Jones: An Interview, February, 1978." In *English 302: An Introduction to Canadian Literature*. Edmonton: Athabasca Univ., n.d., pp. 103–08.

Hutcheon, Linda. *Narcissistic Narrative: The Metafictional Paradox*. Waterloo: Wilfrid Laurier Univ. Press, 1980.

Livesay, Dorothy. Rev. of *Phrases from Orpheus*. *Quarry*, 17, No. 4 (Summer 1968), 41–42.

Mandel, Eli, ed. *Eight More Canadian Poets*. Toronto: Holt, Rinehart and Winston, 1972, p. 74.

New, W.H. "Quelques Arpents de Papillons." Rev. of *Butterfly on Rock*. *Canadian Literature*, No. 47 (Winter 1971), pp. 94–97.

Reaney, James. Rev. of *Frost on the Sun*. *The Canadian Forum*, July 1958, p. 95.

Ross, Malcolm. "Critical Theory: Some Trends." In *Literary History of Canada: Canadian Literature in English*. 2nd ed. Gen ed. and introd. Carl F. Klinck. Toronto: Univ. of Toronto Press, 1976. III, 160–75.

Spettigue, D.O. Rev. of *Butterfly on Rock*. *Queen's Quarterly*, 78 (Spring 1971), 154–55.

Stevens, Peter. "The Poetic Vocation." Rev. of *Phrases from Orpheus*. *Canadian Literature*, No. 39 (Winter 1969), pp. 77–80.

Webb, Phyllis. "Guests and Natives." Rev. of *The Sun Is Axeman*. *Canadian Literature*, No. 12 (Spring 1962), pp. 58–59.

Whiteman, Bruce. "A Riot of Flowers." Rev. of *Under the Thunder the Flowers Light Up the Earth*. *Brick*, No. 4 (Fall 1978), pp. 58–59.

Woodcock, George. "The Garrison and the Wilderness." Rev. of *Butterfly on Rock*. *West Coast Review*, 5, No. 3 (Jan. 1971), 70–71.

———. "Poetry." In *Literary History of Canada: Canadian Literature in English*. 2nd ed. Gen. ed. and introd. Carl F. Klinck. Toronto: Univ. of Toronto Press, 1976. III, 284–317.

———. "Jones, D.G." *The Oxford Companion to Canadian Literature*. Ed. William Toye. Toronto: Oxford Univ. Press, 1983, p. 401.

Patrick Lane (1939–)

GEORGE WOODCOCK

Patrick Lane (1939–   )

GEORGE WOODCOCK

Biography

PATRICK LANE was born in Nelson, in the Kootenay district of inland British Columbia, on 26 March 1939. His elder brother was the poet Red Lane, who died in 1964 at the age of twenty-eight. Early in Patrick's life, the Lane family moved to Vernon in the Okanagan Valley. Here he was educated, leaving school in the late 1950s, and not going on to the university. Instead, he worked as an unskilled labourer in construction, sawmilling, logging, and, as he remarked in a letter to the writer of this essay, "a variety of jobs from fruit-picking to first aid, house-building to hopelessness."[1] He married twice in those early years, and had five children by the two marriages, both of which broke up. He lived in poverty among the poor, in a world that — as he remarked in an interview with Stephen Dale that was published in *Books in Canada* — "in a very odd way, I was a slave to. I accepted that world intrinsically, the world of labouring. I didn't know there was another way. I was mindlessly accepting my poverty and my struggle. I had no intellectual detachment."[2]

Yet beneath this acceptance, there must have been an urge to break free. Lane's brother Red had begun to publish his poems and to associate with other poets in Vancouver, and in the interview with Dale, Lane himself admitted that writing became for him "a way out of poverty" (p. 33). He can hardly have meant that in a material way since he chose the worst-paid kind of writing, poetry, and never attempted to support himself by journalism, literary or other. Indeed, he continued to live by labouring, including work on the building of the Rogers Pass Highway, even after he had started to write poetry, and it was not until the mid-1970s, more than a decade after he had begun to write and publish his verse, that he found the means to escape from the labouring life.

Many of the experiences of that working life and its peripheral incidents—spending nights in jail, living the life of the city streets and slums and the lonely road—have entered deeply into Lane's poetry and helped to create its characteristically plebeian tone. They have also led him to evolve the concept of the poet as outlaw that has influenced his life, the way he looks at the world, and the kind of poetry he writes. In an essay entitled "To the Outlaw," printed in *New: American and Canadian Poetry* in the spring of 1971, he elaborated that concept of the Nietzschean role of the poet:

> Outside the law is a place that is beyond even freedom, for to be free you must be free of something or someone and no-one is free that *must* live. Beyond freedom, beyond all temporal boundaries of ethics and morality is a place called beauty where the outlaw resides in bondage and in that beauty is a burning beyond all knowledge and understanding. It is from there that the poem comes. It is there the outlaw lives.[3]

Lane has never abandoned the wandering life that necessity imposed on him when he was a labourer seeking fugitive employment; he remains one of the most peripatetic poets of Canada and has never established even a place of return like the Roblin Lake house from which Al Purdy makes his journeys. Lane is always on the way or about to leave.

Lane did not begin writing poetry until the early 1960s, though, in the interview with Stephen Dale already quoted, he claimed that he had felt the urge towards a creative life even in his early childhood:

> I do remember when I was a child we had one of those Christmas recording things, one of those huge machines that makes little plastic discs. And somebody asked me what I wanted to be when I grew up. I was six years old and I said I wanted to be an artist. Now how did I know when I was six years old that this is what I'd spend the rest of my life at? I didn't even start writing until I was 23 or 24. (pp. 32–33)

After Patrick Lane began to write poetry, his brother, Red Lane, induced him to move to Vancouver, where he associated with Earle Birney and Milton Acorn, who were then both living in the city. Eventually, with two other young poets, Seymour Mayne and bill bissett, he founded the little press Very Stone House, which began in 1966 and published as one of its first releases Lane's *Letters from the Savage Mind* (1966). Already he had gained a degree of acceptance, not only in Western Canada, where his poems had been published in *Blew Ointment*, *West Coast Review*, and *Talon*, but also in the more easterly provinces, where his work had appeared in *The Canadian Forum*, *The Fiddlehead*, and *Quarry* and been printed by James Reaney in *Alphabet*.

Lane continued to run Very Stone House from Vancouver until 1970. Then his life resumed its wandering course, and the publishing house, never completely abandoned and still run by Lane, was renamed Very Stone House in Transit, issuing its occasional publications from places as far apart as Vernon, Winnipeg, and Montreal. It came to an end in 1980.

In the meantime, Lane published books, pamphlets, and broadsheets of his poems at fairly regular intervals, amassing a total of twenty-three titles by the beginning of 1982. Most of these were little-press publications in small editions that quickly went out of print, and in biographical terms, the most important volumes were probably those that were brought out by established publishers, and which tended to be selections of poems already issued in more ephemeral form. They are *Beware the Months of Fire*, published by the House of Anansi in 1974, *Poems New and Selected*, which was published by the Oxford University Press in 1978 and won the Governor General's Award for poetry in that year, and *Old Mother* (1982), also published by Oxford. For another reason, a fourth collection has a special biographical significance. This is *Unborn Things: South American Poems*, issued by Harbour Publishing in 1975 and inspired by the travels Lane made shortly beforehand in Peru, Ecuador, and Colombia — his first major journey outside North America. *Old Mother* contains a cycle of poems written on a journey to China in 1981.

Lane's work has appeared in most of the Canadian literary journals, from fugitive little magazines to mandarin journals like *The Tamarack Review*, *The Malahat Review*, and *Canadian Literature*, and in magazines abroad like *The Chicago Review* and *The Times Literary Supplement*. He has read his poems often on CBC Radio and other stations, and the double-voiced poem sequence *No Longer Two People*, which he wrote with Lorna Uher, was read by the two poets as a special program on CBC *Anthology* before it was published in 1979 by Turnstone Press.

Unlike many poets, Lane has written little prose, and that in the form of rare reviews. But he has often supplemented his poems by drawings, which have been used to illustrate some of his books, notably *Separations* (1969) and *Unborn Things*. Eight pages of his drawings were also published in the Spring 1971 issue of *Prism International*.

In his 1971 manifesto, "To the Outlaw," Lane remarked that poetry "is not having tenure in a university with a guarantee of $15,000 a year and all the coeds you can fuck" (p.57). But, in fact, his liberation from the labouring life he had felt "a slave to" was achieved largely through the help of institutions like the universities and the arts councils. He has held junior Canada Council arts grants in 1966 and 1970, and senior grants in 1973 and 1976, Ontario Arts Council grants in 1974, 1975, and 1978, and a Manitoba Arts Council senior grant in 1979, while, in addition to the Governor General's Award, he received in 1971 the York University Poet's Award.

"I'm on the writer-in-residence thing now, until that dries up" (p.33), Lane said to Stephen Dale as he was explaining the economics of the modern poet's life in the *Books in Canada* interview. And since 1978, he has in fact been continuously a poet-in-residence, at the University of Manitoba to begin with, then at the University of Ottawa and the University of Alberta, and now, from 1982 to 1983, at the Saskatoon Public Library.

This has not halted Lane's steady production of poems that show great care in the writing, and it is appropriate to end this biographical section with one of the rare glimpses that Lane gives — again it is part of the *Books in Canada* interview — of himself at work as a poet:

> I have to have my cup of coffee and my cigarette burning and the typewriter just right. I could spend three hours

in the morning, which is when I write, going through all the rituals and never getting anything done. Those games every writer goes through. One of the hardest things is to sit down and actually start writing.... When the poem comes, it's great. It's marvellous. It's one of the most beautiful sensations in the world. The act of creation, I think for any artist — and there's an artist in all of us — is one of the most profound experiences a person can go through. As human beings that kind of entrance is a very special one. When the good poem comes, — and you know it's good, that's marvellous. (p. 33)

Tradition and Milieu

Patrick Lane began to publish his work in the little magazines of Vancouver during the 1960s, when the city became one of the most important Canadian centres of poetic activity. Earle Birney, Dorothy Livesay, and Milton Acorn were there, Margaret Atwood and Al Purdy lived in the city for periods during the decade, and among the younger poets who began to emerge in Vancouver at this time were John Newlove, George Bowering, and Red Lane, Patrick's brother, whose career was cut short by his death before the '60s had half ended. It was the decade when the little magazine *Talon* appeared and gave rise to Talonbooks, the leading avant-garde poetry publishing house west of the Rockies, when *Tish* went through its short but brilliant career as the organ of a group of university-centred poets led by Bowering and Frank Davey, and when Patrick Lane himself, with Seymour Mayne and bill bissett, started yet another publishing venture, Very Stone House, which Lane continued in peripatetic style until 1980.

It would be rash to assume that Lane was influenced by, or even sympathetic to, all the poets I have mentioned. For example, he felt little in common with the *Tish* group, who were dominated by the teachings of the American Black Mountain poets and became excessively formalistic in their cultivation of what they considered the basic Canadian speech patterns. Yet he has expressed an admiration for George Bowering, perhaps the most independent, in his eventual development, of all the *Tish*ites. There is no doubt that in his early days Lane was influenced by Milton Acorn, and the affinity between the two as poets of the plebeian life continues. Yet Lane was never swept into committing his poetry to political ends in the way Acorn has done; in fact, he has implicitly detached himself from such poetry, for in one of his most recent collections, *The Measure* (1980), there appears a poem entitled "I Am Tired of Your Politics." Here Lane is explicitly answering Dorothy Livesay's exhortation "be political, impersonal with passion," and he says:

> Lady, I am baffled
> by your care. The mind is
> always a dull thunder.
> Shall we make politics
> out of love?
> . . . .
> Shall we sing other than
> our lives? Peace, wisdom,
> excellence in the small
> affairs of the heart?[4]

It is the singing of our lives to which Lane is devoted, and doing this has brought him into empathy with other poets, though influence may be a more difficult point to establish, except in so far as any poet tends to start off from the milieu in which he first begins to write, where the achievements of other poets come together to form his inspirational launching pad. In this way, one can consider Earle Birney, and Al Purdy, and Irving Layton, to all of whom Lane has dedicated poems, as among his direct predecessors, with Birney as perhaps the most influential in his initial explorations of the British Columbian terrain that has been the site of so many of Lane's experiences and his poetic renderings of them.

But even with the poets he respects most, and from whom he had learned much, Lane is insistent on emphasizing his differences. In his 1971 essay "To the Outlaw," he says:

> "Whatever else poetry is freedom" but I tell you, Layton, poetry is a grand inquisitor waiting in the next cell for your coming — catharsis leading into bondage. "I say the line

never ends" and, Purdy, for once you were right, the poems trailing behind like cast-off clothing, dreams and visions we were never sure of, empty seed pods floating above barren ground, forgotten lovers, promises never made, the substances of fingernails and locks of hair twisted into mud images on the slopes of some Haiti of the mind where the pain returns again and again with each stab of the needle that punctures and threads you onto that clothes-line of latitude that leads to the sun, that line that never ends that you carry with you into the dim serenity of night where monsters and myths as large as continents wait in horror for your arrival. (p. 55)

This passage reflects Lane's most striking difference from Layton, a rigorous self-criticism that has made his production small and has saved him from the rhetorical excess that has marred so much of Layton's work. It also reflects one of his similarities with Purdy — there are others — which is his sense of the fluent movement of colloquial speech, a movement he has controlled and used effectively for his poetic purposes.

Other poets — and these of his own generation — for whom Lane has expressed admiration are John Newlove, Alden Nowlan, and Margaret Atwood. With Atwood, what he has in common is perhaps most of all his need to be an honest, if anguished, witness to the pain of life and his precise and economic use of language and imagery. With Nowlan and Newlove, we come to the more general contexts in which Lane's work can be placed — the plebeian context and the regional context.

For Lane is one of a small group of Canadian poets who have successfully evaded the kind of academic paths to poetry which had their origins in the mythologizing theories of Northrop Frye and in the technocratic experiments of the Black Mountaineers. Purdy, Acorn, Newlove, Nowlan, Lane — they have come from working-class backgrounds and have experienced the working life at its most exacting level, that of the unskilled labourer. They have wandered the country, from the heights of the mountains to the depths of the slums, and they have created a remarkable poetry which is populist in its content and expression yet never licks the dust of vulgar popularization. It is a poetry that speaks out of the actuality of Canadian life.

At the same time, Lane is in the best sense a regionalist in that he is also one of a group of poets who in recent decades have created in Western Canada a poetry of past and place corresponding to the regional fiction that emerged a generation before. Where their pioneer predecessors tended to fight and fear their environment, these poets have sought to live in it and understand it, and in their work the landscape of the Prairies and the Rockies and the Coast has become a living presence as it never was in poetry before. Birney was perhaps the pioneer of this group of poets, with Purdy a kind of visiting apostle, but essentially they consisted of a younger generation among whom Newlove, Dale Zieroth, Andrew Suknaski, Pat Lowther, Sid Marty, Ken Belford, and, of course, Patrick Lane have been the most important. Some of these, notably Ken Belford, have been Lane's close friends. But here it should be noted that friendship and fairly close personal association do not necessarily create mutual literary influences; there is not very much in common between Lane's poetry and that of either Seymour Mayne or bill bissett, though the three collaborated fruitfully in creating the publishing venture of Very Stone House.

However, beyond the obvious regional aspects of Lane's poetry and its roots in Canadian working-class life, there are broader and more cosmopolitan affiliations of which one gradually becomes aware as one reads the poems and appreciates the breadth of Lane's autodidactic reading. (Most self-taught poets are extremely wide readers and tend to acquire an erudition far more extensive, if less specialized, than that of their university-trained counterparts.) And here Lane really belongs to a nihilist tradition whose beginnings can be traced in Baudelaire and among the Decadents and Symbolists, with their fruitful doctrine of correspondences and their restless search for *les diamants dans la boue*. There is the same sense in Lane as there is in these nineteenth-century French poets that the pain and the beauty of life, the filth and the glory, are closely associated and we can never drive them apart. Perhaps the most interesting clue to this link lies in the fact that Lane has written two different poems addressed to one of the most strikingly typical paintings of the Decadent era, *The Absinthe Drinker* by Degas. "I see eternity / of helpless soul," Lane says, addressing the painting and asks, "How many after me / will see your visions / of emptiness...?"[5]

Lane is in many ways a nihilist, yet he goes beyond mere nihilism in his sense of the need to bear witness, even to affirm, which he shares with other nihilistic writers like Henry Miller and Céline, to both of whom he has paid the tribute of using quotations from their writings as epigraphs to his works. In particular, there is the quotation from Céline's *Voyage au bout de la nuit* with which he introduces his first major collection, *Beware the Months of Fire*. It is worth quoting since it so admirably expresses the viewpoint from which Lane approaches his responsibilities as a poet:

> The greatest defeat, in anything, is to forget, and above all to forget what it is that has smashed you, and to let yourself be smashed without ever realizing how thoroughly devilish men can be. When our time is up, we people mustn't bear malice, but neither must we forget: we must tell the whole thing, without ever altering one word, — everything that we have seen of man's viciousness; and then it will be over and time to go. That is enough for a whole lifetime.[6]

Man's viciousness to man and, even more, man's viciousness to other creatures are recurrent themes in Lane's poetry, but one has to ascribe the similarity between his sentiments and Céline's less to the influence of the older writer than to the coming together of similar natures.

Finally, there is no doubt that in terms of experience Lane's travels in South America not only enriched the content of his poems, but also gave his work a philosophic power it had not possessed before. Yet already, before the crucial journey, he had expressed in his "Outlaw" essay of 1971 his admiration for the greatest Spanish American poet of our age, Pablo Neruda; without accepting Neruda's politics, he had found that they shared the sense of a "poetry born in the bondage of experience" (p. 56) and had quoted with approval Neruda's call for

> a poetry impure as the clothing we wear, soup-stained, soiled with our shameful behaviour, our wrinkles and vigils and dreams.... (p. 56)

That is precisely the kind of poetry Patrick Lane has written.

Critical Overview and Context

Only two modest essays, which will be mentioned later in this section, have been dedicated to Patrick Lane's poems; most of the criticisms directed towards his works have been made in reviews of his various volumes as they appeared.

His earliest volumes were scantily noticed, and the reviews that did appear were somewhat tentative. Al Purdy, for instance, writing in *Canadian Literature*, described *Letters from the Savage Mind* as a "reversion to the commonplace," albeit a commonplace "streaked and veined with insights," and expressed in a language that is "straightforward and communicating directly."[7] Of *Separations*, Douglas Barbour remarked in the same journal on the unevenness of the poems, the lack of poetic method, and suggested that "the good poems are accidental" because of the poet's refusal of "the challenge of poetry — to use craft to give specific poetic form to experience."[8] Guilt and loss are the main unifying themes.

Reviewing Lane's first major book, *Beware the Months of Fire*, in *The Globe and Mail*, Gary Geddes recollected the first impression that *Separations* had made on him — that of "a poet untouched by the academy, whose ear was sensitive to rhythms other than those of the computer and metronome, and for whom poetry was more than a hobby."[9] Dealing with *Beware the Months of Fire*, he pointed to the importance of narrative in Lane's work and to the poet's ability to give significant form to his happenings; he also stressed Lane's "poetic image of the tight-lipped loser."[10]

George Melnyk, in the *Edmonton Journal*, saw *Beware the Months of Fire* as "tough, pure, muscular poetry." "He speaks with the voice of withdrawal which in fact only indicates his degree of involvement."[11] Doug Fetherling, writing in *The Toronto Star*, found Lane "one of the authentic voices of the Canadian West, with all the prejudices that position ensures but also the sweep and realism it implies." He noted that Lane is concerned "with craft more than tricks" and suggested that "the centre of his imaginative world is the point at which the urban skid row comes into contact with the outback."[12]

In *The London Free Press*, Stan Dragland saw in *Beware the Months of Fire* "a tough-minded compassion...that is convincing because nothing ugly or offensive is omitted that is part of Lane's picture." He saw a creative tension between many of Lane's subjects "and the sophistication of his language" and discovered "at least two poetic voices. One is matter of fact, understated, sometimes a little sardonic; the other is more 'poetic,' a little more formal and lyrical" and sometimes "sees service in the articulation of myth."[13] Jean Mallinson, reviewing the same book in *The Vancouver Sun*, noted the double reaction the poems evoke: "...we feel delight, because they are beautifully made, the language naturally and artfully arranged, and dismay because of their bleak and unrelieved preoccupation with resigned suffering." Lane, she said, "describes a world seen without the imagination's mercies, things too much as they are to be changed by metaphor."[14] Douglas Barbour, noting the book in *Quill & Quire*, observed that Lane's poems are basically studies in pain and that "the witness they bear to human violence is so complete."[15] And Len Gasparini, discussing the book in *Canadian Literature*, described Lane's style as "an unschooled, street-cool one that serves the purpose of his perception." Lane's "poems are mirrors with the spidery cracks of truth in them." He "transforms the 'I' and gives it an objective dignity. Metaphor and meaning create a kind of magnetic field, and the poet places the 'I' within that space."[16]

Unborn Things attracted more attention than the earlier short books of Patrick Lane. Writing in *Canadian Literature*, I suggested that it established Lane as "a poet unusual in his direct and telling response to experience, whether that experience is a memory of the collective mind or an episode individually lived."[17] Brian Brett in the *Vancouver Province* noted how in this book Lane escapes "the cold realism he has been into lately" and unleashes "his most macabre moods."[18] Len Gasparini in *Books in Canada* remarked on the consistency of Lane's rhythm and imagery and the emotional density of these poems. "*Unborn Things* earmarks Patrick Lane for what is truly great in Canadian poetry."[19]

Lane's next short book, *Albino Pheasants* (1977), aroused mixed critical reactions. Stan Dragland in *Canadian Literature* wrote of the high craftsmanship of these poems. "The form of each poem and the shape of the whole book are carefully considered. All this shaping craft is in the service of releasing something: a spirit, a soul, a bird: mysteries at the heart of things." Dragland noted how "naturally" Lane is now manipulating his increasingly complex formal structures and pointed to his skilful use of metaphor. "It often takes the exterior landscape, and population of the poems and turns them inward, sometimes with the flick of a word."[20] On the other side, *Albino Pheasants* led to a long and uniformly negative review article by Neil Whiteman in *CV/II*. In Whiteman's view, the book is "unpoetical, boring, redundant, and confused." Lane seeks to portray the world as "uniformly vicious."[21] His vision is narrow and his expression is limited, and he repeats himself. Whiteman's review was too badly written to be taken very seriously, and its one positive effect was to provoke a quartet of excellent replies in a later issue of *CV/II* from Jean Mallinson, Howard White, Carolyn Zonailo, and George Amabile,[22] which testified to the respect with which Lane was by now being regarded by his fellow writers.

Other lengthy but less negative considerations of Lane's poetry appeared at this time. In my essay "Poetry of Time and Place: Recent Canadian Trends," I discussed Lane in the context of contemporary Western movements and remarked, "Not merely is the imagery moonlight sharp in Lane's verse, and the language direct yet sufficiently allusive, but there is a remarkable rhythmic control of the longish lines which few poets gain without imposing some kind of metrical regularity."[23]

In the special "West Coast Renaissance" issue of *The Malahat Review* (Jan. 1978), Marilyn Bowering contributed an essay, "Pine Boughs and Apple Trees," on Lane's poems up to and including *Albino Pheasants*. It is a rather disjointedly written piece, relating Lane to two of Bowering's opinions about Western Canadian poetry — that it is dominated by the "spiritual hopelessness bred by exile" with its legacy of "nihility," and that the strongest West Coast poetry "is regional, rooted in particular landscape; place is the measure of certainty."[24] Somewhat cursorily studying a number of key Lane poems, she comes to the conclusion: "At the end of eleven years of published poetry, place and placing remain as essential to Lane as at the beginning....He writes with clarity, with sureness of craft and continues risks with his art. He has maimed if not disabled the habit of self-deceit. His poetry is self-made, self-justified."[25]

The appearance of *Poems New and Selected* led Jean Mallinson to write in *Brick* a long study entitled "A Reading of Pat Lane,"[26] which is the lengthiest piece on him before the present study. Mallinson is a shrewd, observant reader of Lane's poems. The core of her essay is a complex argument trying to prove that Lane as a poet is within the emblematic tradition, and though Mallinson does not make this particular argument wholly convincing to those who regard actuality as an essential element in Lane's poetry, it does give her a framework within which to examine his insights into the human condition and also the metaphoric ways in which he projects them.

Andrew Suknaski, writing in *Canadian Literature*, treated *Poems New and Selected* in terms of the essential Western Canadian myth, but his review was too descriptive in a detailed way to reach a clear theoretical conclusion.[27] Alexandre L. Amprimoz, discussing the book in *Waves*, remarked that "Lane's best poems are those where the purity of the lyric voice reaches the realm of timelessness," and he ended by saying that "through Lane's coherent imaginary universe, the metaphoric process becomes an integral part of his vision: nothing has been constructed here. All has been seen."[28] Edward Prato in *West Coast Review* criticized the inclusion of so many early poems in the collection. Though he spoke with less overt malice than Neil Whiteman, Prato's review was so negative that one can only assume he completely failed to understand Lane's poems or his intentions. "The language...is awkward....The images are overweening, sentimental....The poet offers a self-image of a man who is not only an observer of pain but also an inflictor of it."[29] Mr. Prato is shocked.

Louis Dudek, reviewing *Poems New and Selected* in *The Globe and Mail*, was not much less disturbed than Prato. For him Lane's poetry "reeks of blood and carnage." "More than half...contain brutal images or reference to violence...." And he saw in such developments "a failure of sensibility (good old-fashioned word), a hardening of human nature against the call of humanity or compassion."[30] Dudek had nothing to say about Lane's skills as a poetic craftsman. In a rather similar vein, Norma West Linder in *Canadian Author & Bookman* opined that "...for Lane, no theme is too obscene, no incident too violent, and no subject too distasteful for him to tackle." Lane's work, "though lyrical in form, rarely exhibits an awareness of the mysterious beauty of life."[31]

On the other hand, Rosemary Sullivan, writing in *The Canadian Forum*, saw in *Poems New and Selected* an extraordinary appropriateness to the world from which Lane came. "He writes a tough-minded anecdotal poetry full of narratives of the hard lives of ordinary people. The voice he chooses is often raw and violent, and his best quality is remarkable and moving empathy for all of life that is vulnerable and pained.... Lane has a fine gift for image, and writes of the tragic not histrionically but in understatement, deflecting attention to some small detail that is made to carry the full horror of the situation.... Lane's greatest weakness is posturing; he falls too easily into a highly rhetorical despair."[32] And Doug Beardsley, writing in the *Victoria Times-Colonist*, remarked, "There is nothing compromising about Lane's vision of life and the world in which we live," but added that Lane's best poems occur "when he is able to fuse his love and human compassion with his harsh vision of reality."[33] And Philip Lanthier, reviewing *Poems New and Selected* in *Matrix*, remarked that Lane's poems are "intimate with death and with the language of violent blows:... a raw landscape of hard weather, hard people and hard ground, and one which finds its appropriate locale in the rugged interior of British Columbia or in the fanatical, fantastical worlds of the Spanish Cordillera." At the same time, "Lane faces violence and pain head-on in a laconic, understated fashion.... There is no facile mountainesque afflatus in Lane, no cruising with borrowed mythologies."[34]

At the time of writing this piece, the reviews of Lane's most recent volume, *Old Mother* (1982), can only be anticipated. *The Measure* (1980) received less attention than it deserved, and the reviews, perhaps in reaction against the good reception of *Poems New and Selected*, either were grudging or, if favourable, tended to direct more attention to the mannerisms of the reviewer than to the poetry itself. An example was Ian Sowton's review in *Canadian Literature*, which radiated enthusiasm without convincingly stated understanding. Yet even Sowton hit on a special truth about Lane when he remarked, "*The Measure* ends on a discouraged note. To other perplexities have been added deeper ones: the dark suspicion that it may not be worth going on telling, or even living, is compounded by the compulsion to go on nevertheless in spite of all the waste, violence, trivia and zombyism."[35] And John Cruikshank in *Books in Canada* implied that Lane — at least in *The Measure* — is excessively sententious. "A poet's reflections on life and community are often valuable — perhaps when recounted in memoirs or magazine articles — but when in poems they force the reader to stop in mid-stanza to ask why he is being subjected to this or that opinion, the coherence of the reading experience suffers."[36] Rosemary Aubert, writing in *Quill & Quire*, found three categories of poems in *The Measure*. There are the "philosophical" poems, which are "ponderous and occasionally fall victim to a too-frequent use of rhetorical question." There are the "enriched nature poems," descriptive but also offering comment on what is described, and which Aubert found "reminiscent of fine Oriental poetry." And there are the narratives, which Aubert considered "the real strength of this collection," "vigorous, gripping and nearly unforgettable."[37]

Lane's Works

The list of Patrick Lane's publications is a long one, and it gives at first sight the impression of a prolific and perhaps unself-critical poet rather like Irving Layton. In fact, the list is deceptive and the impression is incorrect. Many of Lane's publications are single-poem broadsheets or brief pamphlets which were later included in small limited-edition volumes; his more substantial volumes tend to consist mainly of poems gathered from the earlier and smaller collections, so that Lane's actual poetic output, for a career lasting almost twenty years, is relatively slight. What does become evident over the years is the steady and conscious development of an individual voice, of a philosophic attitude for dealing with a view of life that is not optimistic, and of a distinctive poetic persona; just as impressive are the growing masteries of form and language that are shown when one compares the early poems of *Letters from the Savage Mind* with the recent meditative poems of volumes like *The Measure*.

In this section, I shall not be dealing separately with the single poems published as broadsheets and later incorporated in collections, but I shall be discussing the smaller volumes since they very clearly mark stages on the road of Lane's development.

The first — *Letters from the Savage Mind* (1966) — consists of fifty-five poems composed in the first three or four years of Lane's activity as a poet. The volume is dedicated to his brother, Red Lane, and the longest poem, "The Carnival Man," is a kind of bizarre elegy on the dead poet, with dreamlike recollections of childhood fairs disguising what is essentially a poem of loss and remembrance, with its frenetic imagery of lights and sounds and childhood wonders quietening down to the last moving threnodic lines:

> I shall search
> in the empty field
> for a puff of dry corn
>
> I shall crawl on the ground
> searching for stones
> among dry hulls of dead lilacs
>
> I shall weave a coat
> from the strands of his red hair —
> it will ride on my shoulders like the night
>   (*LSM*, n. pag.)

There is in these early poems by Patrick Lane a great deal of the rather flat and painful simplicity that characterized so much of his brother's work. In many of the pieces, the imagery is too soft-edged to be apprehended clearly, and the result is often a kind of wavering vagueness out of which no clear intent emerges: for example, the last stanza of the opening poem of *Letters*, "If I Travel Alone":

> If I travel alone
> I'll turn to stone
> and it shall be silently
> without benefit of
> a sun's burning
> or a thousand years
> without a moon
> as a tree walks

into stone and silence
with my hair rustling

(*LSM*, n pag.)

Only five of the fifty-five poems in *Letters from the Savage Mind* were eventually picked for Lane's two more or less definitive collections, and this suggests that he would have us regard most of these early poems as juvenilia, the apprentice work of a writer who developed largely through his inclination towards self-rejection, which may perhaps be regarded as a moral fault but is certainly a poetic virtue. The pieces that have survived in this way are worth special consideration not only because they show that even in his early years Lane was capable of writing the occasional striking poem, but also because they indicate the directions his work was later to follow.

All five are poems that present a situation. We are invited to consider a scene in which the poet is involved; he is there physically and he is moved emotionally, and his feeling is conveyed by an appropriateness of language and a sharpness of imagery that make us sensible that we are at the same time experiencing actuality and living within the poet's imagination, which extends the dimensions of the actuality we see. In this way, a brief poem becomes dense with meaning. Take, for example, "Three Days after Crisis in Cuba":

Looking at cougar tracks
by my back door with Bill;
pads in the mud.
He showed me where grass was bent in soft ground.

Rain on my hard hat,
squatting there among waterpuffed stems.

He shot a crow
from where we sat;
it hangs above his record player —
glass eyes,
black feathers,
it flies on a thread
when you open the door.

(*BMF*, p. 7)

What has all this to do with the crisis in Cuba? Nothing is said about Cuba except in the title: there is nothing that is obviously a metaphor for the crisis. But this is not in the strict sense a metaphoric poem, in which the images can be taken as figures intended to reinforce our perception of what is being told by creating supporting analogies. Rather, it is a symbolist poem, in which we are expected to perceive correspondences rather than figurative likenesses. The cougar and the crow and the arbitrary killing of the crow are images that have nothing to do with the crisis itself, but, because they are images of fear — and particularly fear of the unpredictable — they suggest the state of mind of those who have lived through the crisis, just as the hard hat suggests the futility of human efforts to cope mentally with such situations, and the dead crow that flies, but on a thread, suggests how illusory the hope of escape from the cruel and gratuitous catastrophes of existence.

"Treaty-Trip from Shulus Reservation" is the kind of poem we shall see Lane writing frequently in later years, a poem in which human degradation is evoked with objective honesty yet with a compassion that mingles with pessimism — a pity that what is must be. There are two drunken Indians. The man leans against a dusty wall, struggling with the "...drunken buttons / on his fly."

> His raven woman
> knelt in the dirt
> like some aged black
> supplicant bird.
>
> *(BMF, p. 37)*

She vomits on the man's feet, and he raises his knee to strike her in the face while, apparently unaware of what is going on, an Indian child is wildly bouncing her ball against the same wall. The poet, in his role of agonized witness, contemplates the scene:

> I hung there
> in the sightless night
> like a hooded
> jesse-bound hawk

> my quiet hammered breath
> held in rhythmic beat
> with the bouncing ball
> that neatly caught
> flew out
> from the child's small hand
> to thump on the flat red wall.
>
> (*BMF*, pp. 37–38)

In "Legacies," the poet sits smoking a cigar that is part of the meagre inheritance coming to him from a grandfather he saw only once, yet whom, as he sits and consumes the legacies, he recognizes as

> forebear,
> passing my father to me
> in one sudden moment
> on a prairie night...
> begat
> begat
>
> (*BMF*, p. 9)

There is a sense here of the continuity of human relationships, in the mind at least, that will run right through the line of Lane's poetry as he tells of marriages broken, children lost, friends departed or dead, but all remembered. The continuity is fraught with sadness, for no human relationships are seen as secure, no lives immune from catastrophe. Even in "Act of the Apostles," when Lane writes of three children who have not yet departed (they eventually will), it is the poet seeing his own flaws reflected in his progeny:

> I catch an image
> of myself
> inside their eyes
> and all alone
> I live in fear
> of the sepulchral
> shadow of a tree.
>
> (*BMF*, p. 5)

Another characteristic Lane theme emerges in the fifth of these early poems that he chose to keep, "Loving She Stood Apart." The lover lies watching the woman as she undresses, turned away from him:

> ...afraid she was
> of the wanting to need
> me watching her....

She begs him to turn out the light, and at last he does so, and

> so quietly my mind
> shut out the sight
> and I was blind to
> her but O the night

(*BMF*, p. 13)

Here is a tenderness that seems the opposite of the consciousness of the cruelty in human relationships that pervades so many Lane poems, yet it is a tenderness that recurs, not only in the poet-persona's attitude to women, but also in his gentleness towards those who are wrecked by life. The cruelty appals this agonized witness, but the victims do not, and the moments that are somehow exempt from cruelty are treasured. No critics have been more mistaken than those who have assumed, from the content of his poems, an essential brutality in Lane's vision, a rejoicing in the violence and horror he sees in the world. Rather, like the classic Buddhist, he finds in the recognition of life's horrors, or the terrible things men do to men and even more to other beings, the reason for an ultimate compassion, for a desire to nurture love where it survives.

Separations appeared in 1969, and it shows the growing power and assurance of Lane's poetry. Almost three-quarters of these forty poems eventually emerged in one or other of his definitive collections, and they include some of the poems by which he is now best known, such as "Prospector," "Calgary City Jail," "Elephants," "Wild Horses," "Ten Miles In from Horsefly," "The Water-Truck" and "For Rita — in Asylum."

In *Letters from the Savage Mind*, it was the characteristic Lane themes and the characteristically pessimistic view of life that began to emerge. In *Separations* we encounter, much more often and more pronouncedly, the epiphanic episodes that Lane handles so well. The personal myth of the poet is developed, undoubtedly largely based on an actual life, though that is not what concerns us as readers so much as the mental arrangements of that life which form the armature of the poems. The very titles, as well as the content, of the poems I have mentioned tend to define the perimeters of that myth. It embraces the wanderer, in "Ten Miles In from Horsefly," shovelling manure from a barn to get lodging and food; the worker who is neither efficient nor zealous, in "Elephants" and "The Water-Truck"; the man torn by the suffering of animals yet taking part in their destruction in "Wild Horses"; the enemy of conventional society in "Calgary City Jail"; the sexual predator who yet laments women as the supreme victims of social ills in "For Rita — in Asylum"; and the wondering child (precursor of the suffering man) in "Prospector," a poem centred on an old man who lives in envied rapport with the animal world and so in contrast to the men in other poems who live in enmity with the animals.

What is so compelling about these poems is that they are visual and reflective at the same time. We are shown a scene, an episode, in such a way that we cannot do other than consider its implications, how the particular reflection that emerges from it may affect our view of the life we share with the poet. Lane never offers us an abstract thought; he presents a concrete and particular instance, and from that, if we wish to go such a way, we can abstract our own conclusions, but the act of abstraction is not part of the role the poet accepts.

Yet, as the debris which chokes our memories of the Imagist movement shows, no amount of concrete presentation will have this effect of stirring the mind outside of reason if it does not move on multiple levels of perception and if it is not associated with a technical mastery of the poetic medium. It is for their advances in both these directions that the poems in *Separations* are notable.

To begin there is the development of the multiple perceptions and the ironic juxtapositions which such multiplication inevitably involves. "Elephants" (*BMF*, pp. 39–40) is a work poem in the sense that it presents the poet-narrator in a work situation. But it is not a work poem in the conventional sense of displaying merely the hard life of the toilers. The point it drives at does not, in fact, have much to do with the work situation in which it begins. As it opens, the poet is sitting with two other workers on a road project:

> all of us waiting out the last hour
> until we go back on the grade —

Trying to forget the clatter of machinery

> pounding stones and earth to powder
> for hours in mosquito-darkness
> of the endless cold mountain night

he occupies himself with a slow creative process, a shaping like that of making poetic images, as he sits with his knife and carves out of a chunk of brown soap an elephant, which he intends to give an Indian boy

> who lives in the village a mile back
> in the bush.

As he cuts away and talks to the boy, his mind moves from the work situation — he achieves temporarily the forgetting of the present he desires — and he tells the child, who does not know what an elephant is,

> ...the story
> of the elephant graveyard
> which no-one has ever found
> and how the silent
> animals of the rain-forest
> go away to die somewhere
> in the limberlost of distances
> and he smiles at me

The Indian boy's smile is the ironic turning point of the poem for it brings the fantasies home to roost. What he now tells the poet is of the graveyard where his people have been buried "...so far back / no-one remembers when it started." When the poet asks where the graveyard is,

> ...he tells me it is gone
> now where no-one will ever find it
> buried under the grade of the new
> highway.

And so the wheels have turned full circle. We are all endangered species, our lives likely to be buried by history, and we are all involved in the universal complicity that finds the poet working on the highway that has buried the Indian cemetery at the same time as he is giving the Indian boy a totemic image of the greatest of all animals, doomed for its very greatness.

Perhaps "Elephants" is more complex in its ironies than some of the other poems I have mentioned, and more oblique, for the extinction of the elephants is not linked directly with the actions of men as the destruction of other animals is in "Wild Horses." But even here we are involved in matters which bring us face to face with a crucial question: to what degree is Patrick Lane a moralist poet? Already we have noticed his Nietzschean statement that "...beyond all temporal boundaries of ethics and morality is a place called beauty where the outlaw resides..," and it is from this place outside good and evil that he sees the poem emerging. In fact, evil exists, quite clearly defined, in Lane's poems, and the witness's agony, repeated time and again, represents his judgement and at the same time his acceptance of guilt.

The whole point of "Wild Horses" (*BMF*, p. 46) lies in the poet's involvement as both actor and witness. He sees the gun fired — and he holds it. "Wild Horses" begins obliquely with the expression of a longing for an innocent contact with the free beings of the wilderness — something like the primitive man's encounter with the spirit animals:

> Just to come once alone
> to these wild horses
> driving out of high Cascades,
> raw legs heaving the hip-high snow.
> Just once alone. Never to see
> the men and their trucks.

But in the poem, as in the poet's experience, the men and the trucks are there. The "...stallion with five free mares / rush into the guns." They are all killed.

> Ice bleeds in their nostrils
> as the cable hauls them in.

And then the poem itself bleeds away to human callousness:

> Later, after the swearing
> and the stamping of feet,
> we ride down into Golden:
>
> *Quit bitchin.*
> *It's a hard bloody life*
> *and a long week*
> *for three hundred bucks of meat.*
>
> That and the dull dead eyes
> and the empty meadows.

A similar pattern, of the poet as witness, also taking part in the action, though not initiating it, and then displaying the signs of remorse, occurs in later poems, notably in "Wild Dogs" (*BMF*, pp. 47–49), which first appeared in *Mountain Oysters* (1971). Here the poet begins by talking of the dogs that have run wild in the mountains and formed themselves into packs, which kill the cattle. The mill is shut down in winter, and the poet's mates invite him to join them in killing the wild dogs; though his wife does not like it, he goes, without trying to explain.

> How do you explain
> what men do
>
> there's a special
> hatred for wild dogs
> we go to hunt
> because we were
> their masters

> it's not for food
> we kill them
> or even pleasure
> but the fear
> we thought we'd lost
> so long ago

The dogs are trapped on the road, and the poet thinks of Spartacus and his slaves "free in the hills / of Rome" while he watches the dogs milling round and round "as I wept / and they blew them / to pieces."

There are balancing sentiments at work here. The poet invents a reason in human nature and in men's relation to other creatures to explain the massacre in which he is taking part. But then he suddenly sees the animals as, in their own way, equivalent to human beings who seek their freedom, and in the end *he* weeps as *they* blow them to pieces. In other words, at the very end some impulse within him makes him refrain from taking part in the killing as he had done in "Wild Horses."

Yet the sense of the complicity of the witness remains, and emerges perhaps in its most extreme form in "If," which first appears in *Poems New and Selected* (1978). As he is making love to a woman, the poet remembers a grotesque and terrible scene in Tiajuana, a woman weeping with pain as a burro fucked her on a sideshow stage. Remembering, he no longer wants the woman he is with:

> I am obscene.
> I am one of those who laughed
> when the burro dropped her on the floor.[38]

To see, and to fail in rejection, is to be guilty of whatever you witness; the implication is clear.

It is impossible to consider these as merely poems about the human condition; they are poems making a judgement on mankind's role in the natural world. When Lane quotes Céline in the epigraph to *Beware the Months of Fire*, saying that we must realize "how devilish men can be," and saying also, "...we must tell the whole thing, without ever altering one word, — everything that we have seen of man's viciousness..," he is implying a moral reason for what he writes in his poems. He is not merely saying this is how the human condition is; he is saying also how terrible that it should be so. And so he stands among the pessimistic moralists, like Céline and Swift and Orwell, writers fascinated and horrified by the way in which men have shown themselves more destructive, more gratuitously cruel, than all the animals. If one wants to catch in Lane the opposite vision that also haunts those dark nightmarists, the elusive vision of a world in grace, it exists in the late poem "I Am Tired of Your Politics," which I have already quoted, and in which Lane seems to me to be cautioning himself as well as his readers when he says:

> We must not hide
> our innocence, the distant
> singing we call love.
>
> (M, p. 46)

After arguing that poets should sing of such rare and positive things as "Peace, wisdom, / excellence in the small / affairs of the heart," he goes on to ask, not pity, but respect for living beings, and in the last two excellent verses of the poem — a reflective narrative as so often in Lane — he is really saying that misfortune is inevitable, but the worst crime is to despise those who are unfortunate:

> Listen, once when I was
> young, I knew a woman
> natural as beauty, brave
> with all the mysteries
> she was born to.
> Let us not pity her.
> The sad compassions
> are of little use.
> She left her love
> in a thousand beds
> until she lost her mind
> and fell into the
> dream called death.

Let us respect her now,
give her at least the desire
that she could be in the sun
with her hurt head resting
on her pale white hands.
The will is not holy.
One moves in stillness.
Look, even the birds
are decently silent
while she sleeps.

(*M*, pp. 46–47)

Reading through this series of poems that are clearly related by theme, one is aware of the growing mastery of the craft of poetry that Lane has established. Plainness and the search for the true word were always his virtues as a poet, but in the early works they were accompanied often by an unsought roughness of tone, an unfocused vagueness of imagery, a clumsiness of rhythm. In some ways, what he has achieved is a progression from naïve poetry to a very sophisticated poetry. In the late pieces, one is aware of a constant balancing of the sound and the intent, of the visual element and the thought, and also of a steady moving into the tradition, as a result of which the verbal texture of the poems becomes close-knit yet elastic. There is a careful balancing of syllables in the lines, and a pattern in which the polysyllabic words stand out in emphasis within a basic weave of simple monosyllabic words. Alliteration is modestly present ("left her love," "beauty, brave," "her hurt head," "dream called death"), and in other later poems one finds the occasional rhyme, but just as traditional is the conversational-reflective tone — as old, at least as Wordsworth in its ancestry — that Lane achieves in so many of the later poems. In a poem like "I Am Tired of Your Politics," one is in fact reminded, from the title to the end, of the later Yeats, and a poet who can proclaim such affinities without mere imitation has gone a long way towards maturity.

Mountain Oysters is the volume that perhaps more than any other raises the question of whether Lane is a regional poet, since so many of its pieces spring out of his experiences in the mountain country of British Columbia, where he was born and reared and where he spent a great deal of his working life. Indeed, eighteen of the twenty-one poems would have been impossible without these experiences, and a number of them, like "Wild Dogs," "The Black Colt" (later "The Black Filly"), and "Mountain Oysters," vividly portray episodes in which the poet-persona is directly involved. They are largely poems about violence done in one way or another to animals. The black colt is tethered in an open field during a frightful mountain storm in order to terrify it into submission. In "Mountain Oysters," a sheepherder bites off the balls of his rams, and the poet

> ...enjoyed them with him,
> cutting delicately
> into the deep-fried testicles.
>
> Mountain oysters make you strong
>
> he said
> while out in the field
> the rams stood holding their pain,
> legs fluttering like blue hands
> of old tired men.
>
> (*BMF*, p. 43)

In such poems, the poet is again the witness-accomplice, but there is one poem in which he merges into the animal-protagonist. In "The Dog," the animal is bleeding to death internally because he "...has fed on a flying thing / and the bones are cutting him inside" (*BMF*, p. 18). The dog, without humanity's vaunted intelligence, has committed the sin against his fellow creatures that men are committing all the time in the other poems, and the correspondence that the poet intends becomes evident by the last lines:

> Go now,
> you who would weep at his dying.
>
> His greed has made him feed
> on a flying thing
> and he cannot puke up the bones.
>
> (*BMF*, p. 18)

The dog who feeds on the "flying thing" whose bones destroy him is clearly symbolic of man hastening his own end by destroying the balance of nature.

Dying and living, the bird is an image that recurs throughout Lane's poems, taking various forms — the dead crow in *Letters from the Savage Mind*, the redwing blackbirds in "Fireweed Seeds" (*Separations*), and a number of manifestations in *Mountain Oysters*, including not only the "flying thing" of "The Dog," but also "The God Who Is Goshawk," symbolic of the survival urge with its paradoxical need to destroy, and the blue jay who reaches "unreasonable death," smashing its "fingernail skull" as it hits a boxcar in panic flight:

> Blue wings harden in my hand.
> Bones crack, hollow as the wind
> where it creeps on high snow
> levelling mountains with the land.[39]

In later volumes, the bird dashing itself to death against a wall or a window or dying from cold will become a recurrent image, reaching its climax in "Ice Storm" (*Poems New and Selected*), in which weather, unaided by men, contrives a massacre, and the poet rages, not against his own kind, but against the indifferent cruelty of the universe:

> As if the snow was more than just a prison.
> Ice like an eyelid closing on the birds
> beneath the snow. As I am more than just
>
> the owner of this field, knowing every bird
> I free, I'll find another dozen dead.
> My foot jerks back from cold,
>
> angry now, shaking my fists at the rare
> explosions below me, feet breaking through
> the icy cloud cover of their tombs.
>   (*PNS*, p. 105)

In "The Bird" (*Mountain Oysters*), the implications of this recurrent image are made evident. The poet speaks to a child who has caught a bird and held it in his hands, thinking that in this way he will learn to fly, but the bird dies, and the poet says:

> Only words
> can fly for you like birds
> on the wall of the sun.
> A bird is a poem
> that talks of the end of cages.
>
> (*BMF*, p. 1)

And so the bird becomes a symbol of poetic activity, but also of freedom, as indeed the wild dogs were in other poems, and here the relationship between the poet and the natural world reaches its greatest ambiguity, for it is with the wild things of this world that he senses the greatest affinity—for they, like him, are beyond ordinary human commerce or morality—yet he joins with other men in the destruction of what are, in effect, his totemic counterparts. And here we come to the element of ritual magic in Lane's poems, for he resembles the primitive hunter who will kill a sacred animal, like a bear, for food, but will placate its spirit by apologetic ritual chants.

Into all these poems there enters a vivid sense of the mountain region where the poems take place, and from whose way of life they are derived in theme and imagery alike, and the same happens in the volumes that follow closely after, like *Hiway 401 Rhapsody*, *The Sun Has Begun to Eat the Mountain*, and *Passing into Storm*, except that in these the focus shifts from the hard death of animals to the hard life of men, as in poems like "Thirty Below":

> Men on the pond
> push logs through constant ice.
> Faces stubble with frost.
> No one moves beyond the ritual
> of work. Torment of metal
> and the scream of saws.
>
> (*BMF*, p. 50)

In "Thirty Miles In from the Coast" (*PNS*, p. 55), a man waits with the frozen corpse of his wife stored in a shed until spring;

in "Gerald" (*BMF*, pp. 10–11), a boy is persecuted into insanity by the cruel discipline of his religious fanatic of a father; and in "Sleep Is the Silence Darkness Takes" (*PNS*, pp. 48–50), Lane narrates, as a kind of exemplum of Western Canadian history, the story of a man bred on a hard pioneer farm, growing up to manhood in the hardrock mines, and surviving the war to return "...and pour my soul / into the pocketbooks of others who stole / my brains and used them for their gains / because of privilege, birth or prior right — ". This poem is dedicated to Lane's father, but it is wise when considering any of Lane's narratives to expect a measure of invention. For in another poem, "The Witnesses," also purportedly about his father (this time in the role of a rodeo rider, the McLeod Kid), he says:

What if I try to capture an ecstasy that is not
mine, what if these are only words saying
this was or this was not, a story told to me
until I now no longer believe it was told to me

The witnesses dead, what if I create a past
that never was, make out of nothing
a history of my people whether in pain
or ecstasy, my father riding in the McLeod Rodeo
(*PNS*, p. 101)

But whether the witness evokes an actual incident or an episode conjured by the mind, the faithfulness to place and to historical moment remains in all these poems, and in this way, when he is writing about the interior of British Columbia, Lane does evoke in a convincing way the spirit of a region where he has lived and suffered. The difficulty about classifying him as a regional poet arises when one encounters Lane writing with equal intensity and authenticity about other regions than his native British Columbia. In *Unborn Things: South American Poems* (1975) (some of whose pieces had already appeared in *Beware the Months of Fire* a year before), Lane comes up from an immersion in life along the Andes with a series of splendid and convincing poems, and in his most recent volume, *Old Mother* (1982), the notably dominant region in terms of settings, themes, and recorded experiences is the Prairies, where Lane has been living for the past few years, though this volume also contains a group of poems written on a journey to China.

Unborn Things is a group of threnodies on the lost past of the Incas, alternating with appalled presentations of the here and now in which the descendants of those who created the Andean civilizations survive. In a sense, they are a continuation in another place of Lane's earlier poems recording with mingled delight and anger the splendour of the world and the shame of what man has done to it and to his fellow inhabitants. The difference is that in *Unborn Things* Lane is writing within a context of history and myth that gives his poems a special colour and richness of imagery which his Canadian work, with its faith to place, necessarily lacks.

The heart of the book is a suite entitled "Macchu Picchu," which evokes the past of that lost final fortress of the Inca realm, perched on its splendid crags above the jungle and the rivers. It tells of the departure of Manco Capac, the last Inca, who is to die in a Spanish ambush, of the dying out of the Virgins of the Sun in their mountaintop refuge, and of the fate as an archaeological site and a tourist centre that Macchu Picchu now shares with other tragic loci of history and myth, with Mycenae and Elsinore, with Taxila and Persepolis:

> Today we lay in the Temple of the Virgins
> As centuries filled our mouths with moss.
> They have stripped away the jungle.
> They have torn the winding cloths.
> They have scattered bones to the wind.
>
> Strangers walk through the ruins.
> They talk of where they come from,
> Where they are going.
> As we lay in this roofless room
> They stoned a snake.
>
> It crawled out of the earth
> To lie in the brilliant sun.
> Coils of its body like plaited hair,
> Eyes of cracked stone. They left it
> Broken, draped on a fallen wall.
>
> <div align="right">(<i>PNS</i>, p. 62)</div>

The kind of quasi-Lawrencian transference that equates modern brutality to a snake people fear (there actually are deadly *fer-de-lance* snakes in the Macchu Picchu ruins) with the Spaniards' destruction of a civilization they could not understand is extended to other poems in *Unborn Things*, poems concerning the present-day life of Andean people, and this is not unexpected when one remembers the indictments of the abuse of the will and power of men over other beings in earlier poems like "Mountain Oysters" and "The Black Colt."

"At the Edge of the Jungle" is a poem about disillusionment in a romantically anticipated place. The narrative of horror begins with a dog burying its head in the Amazonian mud to evade the flies that swarm on his sore eyes; it ends with a tethered rooster whose beak children have cut away so that he cannot eat. It is a fine, appalling poem; I recognize its authenticity from having made the same journey over the Andean Sierra and down to the Amazonian headwaters. It ends:

Diseased clouds bloom in the sky.
They throw down roots of fire.
The bird drags sound from its skin.
I am grown older than I imagined:
the garden I dreamed does not exist
and compassion is only the beginning
of suffering. Everything deceives.

A man could walk into this jungle
and lying down be lost
among the green sucking of trees.
What reality there is resides
in the child who holds the string
and does not see
the bird as it beats its blunt head
again and again into the earth.

(*PNS*, p. 81)

There is a curious footnote to be made to this poem and to the title poem of the volume, "Unborn Things." They appeared, as "July" and "June" respectively, in *Beware the Months of Fire*, but they were, as Lane admits in his prefatory note to *Unborn*

Things, "printed in versions where, through changing a few key geographical words, they reflected a British Columbia locale." Lane gives no explanation as to why he made the changes, though he admits it was an "error," as becomes evident when one reads on and encounters a cluster of images that has no imaginable place in a British Columbian locale, but is authentically Latin American:

> a broken melon bleeds a pestilence
> of bees; a woman squats and pees
> balancing perfectly her basket
> of meat; a gelding falls to its knees
> under the goad of its driver.
>
> (BMF, p.79)

Lane's ability to grasp the essential imagery of a series of regions and his power to create a self-consistent myth out of the lost history of the Incas mark him as a great deal more than a regional poet in the way we apply that term to writers whose inspiration comes from a single small area and its traditions, like William Barnes or John Clare. He is on a much wider scale a poet of place and time, committed to considering human communities in relation to their geographical environments and their places in history.

Each of the larger collections of Lane's poems consists mainly of works collected from the smaller earlier volumes, with a few added new pieces — more in the case of *Poems New and Selected* than in the case of *Beware the Months of Fire*. What is most interesting in these books is the method of selection and arrangement. In the case of *Beware the Months of Fire*, both these tasks were apparently done by Margaret Atwood, then the active editor of House of Anansi, which published the book, though it seems unlikely that Lane had nothing at all to do with the process of choice and ordering. In the case of *Poems New and Selected*, Lane seems to have made his own choices, possibly with some advice from William Toye, the editorial director of the Oxford University Press in Toronto.

As I have already remarked, neither of the selected volumes contains much work from Lane's first book, *Letters from the Savage Mind* (only one poem from that book survived into

Poems New and Selected). *Separations* and *Mountain Oysters* are well represented in both books, while almost all of *Unborn Things* (of which a few pieces appear in *Beware the Months of Fire*) and of *Albino Pheasants* (1977) are gathered into *Poems New and Selected* (which, however, drops a number of the pieces from *Beware the Months of Fire* while picking up other poems from *Separations* and *Mountain Oysters* not included there). A close analysis of these various inclusions and exclusions would be a bibliographical task beyond the scope of this essay, but certain general features of the collections should be noted here.

The arrangement of *Beware the Months of Fire* tends to be in thematic groups, which would fit in with Margaret Atwood's critical inclinations at that period. For example, six poems about men's relations with animals are grouped together at one point; these are followed by four poems about experiences connected with work in the interior of British Columbia; next come four poems and a long prose dialogue about the vagabond levels of city life; and then seven love poems of various kinds, followed by five of the poems from South America later included in *Unborn Things*. The arrangement of *Poems New and Selected* is chronological rather than thematic, with groups of poems from the various books following each other in succession, and a group of thirteen previously uncollected pieces bringing the book to an end.

One notices clearly in *Poems New and Selected* the formal change in Lane's poems, the tendency to create fairly regular syllabic structures within traditional stanzaic forms, which becomes evident in the poems of *Unborn Things* and of the year or so immediately preceding that volume, and which accompanies a remarkable advance in poetic skill since the rather loose and unsure poems Lane was writing in the early 1960s. There is also a shift, very perceptible in *Albino Pheasants*, towards a more reflective type of poem, philosophically concerned with human destiny and moving into those verges of the numinous that prose can hardly penetrate. This results in poems quite different in their gravity of tone, in their delicate balancing of correspondences and connotations, and even in their visionary symbolism, from the earlier poems. "Still Hunting" is a fine example, with its contemplative probing of the reality of death:

A single banner of sky between two mountains:
neither the beginning nor the end of clouds.
Somewhere all the animals have happened
and I wait and pray I will know
the difference between the animal and man;
pray for the gift of a death
to break this glacial waste of time —
that when I shoulder the empty body
I will have something to walk with
be it ice, air, stone or man; pray
I will find the road where I left it
in the tree-line far below.

(PNS, p. 83)

And in one of the later, previously ungathered pieces in *Poems New and Selected*, significantly entitled "Wild Birds," the poet sees a flight of crows fighting the wind:

Baffled, returning, knowing the landfall,
they beat their wings against a strength
greater than their own.

(PNS, p. 103)

He goes on to develop his philosophic theme: the way humankind's chaotic nature in a chaotic world frustrates all dreams of order. It is, made clear and articulate, the philosophy that unites Lane's poetry from beginning to end:

    We are all of us

as those birds I saw at sea blown outward
against our will. I read the books
and dreamed the dream that words could change
the vision, make of man a perfect animal
and so transformed become immortal.

What else was there to dream? Not this,
not this beating against the wind. Chaos
is our creation and the god we wished was man:
to turn again into the thing we are, yet be
black cinders lost at sea, the wild birds failing.

(PNS, p. 103)

Since the appearance of *Poems New and Selected*, Lane has published three collections of verse, each with its own special character. In *No Longer Two People* (1979), poems written by Lane and Lorna Uher appear in alternation, and the resultant dialogue marks a departure for a poet who up to now has been a monologist, talking to, rather than with, his readers. Lorna Uher is the speaker as well as the reader; she is the fellow poet, sharer of experience and idea. The result of the collaboration is that in this collection one poet writes at her best and the other seems to move out of his stance as the agonized witness into that of the engaged and involved man, the half of a unity of feeling. It is unnecessary to ask biographical questions. The relationship, so far as the reader is concerned, is one between personae and achieves its validity on that level. As a dialogue of disembodied voices on radio, it found its appropriate medium and was impressive because of the elegiac undertone to its lyrical intensities. *No Longer Two People* builds up to a strange gravity as the speakers see their lives advancing through the debris of the past towards the paradoxical regeneration of winter. Both their final poems evoke the rot of a late garden where the tomatoes hang shrivelled with frost on the black vines. The woman concludes:

> And we await
> the forgiveness of winter: drifts
> to bury all the dead we left behind.
>
> Then we will come to one another
> with the simplicity of trees
> stripped branches holding all
> that will survive.[40]

And the man, more ambiguously, sees himself breaking

> a trail through the snow.
> There is no looking behind.
> Everywhere the wind covers my passing.
>
> (p.51)

Is he really leaving the old past of ruined relationships, as his earlier remark "Now is the time / for patience" (p. 51) suggests?

Or is he just acting once again to the habitual pattern? One suspects the latter when he contradicts the woman by saying:

> There is no forgiveness,
> only a blind woman calling out her dead,
> the snow, the broken earth.
>
> (p. 51)

This stubborn ambiguity takes one back to the relationship between person and persona, and also between animus and anima, and to the ways in which poetic structures become detached from the life they purport to represent, as the Picasso epigraph suggests:

> Though these two people once existed for me, they exist no longer.... They are no longer two people, you see, but forms and colours; forms and colours that have taken on, meanwhile, the idea of two people and preserve the vibration of their life.

The transition to *The Measure* (1980), which is dedicated to the other poet of *No Longer Two People*, is a clear one. For here, as well, Lane is working among the haunting correspondences between art and the actuality that provides its content. His own statement introducing the poems emphasizes this fact. For, beginning with the platitudinous remark that "the old stories aren't dead and neither is the art of telling them," he goes on to say:

> The poems here are mostly narratives, their form a direct result of their content, their content a direct result of a life lived. Even as one allows the poems to be, one selects among the many images in order to find those whose shape will define a way of being alive. There are a number of voices speaking here. Each one struggled into being on its own. If there is a violence reflected among them it is only because I care deeply for the many lives I have seen wasted uselessly. (*M*, cover note)

The intellectual confusion of such a statement is obvious, yet it is a necessary confusion in a poet who has based so much of his writing on actual experiences, and in the end realizes, if the poem is good, it has very little to do with the power of the experience. It is, as he says, a matter of selecting among the images, which means creating an abstract order, an area of detachment among the concrete and particular facts of existence. And this is one of the principal problems and tasks of the narrative as distinct from the epic poet.

For the nonepic writer of narrative poems is dealing, not with the affairs of gods and heroes, but with the affairs of ordinary human beings and perhaps of animals. And the essence of narrative poetry is really trapping those moments in life that are either typical or epiphanous, either that which explains or that which astonishes, and presenting them in a shape that, as Lane remarks, "will define a way of being alive."

A narrative poem need not tell a story at length, as Wordsworth's often do. It can present a single image that portrays or even implies action which reveals through its symbolic power something profound about existence. "Chinook" is the shortest poem of *The Measure*, but the truth it tells is as complex as an ice-flower:

> Beneath the tree, glutted on winter
> apples, seven sparrows lie
> drunk, beating small wings on snow
> as if they could fly into it
> and make of ice an element as free as air.
>
> (M, p. 49)

And a life doomed to loneliness, which many poets would take pages to evoke, is embraced in the hardly longer form of "Coming Home":

> Coming home drunk
> I want you to be
> not there. I want
> the empty in the bottle
> the broken glass
> and the backs of my friends

> as they leave me. But
> most of all I want you
> not to be there.
>
> (M, p. 53)

But by no means all the poems in *The Measure* are as brief or as gnomic in their intent as these. "I Am Tired of Your Politics," which I have already discussed, is one of them; here a general statement is made about the goals of poetry, and the personal history of the "...woman / natural as beauty..." is introduced to illustrate it. In "Blue Valley Night," the poet draws out of the past a recollection of his days as first-aid man at a lumber mill and tells the story of his relationship with alcoholic old Charlie, who gets drunk regularly at the end of the month on lemon extract. The poem is elaborate, building through the savage comedy of human degeneration to the inevitable tragedy when Charlie, putting on what is left of his best clothes, goes out to march into the front of a train. His death creates the merest ripple in the universe:

> In the cedars, crows
> lift in their feathers,
> lift and settle
> in their sleep.
>
> (M, p. 33)

And in "Something Other than Our Own" (M, pp. 34-35), the savage comedy plays out in a different way as the poet and his companions from the bunkhouse watch an enraged husband with a gun stalking his wife's naked lover (armed only with a guitar) through the piles of lumber in the frozen yard. As the naked man stumbles down the railway track into the snowy distance and the husband gives up his hunt, the watchers laugh, and the poet goes back to his bunk to dream of a woman.

Perhaps it is the inevitability of the human comedy, and the strange dignity of those for whom it has turned into tragedy, that is the clearest theme of *The Measure*. If one can talk of the book having a lesson, it is that of respect for life, no matter how ludicrous, how debased, how alien it may seem to us who are observers. It comes round again to the conviction that observation is not enough; there must be the passion and the complicity of witness.

Lane's most recent book, *Old Mother* (1982), is also his most overtly experimental, but this statement immediately involves one in considering what we really mean by terms like *experimental* and *avant-garde* in a country like Canada whose distinctive literature is still young and has only recently emerged from the cautious conservatism of early pioneer writers. I suggest that in such a situation the experimental artist is far less concerned with formal considerations than his counterpart in a country with an established literature. In the arts of a young country, the first task — once the defensiveness of the pioneer has been dissolved — is to define and embrace the land, to understand the interplay of history and geography that has shaped the society for which the poet or the novelist or the painter, each in his special language, speaks. In an old country, it is the shifts of sensibility and perception within an established order that are the concerns of those who move on the forward edge of art. The difference, essentially, is between the process of exploration and the process of invention — between the discovery of what is existing and the creation of what does not yet exist. What the two situations have in common is that they both represent that thrust into the unknown which is the ultimate aim of all true artists.

In terms of these definitions, it seems to me that Lane has always been experimental and always avant-garde since he has been constantly seeking the forms that would most appropriately express a kind of living which has not yet found its place in literature. In such a task, the content often assumes an importance in relation to the form which it may not have in the more abstract and disembodied poetry of older cultures, and this means that very often a stark narrative structure, with a language stripped down to largely monosyllabic simplicity, such as one often encounters in Lane's earlier poetry, is the appropriate and therefore the experimentally correct vehicle.

Nevertheless, Lane's recent work, ever since his visit to the Andes and his encounter with the old cultures of the Incas and the Spanish Americans, has shown a growing complexity, manifested, as we have seen, in the greater sophistication of language and the resort to technically more elaborate forms that are characteristic of poets working in more long-established literary traditions. This echoes a general tendency in Canadian writing — and painting as well — to make the further step, from the stage of exploration to the stage of invention. We see it in the fiction writers who have moved from the naturalism of the early Prairie novelists to the artifice of writers like Timothy Findley and Margaret Atwood, and it appears now among the poets, and in Lane's case within the work of a single poet, so that in *Old Mother* one sees him involved in the exploration of poetic ingenuities in a way that reminds one how much his affinities were always divided between the Canadian poets who explored the immediate environment and the European decadents who were much more concerned with the horror of human existence in any environment.

Already in the naming of a previous volume, *The Measure*, there is a hint of Lane's closer attention to the prosodic aspects of his work, and though the "measure" of the title poem seems to be an existential one —

> What is the measure then, the magpie in the field
> watching over death, the dog's eyes hard as marbles
> breath still frozen to his lips?
>
> (*M*, p.9)

— one soon becomes aware, reading through the book, of the extent to which poetic measures, as well as existential relativities, have become increasingly important to him.

In the first version of Lane's most recent volume, the key word was repeated in the provisional title, "Weights and Measures";[41] later the book was retitled *Old Mother*. The formal concerns of the poet are made very clear in the central sequence of the volume, "The Weight" (meaning the weight of the past, of ancestry), where the second staggered stanza ends:

> which is duty
> not to deny
>   the neck burned
>   calling the dead to come
> eyes buried
>   alive again
>   once more
>   the sprung
> measure[42]

The "sprung measure" is evident throughout this central (in place as well as significance) section of *Old Mother*. It is partly a variant of Hopkins' practice of "sprung rhythm," gaining emphasis through splitting the lines according to the natural pauses and emphases of speech, but it is also a visual element in the layout of the text, which relates it to contemporary "concrete poetry," and it accompanies an associational grouping of concepts and thoughts that reminds one — and not too distantly — of classic modernist works like *Ulysses*, and the *Cantos* of Ezra Pound.

All this may seem to project the image of a Lane coming late to awareness of the variants of poetic post-modernism, and that would be unjust since the erudition that makes him acutely aware of poetic events has long been evident. It is really the content of "The Weight" that has dictated this poly-experimental approach since here, in the grotesque ancestral figure of "old *Jack Lane*," his putative descendant Patrick is enacting — for an audience of poets gathered in by name — Marty, Purdy, Newlove, Suknaski, Kroetsch, etc. — the cruel seeding and subjection of the land. This is poetry that defies exposition, yet — especially in the section of the sequence called "The Dance" — it moves the reader to a strange alternation of bitterness and nostalgia. The past — we are told and believe — was frightful to live through; is beautiful in recollection. And here one lips that paradox which haunts every significant Canadian writer of our generation, the gap between what happened, which was actuality, and what we choose to remember, which is history.

History, in fact, haunts the earlier poems of *Old Mother*, such as "Buffalo Stones" and "Indian Tent Rings," which move Lane out of other pasts linked to a departed present into the prairie of an immediate present. In "Indian Tent Rings," the poet compares his own reactions as a man of the West to the evidences of a past culture with those of the American visitors who relate everything they come across to the archaic remains they have seen in the lands of classical civilizations. Yet in the end he concludes:

> It is enough they are here, the woman
> caught in the circle and the man
> circling below her, his eyes

> trying to find a thing more than an idea,
> a bit of pebble carved into himself.
>
> <div align="right">(<i>OM</i>, p. 15)</div>

In these poems, the relativity of pasts is perhaps the most important theme: the suggestion that the unrecorded histories of peoples without writing may be as important as that of elaborately literate cultures.

At the end of the original "Weights and Measures," the contrast between the primitive and the civilized was emphasized in a cruel sequence, "The Chicken Poems." In *Old Mother* these poems do not stand apart; they are included, and somewhat scattered, in the section called "Prairie Poems." But even in this rearrangement, they stand out for their bleak horror. The intent of these poems is on one level obvious. Chickens bred by modern methods — trapped in their functions of egg-layers and meat-providers — are the ultimate exploitees, the final slaves of human beings. Yet even they have their own orders of domination and subjection, their own mindless cruelties, and here there is a curious series of juxtapositions, with the victor inevitably becoming victim. In "Monarch II," the cock kills an intruding rooster:

> His crowing stuns the air.
> The hens flutter, wings
> cowled and tails held high.
> Monarch stabs at the barred bird
> then stalks toward the garden
> where young worms have risen after rain.
>
> <div align="right">(<i>OM</i>, p. 25)</div>

In "Monarch IV," the same cock is crippled because he twisted his tendons during the fight. Detecting his sickness, his own hens attack him. It is left for the lowest in the pecking order, a bird almost deprived of plumage, to deliver the *coup de grâce*:

> She circles carefully
> as if her scabs might crack,
> and keeping safe from her white sisters
> stands above her king. The rooster

twitches and his one eye opens
to a sky whose sun has gone.
With a stab she returns him to the dark.
(OM, p. 31)

In Lane's early poems, the bird was always the image of flying free, of liberation. But in "Archaeopteryx," another poem of *Old Mother* that appeared in the original "Chicken Poems" sequence, the prehistoric creature is

...the bird of aeons.
The thing you kill.
(OM, p. 43)

The chickens are all victims as distinct from free flyers. Yet a human being is shown as no better or more fortunate than the bird victims, for at the end of another poem, "Wings":

The hawks have flown the sky,
following a darker wing.
I stand alone, a thing of bones,
a wingless thing who cannot find the wind.
(OM, p. 42)

Old Mother ends with the sequence "China Poems," written as a result of Lane's visit, with a group of other Canadian writers, to China in 1981. A version of it appears in *Chinada: Memoirs of the Gang of Seven*, written by the members of the group and edited by Gary Geddes. Lane's poems were by far the best writing to come out of the venture; in them he shows the same power of empathizing with a strange landscape and of catching the resonances of another people's history as he did in Peru. "Silk Factory" is a good example; it shows admirably the way the patterns of the past — dragon and phoenix in the white brocade woven in the factory — survive in modern China, and not only in artefacts but also in the human condition exemplified in the lives of the silk weavers:

A weaver-girl
laughs at a young man and he trips on nothing.

> When she moves he cannot see where he is going.
> Grey with silk dusk, windows rattle
> and the glass is frosted with snow.
> The bitterness of Ch'en T'ao is long ago
> and the shuttles are no longer lumps of ice.
> Still, the brocade the weaver-girl makes
> is not for her, and the young man, though
> he labours for many years, will never buy
> the white silk she works so hard to weave.
>
> (*OM*, p. 81)

The human condition, Lane is suggesting in these poems, modifies and largely frustrates all political hopes. The "China Poems" accept no ideology; they do accept friendship, human warmth, and there is a tenderness to their tone that is in striking contrast to the ferocity with which, in the chicken poems, Lane handles the fates and the natures of both beasts and men trapped in unnatural ways of existence, whether as exploiters or exploited. In the "China Poems," birds return to their role of flying free, like the swallows in "Over the Slow Rivers":

> Sing to me of the tireless, the endless,
> the coming and the going that are leaves:
> sing the female and the male of things
> among the empires of the air, bright warriors,
> none as swift as you in the blue worlds.
>
> (*OM*, p. 85)

NOTES

[1] Letter received from Patrick Lane, n.d.

[2] Stephen Dale, "Interview," *Books in Canada*, Dec. 1981, p. 33. All further references to this work appear in the text.

[3] Patrick Lane, "To the Outlaw," *New: American and Canadian Poetry*, No. 15 (April–March 1971), p. 58. All further references to this work appear in the text.

[4] *The Measure* (Windsor, Ont.: Black Moss, 1980), p. 46. All further references to this work (*M*) appear in the text.

[5] "The Absinthe Drinker," in *Letters from the Savage Mind*

(Vancouver: Very Stone House, 1966), n. pag. All further references to this work (*LSM*) appear in the text.

[6] *Beware the Months of Fire* (Toronto: House of Anansi, 1974), n. pag. All further references to this work (*BMF*) appear in the text.

[7] Al Purdy, "Other Vancouverites," rev. of *From the Portals of Mouseholes*, by Seymour Mayne, *Fires in the Temple*, by bill bissett, *Letters from the Savage Mind*, by Patrick Lane, and *The Circus of the Boy's Eye*, by Jim Brown, *Canadian Literature*, No. 35 (Winter 1968), p. 84.

[8] Douglas Barbour, "The Common Craving," rev. of *Separations*, and six other books, *Canadian Literature*, No. 48 (Spring 1971), p. 72.

[9] Gary Geddes, "Tight-Lipped in a Brutal World: Lane Close to the Boards," rev. of *Beware the Months of Fire*, *The Globe and Mail*, 18 May 1974, p. 37.

[10] Geddes, p. 37.

[11] George Melnyk, "The Social and Personal Views of Poets," rev. of *Poems Selected and New*, by P. K. Page, *Beware the Months of Fire*, by Patrick Lane, and *For and Against the Moon*, by Tom Wayman, *Edmonton Journal*, 27 July 1974, p. 72.

[12] Doug Fetherling, "Poet Stands Out like a Mountain Peak," rev. of *Beware the Months of Fire*, by Patrick Lane, and *For and Against the Moon*, by Tom Wayman, *The Toronto Star*, 8 June 1974, Sec. F, p. 7.

[13] Stan Dragland, rev. of *Beware the Months of Fire*, by Patrick Lane, and *Achilles' Navel: Throbs, Laments and Vagaries*, by Doug Fetherling, *The London Free Press*, 17 Aug. 1974, p. 47.

[14] Jean Mallinson, "Tones of Gloom," rev. of *Beware the Months of Fire*, by Patrick Lane, *Leaving*, by Andrew Suknaski, and *Living with th Vishyun*, by bill bissett, *The Vancouver Sun*, 12 July 1974, Sec. A, p. 33.

[15] Douglas Barbour, rev. of *Beware the Months of Fire*, *Quill & Quire*, June 1974, p. 12.

[16] Len Gasparini, "One Plus Three," rev. of *Beware the Months of Fire*, by Patrick Lane, *Leaving*, by Andrew Suknaski, *Snakeroot*, by Gary Geddes, and *Sullen Earth*, by Brenda Fleet, *Canadian Literature*, No. 63 (Winter 1975), pp. 92, 93.

[17] George Woodcock, "Playing with Freezing Fire," rev. of *Unborn Things: South American Poems*, and seven other books, *Canadian Literature*, No. 70 (Autumn 1976), p. 88.

[18] Brian Brett, rev. of *Unborn Things: South American Poems*, *Vancouver Province*, 9 April 1976.

[19] Len Gasparini, "Exile and Exhumation," rev. of *Unborn Things: South American Poems*, by Patrick Lane, and *The Shrouding*, by Leo Kennedy, *Books in Canada*, April 1976, p. 21.

[20] Stan Dragland, "Bone-Structures," rev. of *Free Time*, by Tom Wayman, and *Albino Pheasants*, by Patrick Lane, *Canadian Literature*, No. 84 (Spring 1980), pp. 125, 126.

[21] Neil Whiteman, "A Left to the Mind: The Poems of Patrick Lane," *CV / II*, 3, No. 4 (Summer 1978), 52.

[22] *CV / II*, 4, No. 1 (Winter 1979), 52–56.

[23] George Woodcock, "Poetry of Time and Place: Recent Canadian Trends," *Pacific Northwest Review of Books*, May 1978; rpt. in George Woodcock, *The World of Canadian Writing: Critiques and Recollections* (Vancouver: Douglas & McIntyre, 1980), p. 247.

[24] Marilyn Bowering, "Pine Boughs and Apple Trees: The Poetry of Patrick Lane," *The Malahat Review*, No. 45 (Jan. 1978), p. 25.

[25] Bowering, p. 33.

[26] Jean Mallinson, "A Reading of Pat Lane," rev. of *Unborn Things: South American Poems, Albino Pheasants*, and *Poems New and Selected, Brick: A Journal of Reviews*, No. 7 (Fall 1979), pp. 5–8.

[27] Andrew Suknaski, "A Saving Grace," rev. of *Poems New and Selected*, by Patrick Lane, and *Anniversaries*, by Don Coles, *Canadian Literature*, No. 86 (Autumn 1980), pp. 130–33.

[28] Alexandre L. Amprimoz, "Fear and Experience: The Poems of Patrick Lane," rev. of *Poems New and Selected, Waves*, 7, No. 3 (Spring 1979), 69, 71.

[29] Edward Prato, rev. of *Two-Headed Poems*, by Margaret Atwood, and *Poems New and Selected*, by Patrick Lane, *West Coast Review*, 14, No. 1 (June 1979), 46.

[30] Louis Dudek, "The Poet as Rapist," rev. of *Poems New and Selected*, by Patrick Lane, *Albino Pheasants*, by Patrick Lane, *The Salmon Country*, by Greg Gatenby, and *Moon without Light*, by Len Gasparini, *The Globe and Mail*, 27 Jan. 1979, p. 42.

[31] Norma West Linder, "Starkness and Sensibility," rev. of *Poems New and Selected*, by Patrick Lane, *Sunblue*, by Margaret Avison, *Fall by Fury*, by Earle Birney, and *Intrigues in the House of Mirrors*, by Mike Zizis, *Canadian Author & Bookman*, 54, No. 3 (May 1979), 28.

[32] Rosemary Sullivan, "Staying Power," rev. of *Poems New and Selected, The Canadian Forum*, March 1979, p. 34.

[33] Doug Beardsley, "Pat Lane: Time to Honor a Top-Rank Poet," rev. of *Poems New and Selected, Victoria Times-Colonist*, 22 Dec. 1978.

[34] Philip Lanthier, "Careful Talk," rev. of *Poems New and Selected*, *Matrix*, No. 9 (Spring–Summer 1979), p. 81.

[35] Ian Sowton, "North-Northwest," rev. of *The Measure*, *Canadian Literature*, No. 91 (Winter 1981). p. 104.

[36] John Cruikshank, "Precious Little," rev. of *The Measure*, *Books in Canada*, Aug.–Sept. 1981, p. 18.

[37] Rosemary Aubert, rev. of *The Measure*, *Quill & Quire*, Feb. 1981, p. 48.

[38] *Poems New and Selected* (Toronto: Oxford Univ. Press, 1978), p. 98. All further references to this work *(PNS)* appear in the text.

[39] "Loading Boxcars," in *Mountain Oysters* (Montreal: Very Stone House in Transit, 1971), n. pag.

[40] Patrick Lane and Lorna Uher, *No Longer Two People* (Winnipeg: Turnstone, 1979), p. 49. All further references to this work appear in the text.

[41] I am indebted to Patrick Lane for having allowed me to read a typescript of this early version of the book that eventually became *Old Mother*.

[42] *Old Mother* (Toronto: Oxford Univ. Press, 1982), p. 48. All further references to this work *(OM)* appear in the text.

SELECTED BIBLIOGRAPHY

Primary Sources

Lane, Patrick. *Letters from the Savage Mind.* Vancouver: Very Stone House, [1966].

———. *Newspaper Walls* [broadsheet]. Vancouver: Univ. of British Columbia, 1967.

———, and Seymour Mayne, eds. *Collected Poems.* By Red Lane. Vancouver: Very Stone House, 1968.

———. *Sunflower Seeds* [broadsheet]. [Vancouver]: n.p., [1968].

———. *For Rita — in Asylum* [broadsheet]. Poster Poem, No. 3. Vancouver: Very Stone House, 1969.

———. *Calgary City Jail* [broadsheet]. Poster Poem, No. 6. Vancouver: Very Stone House, 1969.

———. *Separations.* Trumansburg, N.Y.: New / Books, 1969.

———. *On the Street.* [Vernon, B.C.]: n.p., 1970.

———. *Hiway 401 Rhapsody.* [Winnipeg]: Very Stone House in Transit, 1971.

———. *Mountain Oysters.* [Montreal]: Very Stone House in Transit, 1971.

———. "To the Outlaw." *New: American and Canadian Poetry,* No. 15 (April–March 1971), pp. 54–58.

———. *The Sun Has Begun to Eat the Mountain.* Montreal: Ingluvin, 1972.

———. *Passing into Storm.* Vernon, B.C.: Traumerei Communications, 1973.

———. *Beware the Months of Fire.* Toronto: House of Anansi, 1974.

———. *Certs* [broadsheet]. Prince George, B.C.: College of New Caledonia, 1974.

———. *Unborn Things: South American Poems.* Madeira Park, B.C.: Harbour, 1975.

———. *For Riel in That Gawdam Prison* [broadsheet]. White Rock, B.C.: Blackfish, 1976.

———. *Albino Pheasants.* Madeira Park, B.C.: Harbour, 1977.

———. *Poems New and Selected*. Toronto: Oxford Univ. Press, 1978.
———, and Lorna Uher. *No Longer Two People*. Winnipeg: Turnstone, 1979.
———. *There Are Still the Mountains* [pamphlet]. Winnipeg: Very Stone House in Transit, 1979.
———. *The Garden* [pamphlet]. Toronto: League of Canadian Poets, 1980.
———. *The Measure*. Windsor, Ont.: Black Moss, 1980.
———. *Skull* [pamphlet]. Madeira Park, B.C.: Harbour, 1980.
———. *Old Mother*. Toronto: Oxford Univ. Press, 1982.

Secondary Sources

Amabile, George. Letter. *CV/II*, 4, No. 1 (Winter 1979), 55–56.
Amprimoz, Alexandre L. "Fear and Experience: The Poems of Patrick Lane." Rev. of *Poems New and Selected*. *Waves*, 7, No. 3 (Spring 1979), 68–71.
Aubert, Rosemary. Rev. of *The Measure*. *Quill & Quire*, Feb. 1981, p. 48.
Barbour, Douglas. "The Common Craving." Rev. of *Separations*, and six other books. *Canadian Literature*, No. 48 (Spring 1971), pp. 70–74.
———. Rev. of *Beware the Months of Fire*. *Quill & Quire*, June 1974, p. 12.
Beardsley, Doug. "Pat Lane: Time to Honor a Top-Rank Poet." Rev. of *Poems New and Selected*. *Victoria Times-Colonist*, 22 Dec. 1978.
Bowering, Marilyn. "Pine Boughs and Apple Trees: The Poetry of Patrick Lane." *The Malahat Review*, No. 45 (Jan. 1978), pp. 24–34.
Brett, Brian. Rev. of *Unborn Things: South American Poems*. *Vancouver Province*, 9 April 1976.
Cruikshank, John. "Precious Little." Rev. of *The Measure*. *Books in Canada*, Aug.–Sept. 1981, p. 18.
Dale, Stephen. "Interview." *Books in Canada*, Dec. 1981, pp. 31–33.
Dragland, Stan. Rev. of *Beware the Months of Fire*, by Patrick Lane, and *Achilles' Navel: Throbs, Laments and Vagaries*, by Doug Fetherling. *The London Free Press*, 17 Aug. 1974, p. 47.
———. "Bone-Structures." Rev. of *Free Time*, by Tom Wayman, and *Albino Pheasants*, by Patrick Lane. *Canadian Literature*, No. 84 (Spring 1980), pp. 124–26.

Dudek, Louis. "The Poet as Rapist." Rev. of *Poems New and Selected*, by Patrick Lane, *Albino Pheasants*, by Patrick Lane, *The Salmon Country*, by Greg Gatenby, and *Moon without Light*, by Len Gasparini. *The Globe and Mail*, 27 Jan. 1979, p. 42.

Fetherling, Doug. "Poet Stands Out like a Mountain Peak." Rev. of *Beware the Months of Fire*, by Patrick Lane, and *For and Against the Moon*, by Tom Wayman. *The Toronto Star*, 8 June 1974, Sec. F, p. 7.

Gasparini, Len. "One Plus Three." Rev. of *Beware the Months of Fire*, by Patrick Lane, *Leaving*, by Andrew Suknaski, *Snakeroot*, by Gary Geddes, and *Sullen Earth*, by Brenda Fleet. *Canadian Literature*, No. 63 (Winter 1975), pp. 92–95.

——. "Exile and Exhumation." Rev. of *Unborn Things: South American Poems*, by Patrick Lane, and *The Shrouding*, by Leo Kennedy. *Books in Canada*, April 1976, pp. 21–22.

Geddes, Gary. "Tight-Lipped in a Brutal World: Lane Close to the Boards." Rev. of *Beware the Months of Fire*. *The Globe and Mail*, 18 May 1974, p. 37.

Lanthier, Philip. "Careful Talk." Rev. of *Poems New and Selected*. *Matrix*, No. 9 (Spring–Summer 1979), pp. 81–83.

Linder, Norma West. "Starkness and Sensibility." Rev. of *Poems New and Selected*, by Patrick Lane, *Sunblue*, by Margaret Avison, *Fall by Fury*, by Earle Birney, and *Intrigues in the House of Mirrors*, by Mike Zizis. *Canadian Author & Bookman*, 54, No. 3 (May 1979), 28–29.

Mallinson, Jean. "Tones of Gloom." Rev. of *Beware the Months of Fire*, by Patrick Lane, *Leaving*, by Andrew Suknaski, and *Living with th Vishyun*, by bill bissett. *The Vancouver Sun*, 12 July 1974, Sec. A, p. 33.

——. "A Reading of Pat Lane." Rev. of *Unborn Things: South American Poems*, *Albino Pheasants*, and *Poems New and Selected*. *Brick: A Journal of Reviews*, No. 7 (Fall 1979), pp. 5–8.

——. Letter. *CV/II*, 4, No. 1 (Winter 1979), 53–55.

Melnyk, George. "The Social and Personal Views of Poets." Rev. of *Poems Selected and New*, by P. K. Page, *Beware the Months of Fire*, by Patrick Lane, and *For and Against the Moon*, by Tom Wayman. *Edmonton Journal*, 27 July 1974, p. 72.

Prato, Edward. Rev. of *Two-Headed Poems*, by Margaret Atwood, and *Poems New and Selected*, by Patrick Lane. *West Coast Review*, 14, No. 1 (June 1979), 43–46.

Purdy, Al. "Other Vancouverites." Rev. of *From the Portals of Mouseholes*, by Seymour Mayne, *Fires in the Temple*, by bill bissett,

Letters from the Savage Mind, by Patrick Lane, and *The Circus of the Boy's Eye*, by Jim Brown. *Canadian Literature*, No. 35 (Winter 1968), pp. 83–85.

Sowton, Ian. "North-Northwest." Rev. of *The Measure*. *Canadian Literature*, No. 91 (Winter 1981), pp. 102–04.

Suknaski, Andrew. "A Saving Grace." Rev. of *Poems New and Selected*, by Patrick Lane, and *Anniversaries*, by Don Coles. *Canadian Literature*, No. 86 (Autumn 1980), pp. 130–33.

Sullivan, Rosemary. "Staying Power." Rev. of *Poems New and Selected*. *The Canadian Forum*, March 1979, p. 34.

White, Howard. Letter. *CV/II*, 4, No. 1 (Winter 1979), 55.

Whiteman, Neil. "A Left to the Mind: The Poems of Patrick Lane." *CV/II*, 3, No. 4 (Summer 1978), 49–52.

Woodcock, George. "Playing with Freezing Fire." Rev. of *Unborn Things: South American Poems*, and seven other books. *Canadian Literature*, No. 70 (Autumn 1976), pp. 84–91.

———. "Poetry of Time and Place: Recent Canadian Trends." *Pacific Northwest Review of Books*, May 1978. Rpt. in *The World of Canadian Writing: Critiques and Recollections*. Vancouver: Douglas & McIntyre, 1980, pp. 241–49.

Zonailo, Carolyn. Letter. *CV/II*, 4, No. 1 (Winter 1979), 52–53.

Dennis Lee (1939–)

T. G. MIDDLEBRO'

Dennis Lee (1939-   )

T. G. MIDDLEBRO'

Biography

DENNIS LEE was born in Toronto on 31 August 1939 and attended Kingsway Lambton Public School, Etobicoke, and the University of Toronto Schools. In 1957 he enrolled in honours English at Victoria College of the University of Toronto. As an undergraduate, he was active with the Student Christian Movement, with the Victoria College literary review *Acta Victoriana*, and in theatre. Lee published one short story and fifteen poems in *Acta Victoriana* between 1959 and 1964 and, in addition, collaborated with Margaret Atwood in writing a regular humorous column over the signature "Shakesbeat Latweed." In theatre, he wrote the lyrics to accompany the music of Peter Grant for two productions of the annual college review, *The Bob*. His interest in this field was to lead later to his writing the libretto for John Beckwith's cantata *Place of Meeting*, a work commissioned by the Toronto Mendelssohn Choir for premier performance in 1967.

Lee graduated in 1962. After spending a year in England, he returned to the University of Toronto for graduate work and received an M.A. in 1964. His thesis was on the American fascist[1] poet Ezra Pound. He taught English literature at Victoria College, then at the Rochdale Cooperative and York University. His interest in literature and education led him to coedit, with Roberta Charlesworth, two secondary-school verse anthologies, *An Anthology of Verse* (1964) and *The Second Century Anthologies of Verse* (2 vols., 1967-69), both published by Oxford University Press.

In 1967 Dennis Lee and Dave Godfrey founded the House of Anansi Press. The first volume published was Lee's collection of irregular sonnets, *Kingdom of Absence*. Individual poems by Lee had begun to appear in various periodicals late in 1963, and in

April 1966 a sequence of sixteen sonnets was published in *The Canadian Forum* under the title "Kingdom of Absence." The book with that title contains forty-three sonnets. In 1968 the House of Anansi published the first version of Lee's *Civil Elegies*. The revised version of 1972 won the Governor General's Award.

Lee worked as chief editor with Anansi for six years. The press published mainly prose; however, in 1968 it published *T.O. Now: The Young Toronto Poets*, an anthology of thirteen young poets with an introduction by Lee. In it he wrote:

> ...the city's aesthetic puritanism, which surfaced in many of its writers as an inability to write convincingly of the *polis*, as gaucherie in any sphere between the private and the metaphysical — that puritanism is becoming something of an asset as it recedes. For while many of these poets now write with an unforced sense of their own time and place as a public arena, they seem to retain the sense that decisions about starting-point and direction originate in the space that they occupy as private men and women.[2]

Whatever its applicability to the anthologized poets, the statement does give Lee's own goal as a poet.

During his time at Anansi, Lee wrote a number of brief prose articles, such as a review of Al Purdy's poetry, "Running and Dwelling: Homage to Al Purdy," published in the July 1972 issue of *Saturday Night*, and the essay "Modern Poetry" for *Read Canadian: A Book about Canadian Books* (1972), edited by Robert Fulford, Dave Godfrey, and Abraham Rotstein. His major prose work was the autobiographical essay "Cadence, Country, Silence," first published in *Liberté* in 1972, then republished, slightly revised throughout and with an altered conclusion, as "Cadence, Country, Silence: Writing in a Colonial Space," in the Fall 1973 issue of *Open Letter*. Later, after leaving Anansi, Lee published his most important critical essay to date, *Savage Fields: An Essay in Literature and Cosmology* (1977). It is a study of Michael Ondaatje's *The Collected Works of Billy the Kid* and Leonard Cohen's *Beautiful Losers* and has been as important to its time as John Sutherland's critical book on E.J. Pratt was to his. Like Sutherland's work, Lee's study is open to the charge that it is a thesis statement and that the thesis predetermines the critical literary analyses. Lee responded to this and other criticisms in the essay "Reading *Savage Fields*," which first appeared in the Summer 1979 issue of *Canadian Journal of Political and Social Theory*. It was reprinted, with some of the debate with Godfrey's criticism omitted, in the Fall 1981 issue of *Brick*. A subsequent essay, "Polyphony, Enacting a Meditation," first published as an interview in 1979 and then revised as a sequence of aphorisms on some themes from the earlier "Cadence, Country, Silence," appeared in *Tasks of Passion: Dennis Lee at Mid-Career* (1982).

In 1970 Lee published the first of his books of children's verse, *Wiggle to the Laundromat*. There were three immensely popular successors: *Alligator Pie* (1974), *Nicholas Knock and Other People* (1974), and *Garbage Delight* (1977), all published by Macmillan, with illustrations by Frank Newfeld. *Jelly Belly* (1983) was illustrated by Juan Wijngaard. His most recent collection of adult poetry, *The Gods*, appeared in 1979.

Lee has continued to work in publishing, first with Macmillan of Canada, then with McClelland and Stewart. In 1961 he married Donna Youngblut, and the couple had two children before being divorced in 1976.

Tradition and Milieu

Dennis Lee enrolled as an undergraduate at Victoria College in the University of Toronto shortly before Professor Northrop Frye, with his recently published *Anatomy of Criticism* (1957) and an earlier study of William Blake to his credit, became principal of the college. Victoria's most revered poet, E.J. "Ned" Pratt, had retired serveral years earlier, but his presence was still felt, and the recent publication of Jay Macpherson's startling *The Boatman* (1957), with its dedication to Northrop and Helen Frye, seemed to assert that Victoria College would continue to be the centre of the University's artistic life.

Beyond college walls was a nation still bemused at the new Conservative government under the leadership of John Diefenbaker, and the almost complete eclipse of the Co-operative Commonwealth Federation. The latter was to have important implications for Lee and his fellow students at Victoria College, traditionally a stronghold of Christian radicalism of the social gospel variety: with the demoralized indigenous left preoccupied with the administrative task of creating a new party, there was an intellectual vacuum on campus. The radical impulses of the next decade would come from abroad. And when, late in the next decade, Lee was to feel the need to act against the impulses that peripheralized his nation by locating himself in space, it was not to the reconstructed Canadian left he turned, but to the red Tory eulogist for John Diefenbaker, George Grant.

Authors then popular on campuses were J. D. Salinger, William Golding, and Samuel Beckett, each active in his own way in wresting Nothingness from the clasp of Marxist existentialist Jean-Paul Sartre and serving it up as a suitably fashionable middle-class complaint. One can assume that a serious young undergraduate with his eyes on the United Church ministry would be familiar with these writers and their diagnoses of the moral emptiness at the core of prosperous middle-class complacency.

In the fall of 1958, Lee's name was printed on the staff list for the college literary magazine *Acta Victoriana*, and issues appearing during the next two years contained a short story of his and four humorous columns he co-wrote with Margaret Atwood, but his first poems were not published until the November 1960 issue. These were "Song of Seasons," "Titanic," and "Dirge at a Wake." All are slightly irregular sonnets. "Song of Seasons" and "Dirge at a Wake" are romantically spiritualized death-resurrection/cycle-of-seasons poems, offspring of Sir James Frazer's *The Golden Bough*: they would fit easily into Leo Kennedy's *The Shrouding* (1933). "Titanic" is more interesting, if less successful: the metre is more experimental, and the diction is made challenging with newly compounded words. E. J. Pratt's *Titanic* has collided with G. M. Hopkins' *Deutschland*.

The February 1961 issue of *Acta Victoriana* contained three more sonnets by Lee: "Tigerlily," "The Fire of Eros," and "Anima." The first two are explicitly Christian: "Tigerlily," for example, concludes, "O Tigerlily, men make Christ your name: / O, roar in mildness, bud in darkling flame."[3] T. S. Eliot, W. B. Yeats, John Keats, William Blake, the English metaphysicals — the influences are obvious, and expected, given the

University of Toronto honours English curriculum of the time. Later contributions were to include a couple of love poems and some lyrics from the college review, but by the time of his graduation Lee could be classed as a competent minor figure in the school labelled by Montreal critic and poet Louis Dudek "Toronto transcendental," itself a variety within the postwar Romantic movement which arose to release the springs of feeling in an emotionally numbed population and which, in English literature, is usually associated with the Orphic figures Dylan Thomas and Malcolm Lowry.

The sonnet sequence *Kingdom of Absence* (1967) marks Lee's break with the school. Although it was his first volume of poetry to be offered to the general public, it should be seen as a transitional work. The poet may complain of being "hung between styles,"[4] but the book marks his attempt, aided by his knowledge of German literature and sparked by his interest in the theology of Martin Heidegger, to develop an intellectually tough poetic style that will permit his own voice to come through.

In 1968 Lee noted in his introduction to *T.O. Now: The Young Toronto Poets* that the one identifiable group were the Victoria College poets Greg Hollingshead, Robert Read, Charles Douglas, Eldon Garnet, and Ian Young. There are individual differences among these poets, of course, but generally speaking one is always aware of the pastiche of influences: James Reaney and Jay Macpherson (and, behind them, Northrop Frye); Margaret Avison, Samuel Beckett, James Joyce, and the rest. Reading these five poets, one can see why Lee found it necessary to make a break. Take, for example, Greg Hollingshead, represented in *T.O. Now* by a dozen poems that too often fail to live up to their opening lines: "Free-Fall Lovers," a lyric of two seven-line stanzas, begins, "The Void refuses to take us for an answer,"[5] and then falls into pedestrian attempts at deadpan humour juxtaposed with tired Romantic clichés. This is a flaw occasionally found in Lee, as well, introducing a few false notes into "The Death of Harold Ladoo"[6] and weakening the lyric "Song: Lay Down," which reads like a promising first draft, although it had appeared in Sheila Watson's journal *White Pelican* five years before its publication in *The Gods* (1979). But normally, Lee is in control of the tone of his poetry and can move confidently through a wide emotional range.

Critical Overview and Context

The reviews of Dennis Lee's first book of poetry, *Kingdom of Absence*, were neither numerous nor favourable. Lionel Kearns in *Canadian Literature* simply dismissed the volume as the work of an incompetent disciple of A.J.M. Smith.[7] Al Purdy, in a review of twelve books of poetry for *The Tamarack Review*, devoted one brief paragraph to *Kingdom of Absence*, calling it "perhaps a little too clever."[8] The book received more serious consideration in reviews by Eric Thompson for *The Fiddlehead* and George Bowering for *Canadian Dimension*. Both acknowledged the serious intent of Lee's work, but Bowering objected to the "continual abstraction" and the diction. He singled out "'lambent' and 'impinge' and 'ken'" for comment.[9] Thompson put it more generally: "By aligning himself in both a real and fancied way with those who experienced the mystery and chaos of existence, Mr. Lee hopes to clarify man's essential problems in poetic terms. The only trouble is that he doesn't appear to know the difference between rhetoric and poetry."[10] A more favourable notice appeared in Hugh MacCallum's survey — for the "Letters in Canada" issue of the *University of Toronto Quarterly* — of poetry published in 1967.[11]

The first edition of *Civil Elegies* received a brief but favourable comment from Ann Montagnes in a *Saturday Night* review of seven poets.[12] Mary Keyes gave it favourable notice in her *Canadian Forum* review of three poets: "The seven shaped meditations on being political, being Canadian, being confused and thwarted in our times, being ashamed of and glorying in being human, are a real contract with an extremely honest and maturing personality searching and working to grow."[13] Hugh MacCallum, in his "Letters in Canada" survey of poetry published in 1968, thoughtfully commented that "... whereas the sequence purports to be about the membership of the individual in the body politic, its public intention is eroded by private obsessions."[14] I would prefer "religious concerns" to "obsessions," but it is true that the religious and national strands were not sufficiently distinguished and balanced: Lee proceeded to do just this for the much improved second edition of 1972. MacCallum also commented on the language: "The slow, grave rhetoric is often persuasive, and the best passages are those which reveal Lee's control of the casuistry of self-abnegation."[15]

When the revised *Civil Elegies and Other Poems* appeared in 1972 and won the Governor General's Award, it and Lee received a number of brief favourable notices. Doug Fetherling in *Saturday Night* compared Lee as a poet-publisher to Louis Dudek of Montreal and Fred Cogswell of Fredericton.[16] Andreas Schroeder, in a review article "Difficult Sanities" for *Canadian Literature*, praised Lee for his honesty and "compelling desperation" in tackling the themes of national and personal rebirth.[17] About the only denigrating review was that of David Helwig, in the form of a letter to Lee, published with Lee's answer in *Quarry*. Helwig did not like the marriage poems and felt the revisions in *Civil Elegies* did not improve it.[18]

Lee's established stature as a poet was recognized, in the usual way, by inclusion in reference books. In the *Supplement to the Oxford Companion to Canadian History and Literature* (1973), Gary Geddes wrote, "In his cultural concerns [Lee] is a sort of Canadian Matthew Arnold, unbearably conscious of our discontinuity with the past, of our loss of faith in God and in human values and institutions."[19] Geddes made the familiar objection to "too much abstraction" but hoped to see Lee work free of the vice. Frank Davey in *From There to Here: A Guide to English-Canadian Literature since 1960* (1974), the second volume of *Our Nature — Our Voices*, launched a much stronger attack on the same perceived flaw: Lee must learn that "...the power of art is based on its particularity and vividness, and not on its grasp of abstract issues...."[20] Davey's antithesis is a false one, of course, but more than that it is another prime example of provincial Canadian anti-intellectualism. Dennis Duffy, in *Gardens, Covenants, Exiles: Loyalism in the Literature of Upper Canada/Ontario* (1982), treated the religious and nationalist concerns of Lee's poetry in the context of the vestiges of the Loyalist myth of defeat and violent expulsion, exile, and reconciliation to a new land made possible by the initial act of loyalty. This myth of exiles making from their northern wilderness a new garden, Duffy feels, quoting George Grant, was always flawed; for the Loyalists carried within not only their commitments but also the weed seeds of modernity, as they, like those they unsuccessfully fought, were children of the Enlightenment. Thus Lee's anguish for a nation that cannot protect itself from the virulent technological form of modernism dominant in the United States because of inner inconsistencies, self-doubt, and loss of courage —

> The dream of Tory origins
> Is full of lies and blanks,
> Though what remains when it is gone,
> To prove that we're not Yanks?
> ("When I Went Up to Rosedale," in *The Gods*, p. 17)

— can be seen as a late questioning within a myth of declining significance. Duffy's treatment of Lee, necessarily brief and tentative in a thematic survey of this type, is useful since it provides a setting that both illuminates and is illuminated by Lee. Too often Lee has been regarded as an exotic accident in Canadian poetry.

The reviews of *The Gods* were more varied in tone and generally of a higher quality. In a review "Loss and Confusion" for *The Canadian Forum*, Dennis Cooley attacked Lee for his recurring stylistic weaknesses, "his addiction to abstraction, declamation, humourless exaggeration, and high-flying rhetoric."[21] However, Cooley declared, Lee was better when he used a domestic voice and avoided the role of "stricken prophet" of his generation. Paul McNally, in a review in *Queen's Quarterly*, attacked the substance — "the book shares with other postmodernist poetry the vacuity of a prolegomenon to silence" — but praised Lee's continued, muted quest for human space.[22] Ian Pearson in *Quill & Quire* singled out "The Death of Harold Ladoo," from *The Gods*, as the "most important Canadian poem of the decade."[23]

Although Lee's three volumes of adult poetry were reviewed as they appeared and a number of interviews with him have been published, his adult poetry as a whole was not subjected to much scholarly critical investigation until the publication in 1982 of *Tasks of Passion: Dennis Lee at Mid-Career*, a collection of essays on Lee's works edited by Karen Mulhallen, Donna Bennett, and Russell Brown. D.G. Jones, in "In Search of Canada: Dennis Lee's Ironic Vision,"[24] had looked at *Civil Elegies* and the essay "Cadence, Country, Silence: Writing in a Colonial Space" to place Lee in the current controversy about humanism and modernism. Jones finally located Lee as a modernist qualified by the ironic refusal to abandon history for myth, society for nature, or the mundane for the visionary. Jones found this precarious position necessarily typical for the writer in our country with its many internal contradictions. But the publication of *Tasks of Passion*, with its essays on Lee as editor, poet, and critic, and its provision of a bibliography, marks an end to the puzzled interrogations and the beginnings of the shaping of a critical consensus on the nature and value of Lee's work. The volume requires separate treatment, which I shall postpone until after looking at contemporary responses to Lee's *Savage Fields*.

Lee published his first critical prose book, *Savage Fields: An Essay in Literature and Cosmology*, in 1977. The bleak, claustrophobic vision of the work aroused a good deal of controversy. The *Canadian Journal of Political and Social Theory* (Spring–Summer 1979) contained two articles critical of Lee, Leah Bradshaw's "A Second Look at *Savage Fields*" and Dave Godfrey's "On *Savage Fields* and the Act of Criticism," and Lee's defence, "Reading *Savage Fields*." *Brick: A Journal of Reviews* (Winter 1981) also published two critical articles, by Douglas Barbour and Peggy Dragišić;[25] Lee's "Reading *Savage Fields*," revised to meet the new attacks, was reprinted in a subsequent issue.[26]

Savage Fields also received a number of thoughtful reviews in such journals as *The Canadian Forum*, *Books in Canada*, *Canadian Literature*, *Saturday Night*, *Dalhousie Review*, and the *University of Toronto Quarterly*. R. P. Bilan, in his review article "Canadian Poet-Critics" (in the *Dalhousie Review*) on Eli Mandel's *Another Time* and Lee's *Savage Fields*, first praised both writers for stepping beyond a preoccupation with national identity, then faulted Lee for a sentimental conception of "earth" derived from D. H. Lawrence.[27] J. M. Kertzer in the *University of Toronto Quarterly* also noted the influence of Lawrence, but noted a more specific debt to Northrop Frye's "garrison mentality" and kinship to Margaret Atwood's *Survival*.[28] Doug Fetherling in *Saturday Night* had high praise both for the book and for the author as a 1960s radical who, unlike his predecessors of the 1930s, did not give up the radical quest when circumstances changed.[29]

Part of the difficulty arose from not knowing whether *Savage Fields* should be taken as a piece of objective criticism or a poet's prosaic manifesto. There is a significant difference. As anyone who has read W. B. Yeats' *A Vision* knows, a poet's prosaic declarations can be both intrinsic nonsense and an ideal glass for his El Greco vision. T. S. Eliot to the contrary, I do not think that poets necessarily make the best critics — and, incidentally, I hold against Eliot the proliferation of bad poetry by would-be critics trying to establish credentials. I shall argue in the main body of this essay that the *Titanic*-iceberg analysis of reality Lee has formulated may have fostered his poetic development: here I want to deal with the prosaic nonsense. It may seem unfair to so cavalierly dismiss Lee as a detached intellectual for he was one of the first in Canada to recognize the central importance to our century of the theology of Martin Heidegger. Heidegger is one of those intellectuals who, like Carl Jung, gave humanity a map for the future. Also, like Carl Jung, he failed his own time by failing to diagnose and loudly warn against the evil thereof, the rise of Adolf Hitler's National Socialist Workers' Party. Lee in *Savage Fields* has given us a far-off forecast of the need to become reconciled to our earthly Being. But on our immediate problem, two worldly ideologies prepared, like the gingham dog and the calico cat, to eat each other up, he is of little use. He seems not to have noticed.

In *Savage Fields*, Lee defines the basic reality of our planet as the conflict between "world," essentially instrumental consciousness, and "earth," brute facticity and instinct. Thus he is in the good Canadian tradition of Harold Innis and the Laurentian school of selecting as basic the relation of human beings to nature. But Lee's variant paradigm is strangely restrictive: if instrumental consciousness — Aristotle's practical reason — is here, speculative reason is absent. Mind as awareness, as imagination, has disappeared—there is consciousness as agent of will, but not self-consciousness, the Greek virtue of philosophic detachment which, in its Christian form as devout meditation, George Grant has laboured to reinstate in our practical nation. The image of "earth," with the implication that the instinctive life only turns brutal in response to world's aggression, is a form of "ape with angel glands" romanticism. Since the writings of Charles Darwin, we have known that in nature to survive is to dominate. As John Stuart Mill noted, "If the artificial is not better than the natural, to what end are all the arts of life?"[30] In his essay "Nature," from which this quotation is taken, he goes on to elaborate:

> In sober truth, nearly all the things which men are hanged or imprisoned for doing to one another, are nature's every day performances. Killing, the most criminal act recognized by human laws, Nature does once to every being that lives; and in a large proportion of cases, after protracted tortures such as only the greatest monsters whom we read of ever purposely inflicted on their living fellow-creatures.[31]

Nature is systematically exploited by humanity from two motives: to free men and women from pain and increase human well-being in the service of love; and to increase the means of manipulating or killing other humans in the service of power. It is hard to separate the two as they act in time for the will to power usually masquerades as the defence of love. However, to lump the two together under the label "systematizing" is morally irresponsible.

The flaws in Lee's thought show most starkly in the third part of *Savage Fields*, "Interlude." Here he glances at the scientific work done on the brain as an object of investigation, and he concludes that liberalism has, by treating the brain as an object, destroyed one of its supporting pillars, consciousness (the other being the universe as value-free raw material). However, one of the most fascinating areas for the exploration of the problem our language externalizes — that we know ourselves both as "I" and "me," subject and object — is in the relation of mind to brain. Mind is, to use Arthur Koestler's suggestive phrase, the ghost in the machine. To stay within the Canadian context, we know from the work of Dr. Wilder Penfield that in a child whose brain has been injured by epilepsy, the mind can reassign functions to uninjured parts of the brain. We know that there are mental illnesses with no organic cause, that leave no lesions on the brain. Lee simply identifies mind and brain, and then claims it is liberalism that has collapsed the "I" into the "me."

Lee's treatment of the two literary texts is partial. As Leah Bradshaw pointed out in her review, the conflict in *The Collected Works of Billy The Kid* includes Billy's struggle for domination and recognition with the law and its representative, Pat Garret;

or, in Lee's terms, world against world. From the time people of the Stone Age threw rocks at one another, the exploitation of nature has been a means to strengthen the arms of men divided into savagely warring groups by family, tribe, nation, race, class, religion, ideology, etc. As group membership with all its dangers is essential to human identity, humankind is presented with critical problems that must be faced. Lee's model does not help us to do so. For Lee's starting point is different: he makes the Protestant assumption that if one can come to terms with God and oneself, loving one's neighbour will naturally follow. As a critical position for the objective analysis of secular literature, the assumption may have limits, but it does give Lee a poetic dwelling. He is essentially a religious poet, and as such should be evaluated.

Tasks of Passion, a volume of essays devoted to an appraisal of the accomplishments of Dennis Lee, is a useful place to conclude our overview of the development of his reputation, for it marks scholarly acceptance of his writings into the canon of significant Canadian literary works. Such an attained status is to be welcomed, for it means that his writings will be subjected to thoughtful, informed analyses and evaluation. But no gain is unalloyed; despite the volume's title, there is more urbanity than passion in most of the articles contributed, which include tributes to Lee as editor as well as scholarly studies.

The most significant scholarly contributions to *Tasks of Passion* are the five articles by Ted Blodgett, Robert Bringhurst, Sean Kane, Ann Munton, and Stan Dragland. Blodgett concentrates on the prose, and the other four examine the poetry, but all give primacy to Lee the poet. Thus Blodgett, while complaining of the "totalitarian" paradigm Lee establishes in *Savage Fields*, is more interested in that work for the light it sheds on Lee's own attitude to language and practice as a poet than he is in its value as literary criticism. Bringhurst, in his essay "At Home in the Difficult World," sympathetically examines the multiplicity of selves Lee presents in the different voices within his poetry. Sean Kane, in his essay about the influence of Heidegger on Lee, lucidly summarizes the relevant elements in Heidegger's thought, including his interpretations of the poets Hölderlin and Rilke, then demonstrates their presence in Lee's poetry. Munton's essay, "Simultaneity in the Writings of Dennis Lee," is a more specialized study of the influence on Lee of Rilke and, in particular, of Rilke's approach to the problem of the debasement of language. And Dragland places Lee in the context of Canadian poetry: James Reaney, Earle Birney's "Bushed," Margaret Atwood, E. J. Pratt. In all these critics, there is an acceptance of the legitimacy of Lee's particular approach, his passionate meditations. He is no longer scolded for bringing a philosophic mind to the composition of poetry.

Lee's Works

In an essay entitled "Getting to Rochdale," published in *The University Game* (1968), Dennis Lee wrote:

> How create a radical institution? My own answer is that we can come to share the experience of impoverishment and detachment, that we can discover the mutuality of our ignorance and our inauthenticity; and that because this ground is really common — it is not something we have to persuade ourselves of — we can build upon it.[32]

These expectations for Rochdale Lee transferred to his country, Canada, in *Civil Elegies*, first published in 1968 and republished, slightly revised and with two additional elegies, in 1972. Lee had issued one previous collection, *Kingdom of Absence* (1967), and has since published *The Gods* (1979). In all these writings, the influence of the theology of Martin Heidegger is evident. Heidegger provides not only the concerns, and in particular the problem of investing the phenomenal universe with meaning, but also much of the attendant vocabulary: Being, authenticity, ground, absence, void. These are rather intractable terms, and Lee's development as a poet can be seen in his struggle to reconcile them to the sensualities of verse. The nature of his self-imposed task can be seen in his first book, *Kingdom of Absence*.

Kingdom of Absence is made up of a sequence of forty-three very irregular sonnets, in seven sections. "Muskoka Elegiac," the first section of five poems, starts with an apparently Wordsworthian contrast between the hysteric urban and the pastoral rural. Nature, love, childhood — all the Romantic themes are here. But a few details — "I keep on falling through cement" (p.3) — suggest what is elaborated on in the eleven poems of the next section, "Cities of the Mind Interred," that "urban" is no longer simply a setting, it is a pervasive cast of mind, in which all nature is perceived as simply real estate, raw material whose only value is what the mind imposes. The sense of the sublime, of an unalterable otherness in nature, has vanished. Lee identifies the Renaissance as the start of the last phase in the development of the corrosive intellect which dissolves all external values to leave nature as raw material for the mind's exploitation:

> The trumpets of the randy Renaissance
> came blowing wind and integers, blew news
> high to the good old concert of the spheres:
> linear mind is the measure of all things.
>
> Newton played his scrawny masterpiece
> upon that single string. René Descartes
> heard one vibration twanging through his brain,
> intoxicating monotone, until
>
> he cried that only measurement is real
> and the measuring mind; and with that declaration
> shrunk the universe to three dimensions,
> drubbed it down to fit the bed of the mind.
>
> Crumpled through the slot of single vision
> van Gogh bleeds his sanity away.
>
> (p. 13)

Other poems in this section chart the personal sense of loss with the collapse of traditional value systems. The six poems of the next section, "Annex Elegiac," record the frantic failures in the lives of acquaintances.

The central section of the book, "Kingdom of Absence," is a dream sequence in which individuals are imaged as each trapped on an individual ice flow. The choice of this image to portray mass alienation appears arbitrary; worse, the ice lacks iciness. E.J. Pratt never made that error. The final three sections are rather a mixed bag: "The Acrobat," three poems about Lee's poetic predecessors in bearing witness to the wasteland; "Lady," which attempts to combine celebrations of love with his dominant theme, that reality as experienced by the modern mind is pretty thin gruel; and "Accessions," eight metaphysical poems. One example should illustrate the problem with these final poems and their muted consolation with facing up to emptiness:

> Until God riddle our cankered souls with light
> and ply the sweet eviction, till the day
> men babbled in our pious adolescence,
> until the holy stoning, when the tug
> of love and stark cessation that divide
> the earth between them — till their fission catch
> and be consumed into the last barrage and wooing,
> the quest of Being for its diminutives,
> we wander disinherited.
>   And if
> we flare and gutter into darkness, if
> the ground, the unimaginable deprivation
> be not into the One and we dissolve
> pointblank to zero, let that knowledge come
> as costly triumph at the razor's edge.[33]
>
>   (p. 56)

The basic theme, a kind of Pascalian wager that the fact of being verifies a teleology of love, is clear enough. But the tone is wrong: the poem starts off sounding like Henry Vaughan and ends with an echo of Somerset Maugham. A line like "the quest of Being for its diminutives" can only make sense to one well grounded in Heidegger. For Heidegger, Being, Willing, and Knowing make up a kind of trinity. Willing is presupposed in there being Being (as witnessed in particular beings), as apart from the terrifying emptiness of nonbeing — an emptiness that intrudes as time. The third term, Knowing, has in humanity, as its main instrument, language. Language partakes of both Willing and Being, or should: in our particular Western culture, since the time of classical Greece, the balance has been lost and Knowing has become identified with Willing in the form of manipulating objectified reality. To rectify the balance, language, the Word, must return to the first fiat, "Let there be." The octave tells us, in four or five ways, that until the day of judgement we wander disinherited. To restate a theme in various ways is traditional poetic technique — Shakespeare's sonnets are often structured in this way — but the restatements ought to have a cumulative effect; here they merely jostle. The terminology, too, creates unnecessary difficulty. For example, in Christian thought, God is thought of primarily as Energy, a Will to which all individuals should align their wills. In Hindu thought, God is Being, to which separated beings hope to be reunited. Is the One of line 12 God as Being? If so, then why use the images of light and love — both traditionally metaphors for the Divine force? Lee might respond that his concept of Being is derived from Heidegger, not Hinduism; but, if so, the poem must carry the frame of reference, not leave us groping. A poet may well introduce his own philosophical or religious ideology, as A. M. Klein used the kabbalah, but the ideology must be incarnate within the poem, not a spectre hovering off-stage. And does not the whole drift of the octave clash with the Promethean humanism of the sestet? For the sestet attributes final value only to the mind's knowing — the very trap that elsewhere the poet savaged.

I am aware that one person's complexity is another's confusion and do not wish to be harsh. The inauthentic sonnet provides a formal analogy for a portrayal of a state removed from, yet aware of, fullness of Being. The device of writing a free-verse approximation of a traditional form works better in the elegies for there the hexameter echoes go back to the Greek choral odes; whereas the sonnet form seems arbitrary, too closely tied to the "randy Renaissance." The interest in juxtaposing various levels of language — philosophic, conversational, slang — which gives Lee's later poetry much of its appeal, is already evident here. But, lacking coherence of thought or emotional consistency of image, the poem remains poor rhetoric.

Lee's subject, alienation (although filtered through the Heidegger lens), has been a stock one in English-language poetry at least since Matthew Arnold. It is only when Lee, under the influence of George Grant, sheds his individualist frame and looks at the collectivity, Canada, in *Civil Elegies*, that he contributes something new and of interest.

Traditionally the elegy is a public meditation on serious issues such as death, and among English poets it has most often been inspired by the death of a particular friend: Milton's "Lycidas," Shelley's "Adonais," Arnold's "Thyrsis." The more general meditation, such as Gray's "Elegy Written in a Country Churchyard" or perhaps Tennyson's *In Memoriam*, is less common in English, and Lee seems to have learned more from the *Duino Elegies* (1923) of the German poet Rainer Maria Rilke.[34] Rilke's elegies, in part, derive their approach from the Romantic adaptation of the form to a lament for past youth — Charles G. D. Roberts' "Tantramar Revisited" is of this type — but go beyond it to present lament and affirmation for realized humanity in life and death. However, the civic dimension, normally present in English poetry, even in such pointedly spiritual works as T. S. Eliot's *Four Quartets*, is conspicuously absent in the German poet; and the influences at work in Lee in his poetic handling of this dimension are much more diffuse. The political substance, Lee has affirmed in his essay "Cadence, Country, Silence: Writing in a Colonial Space," is derived from the writings of George Grant.

One has to be careful here. George Grant's political vision has Loyalist roots and contains an indulgent nostalgia for the impossible ideals of the Tory Anglican cavalier. Lee lacks this, as is made clear in the first elegy where the Loyalist opponents to William Lyon Mackenzie's rebels share the poet's contempt at the "spontaneous mutual retreat"[35] during the 1837 uprising. Interestingly, the lines in praise of Sir John A. Macdonald in the last elegy of the first edition of 1968 disappeared in the revised version of 1972, perhaps reflecting the decline in influence of that early nationalist mentor and biographer of Macdonald, Donald Creighton, after his late fulminations against French-speaking Canadians. The effect of the Conservative views of George Grant was as much iconoclastic, breaking the hold of the "single vision" to allow Lee to find his own voice, as it was substantial.

George Grant singles out John Locke, Descartes' English contemporary, as the "architect" of progressive modern liberalism.[36] Locke takes as his starting point the individual happily wresting a living from a benevolent nature — an economic equivalent of Descartes' epistemological isolation. Political associations are formed only when individuals find it expedient to do so in order to guarantee the uninterrupted enjoyment of their wealth. Political structures are, then, secondary conveniences, subservient to economic self-interest. By abandoning both the Aristotelian view that the chief end of the political state is to enable both individuals and community to share in the good life and the Conservative Christian view that the state is analogous to the family and ordained by God, Locke accelerated the process of desacralizing all human relationships to leave intact only the naked human will facing the exploitable raw material of nature.

But if Locke's political state was only instrumental, it was also seen as benevolent. The point is made by Charles Taylor in his book on Hegel:

> The label "liberal" is uncommonly broad and loose, but there is a central tradition which has regarded individual liberty, equality (including the sweeping away of unearned privileges), and the responsibility of government to the governed as the three essential properties of a legitimate policy.... The underlying belief of the liberal tradition is that these values were the sufficient basis for a viable society. That is, a society which embodied these should command the loyal co-operation of its members. It was believed either that men would be satisfied with the inherent justice of such an arrangement; or that enlightened men would see the utility of such a society and so play by its rules; or that men would identify with a society in which they were free and sovereign and consider it their own.[37]

Since the liberal successors to the Enlightenment had reason on their side, the Romantic reaction against the sensed individualistic sterility of liberalism was irrational, muddled, reactionary, religious, sexual, revolutionary — and ultimately coopted by its enemies. To again quote Charles Taylor:

> Modern civilization has thus seen the proliferation of Romantic views of private life and fulfilment, along with a growing rationalization and bureaucratization of collective structures, and a frankly exploitative stance towards nature. Modern society, we might say, is Romantic in its private and imaginative life and utilitarian or instrumentalist in its public, effective life.[38]

If in the liberal view nations and their boundaries are simply conveniences in the service of basic economic goals, and if Canada is now economically integrated to the American empire, can Canada be taken seriously as a homeland worthy of living and dying in? Or is it too late for even the question to make sense? *Civil Elegies* is Lee's attempt to grapple with this problem.

Civil Elegies is prefaced by two quotations: one from George Grant's essay "Canadian Fate and Imperialism" (which is included in his *Technology and Empire*), indicating the public themes of early odd-numbered elegies; the other from the eleventh-century Buddhist mystic Saraha, indicating the quest for private values in the even.[39] The climax, public despair in the fifth and private retreat in the sixth, is followed by a meditation on love in the seventh, which unites the failures in public and private realms. With the rejection in the eighth elegy of the way of negation and withdrawal lived by the poet Saint-Denys-Garneau, the way is left for the muted positive assertions of the closing elegy. Keeping this general framework in mind, let us look more closely at the individual elegies.

The setting for the first elegy is Nathan Phillips Square, in front of Toronto's new city hall, with Henry Moore's abstract statue, *The Archer*, in its midst. The statue is important for in the third elegy it will take on the function Rilke assigned to his angels, a steadfast statement of Being. But the first elegy is haunted by spectres, the spirits of those who, "...never at / home in native space and not yet / citizens of a human body of kind..." (p.33), can neither live nor die in the limbo that is Canada, past and present. The predicament is political for neither the patricians of muddy York who "made their compact together" (p. 33) nor their opponents under Mackenzie left their successors a satisfying inheritance. It is also economic for our forefathers treated the difficult land as an exploitable resource: it was a means, and Canada a house that was never home. Thus our cities perch like strangers on the land, the architecture stamped with the look of the temporary and the transient. The English art critic John Ruskin had noted that the architecture of a society is an indicator of the quality of life in that society. In Toronto's polluted central square, the poet is led to the conclusion that "...not / one countryman has learned, that / men and women live that / they may make that / life worth dying" (p.36). The terminology is typically Heideggerian, but behind that theologian for a diminished age lies a long, rich tradition of Christian meditation on death.

The second elegy, to my mind the most satisfactory as a poem, is a lament and a plea at the loss of the religious dimension in the modern world. The poet feels a sense of emptiness at the withdrawal of the religious value system that gave both individual and social existence meaning. The theme is hardly new — Matthew Arnold in "Dover Beach" lamented the ebbing of faith — but Arnold with his classical stoic stance could treat the subject as a historical phenomenon; for Lee, it is a personal predicament. The final line, "The poets spoke of earth and heaven. There were no symbols" (p. 38), by making symbols (like clothing) badges of our lost innocence, makes clear that the loss of the experience of the divine has meant a loss of the experience of the secular, earth. The garden is a symbol to those no longer in it.

The third elegy returns to the public and is a sad reflection on the defeat of a people by the land. It opens with a description of an epiphany inspired by Moore's *Archer* — a work that in sublimely asserting itself asserts all Being. Then follows a verse-paragraph that reminds one of Margaret Atwood's "Progressive Insanities of a Pioneer" in its delineation of the failure of the settlers' minds to adapt to a new land. This is again followed by a contrast, the painter Tom Thomson, who did receive "the radiance of the renewed land" (p. 41). But he has gone, we cannot "malinger among the bygone acts of grace" (p. 41) and must accept as starting point our spiritual bankruptcy.

Lee has here identified, even if negatively, the artist and the man of God. From the beginning of the Romantic movement late in the eighteenth century, the artist, feeling himself without a valid class base, has been attracted by two roles: he could see himself as the aristocrat of a democratic age, asserting even in the late shabby bohemian versions the aristocrat's self-justifying Being — a gentleman *is*, a bourgeois *does* — or he could see himself as a member of a new secular priesthood, providing the moral and spiritual insight which once was the prerogative of the clerical pulpit. The first of these roles could have little attraction for Lee, who could not see in the Tory Anglican gentleman the lineaments of a valid aristocracy worth saving, but the second offers problems, as well, for the rise in the value placed on the artist is itself a symptom of the desacralizing of the human which has accompanied the decline of traditional Christianity. With a few significant exceptions, most so-called artists are part of the amusement industry. The few Canadian artists singled out by Lee for mention — Tom Thomson, Saint-Denys-Garneau — could hardly compose a Canadian pantheon. In his prose work *Savage Fields*, Lee falls back on the concept of artist as diagnostician, presenting without intrusion the fever chart of a sick society. "L'esprit d'observation succède à celui de transfiguration."[40] Lee notes the deterioration in art — "many are called but none are chosen now" (p. 41) — and then turns to try to make a virtue of negation: "it is time to honour the void" (p. 42). Such a stance once attracted Lee and found expression in the lyrics he wrote to accompany John Beckwith's musical *Place of Meeting* (1967). But it is a form of metaphysical suicide, as becomes clear in the fourth elegy. As often in Lee, the movement of thought is dialectical: statement, then counterstatement. The elegy opens with Lee wondering if the path of negation should be his vocation. He notes the pain in the cumulative losses wrought by time, by the cancerous growth of the city, and by the assimilation of Canada into the American empire, then wonders if he willingly accepted, would there be a breakthrough to a new beginning? But "meanwhile the country is gone" (p. 45). Yet the alternative is the heroic and foolish gesture. The dilemma is not resolvable in these terms and leads to the despair of the next elegies.

Whereas the farewells in the fourth elegy were to disassociated hopes, fears, desires, and hurts — fragments unable to shore up — the fifth begins with a statement, "It would be better maybe if we could stop loving the children" (p. 46), which, followed by several lines that give the children vivid existence apart from the poet's self-absorption, implicitly poses the question, Are we involved in a society we are not ashamed to pass on to them? It is followed by a chronicle of the evils of appeasement in our time, whether by statesmen at Munich, by good Germans who chose inner exile during Hitler's time, or by Canadians who chose acquiescence to American imperial necessity despite the napalm evidence of where that criminal, technologically armed will to Power was leading. But while the final judgement of Canada, "burning kids by proxy" (p. 48), is terrible, at least in the movement of mind from the subjective narcotic haze of the opening elegy to the lucid objective nadir of the central fifth elegy there is the latent possibility of the self-assessment that precedes affirmation. The self-assessment takes place in the brief sixth elegy, where the speaker, unable to become more than a shadow of the imperial power he obsessively criticizes and haunted by "continental drift to barbarian normalcy," admits he "cannot get purchase on life" (p. 49). Incidentally, "get purchase" is a good example of Lee's mastery of diction; it sounds so jocularly modern, yet "purchase" is a word rich in biblical connotations: God's relations to his people (Psalms lxxiv.2), Christ's redemption of humanity (Ephesians i.14; Acts xx.28). Yet the theme is a local, particular, and personal version of the cry of Paul-Emile Borduas in "Refus Global": "L'écartèlement entre les puissances psychiques et les puissances raisonnantes est près du paroxysme."[41]

In the seventh elegy, the public and private themes come together within what S. T. Coleridge called "the circle of affection." For role playing can be played naked: a home, like a homeland, can be sought out of personal inadequacy. In Canada, lovers and leaders are chosen who will act out the voluntary betrayal. With this self-knowledge, the poet can go on to his eighth meditation, on Saint-Denys-Garneau, "our one patrician maker" (p. 53), who embraced and created his art from the fear of life. Lee's interpretation of Garneau's life and art is akin to that of Jean Le Moyne,[42] but more than that, Garneau provides Lee with the means for looking impersonally at very personal concerns. For Garneau was a Canadian artist haunted by the withdrawal of value and joy from life; he functions as an alter ego from whose dedication to language Lee can learn and whose rejection leaves Lee free to make his limited assertion of the final elegy. The assertion is an act of commitment which, like Pascal's wager, encompasses rather than avoids doubt: there is nothing to lose.

> Earth, you nearest, allow me.
> Green of the earth and civil grey:
> within me, without me and moment by
> moment allow me for to
> be here is enough and earth you
> strangest, you nearest, be home.
>
> (p. 57)

The longest poem in *The Gods* is also, in more modern form, an elegy, "The Death of Harold Ladoo." Lee was working with the House of Anansi press when he met Ladoo, who came to him with the manuscript of his first novel. Anansi ultimately published two of Ladoo's novels, *No Pain like This Body* (1972) and *Yesterdays* (1974). He was murdered on a trip home to Trinidad in 1973.

No Pain like This Body is set in a poor Hindu settlement in Trinidad and tells the story of a brutal drunken father who drives his wife and four children, Balraj, Sunaree, and the eight-year-old twins Rama and Panday, out of the house into the night rain. As a consequence, Rama dies in hospital of a scorpion sting and pneumonia. The novel builds up to the central sixth chapter, the drunken funeral for the child, then concludes with the grief-stricken mother's growing madness. The point of view is supposedly omniscient, yet it takes the diction and perspective of the children, so that the mother and father appear as larger than life. In structure, the novel resembles Roch Carrier's *La Guerre, Yes Sir!*. There is anger and pain in the novel, but the figures presented are capable of villainy and heroism. Ladoo's second novel, *Yesterdays*, has much the same setting, but the whole cast of characters is treated with denigrating contempt. It is a distasteful work, in which the writer deliberately fouls his own origins. While the evidence is too scanty to give any kind of certainty, one's impression is that something had gone wrong in Harold Ladoo's artistic development.

Lee's elegy "The Death of Harold Ladoo" is in two parts. The first deals with Ladoo as an individual, a writer, a friend living his doomed career. The second deals with Ladoo as a representative of larger forces let loose in the world.

The elegy opens quietly with the poet, now in pastoral suburbia, reflecting on his need to pay tribute to his dead friend, the writer Harold Ladoo. After giving his present setting in four brief sentences, the poet then catalogues his reasons for wishing to salute his dead friend in a twenty-six line sentence, reasons which all fit within the decorum of literary elegy.

Lee then proceeds to record his memory of his first meeting with Ladoo and his subsequent memories of their intense debates. Although we only see Ladoo in relation to Lee's strong emotional response to him, enough particular details are given for us to visualize him as an individual: "skinny brown man" (p. 40), "swagger of tricky humility" (p. 43), "those liquid eyes unhooding" (p. 40), "sideways grin" (p. 48). For Lee, however, it quickly becomes obvious that Ladoo is more than a fascinating indivudual; in his compulsions, he becomes a type for a brief hectic era. And as the recording brings back a flood of memories, the poet becomes first uneasy, then angry — he comes more and more to sense that he has been used, and so "Ladoo, you bastard, goodbye: you bled me dry" (p. 44). Such a sterile response leaves Lee in a cul-de-sac, and so he starts anew: the Anansi years, Harold Ladoo, his own need for vicariously venturing all — he has used Ladoo, become in fact Baudelaire's *hypocrite lecteur*. From such contraries, Lee attempts to salvage common ground. The first claim is to fellowship, "the deep unscheduled ground of caring" (p. 49), for Lee had noted how writers shield one another. It is not sufficient for Ladoo no longer shares the fellowship of the living. He is dead. And what that means, Lee can neither comprehend nor imagine.

In the second part of the elegy, Lee attempts to come to terms with Harold Ladoo, not as a particular individual, but as an embodiment of larger forces, as an agent of the gods. For if Harold Ladoo was a "routine megalomaniac" (p. 44), with the artist's version of *Götterdämmerung* in his bones, Orpheus dismembered, and if he was one of those who "... carry this century / malignant in their cells from birth / like the tick of genetic stigmata" (p. 57), then this century is under the sign of the Great Nihilist, with Ladoo one of the Fallen Angel's minor prophets, as Adolf Hitler was one of his major. Lee's thesis is that the only transcendent forces now at work in the world are malignant. Such a prognosis may provide an apologia for Ladoo, but there is little consolation in it for the rest of us. And for Lee as an artist dealing with Ladoo as another, the predicament faced by the artist as one granted the power of words is critical. It is a predicament that has gone beyond Hölderlin's "What good are poets in a time of dearth?" for the dearth has gone cancerous. What is the artist of today who does not wish to either retreat to an arid formalism or endlessly dissect the body of a moribund society to do? Lee's answer, to bear witness to the holy absence while maintaining a humble humanism, is not altogether satisfactory. Here are his lines, the concluding ones of the elegy:

We must withstand the gods awhile, the mutants.
And mostly the bearers of gifts, for they have
singled us out for unclean work; and supremely
those who give power, whether at words or
the world for it will bring
criminal prowess.
But to live with a measure, resisting their terrible inroads:
I hope this is enough.
And, to let the beings be.
And also to honour the gods in their former selves,
albeit obscurely, at a distance, unable
to speak the older tongue; and to wait
till their fury is spent and they call on us again
for passionate awe in our lives, and a high clean style.
(p.59)

It is a passive defensive stance, and I want to examine its adequacy. But first, having looked at Lee's elegies, let us glance at his love poetry and odes.

Civil Elegies and Other Poems and *The Gods* contain about eighteen love poems. The classification is a little arbitrary for the poems focus so completely on the lover's response to the woman that they become introspective lyrics — only in a few, or in throw-away lines, does the woman take on any independent personality. This is reinforced by Lee's emphasis on moments of stasis: like his friend the painter Alex Colville, he strives for the epiphany of luminous repose — not the rumpling of the sheets and the singing of the choir, but the ink-pot on the sheets and the levelling of the quire. This is not to say that all love poetry must be, to quote the immortal Joe Wallace, "from bed to verse";[43] all love poetry is before or after the fact for, betwixt, the lovers' minds are otherwise engaged. But a lover engagé writing verse should strive to decrease the distance — there are experiences for which recollection in tranquility is inappropriate. Few referees become good sportswriters. The following are the poems by Lee in which passion maintains itself against self-analysis: "When It Is Over," "Of Eros, in Shiny Degree," and "Remember, Woman," in traditional stanzas; and "High Park, by Grenadier Pond," "Brunswick Avenue," "Song," and "You Can Climb Down Now," in free verse. To these one could add "Summer

Song," which uses lover's terminology for a lighthearted hymn to being. As a group, they show again Lee's ear for language, rhythm, and sound; his almost painful honesty; his intellectual energy.

One additional poem should be considered here, "Riffs,"[44] a dramatic monologue spoken by a lover reliving his passion for a temporarily absent mistress. But, while looking forward to reunion and consoling himself with drink, the lover senses their coming permanent separation. The stanzas are carefully numbered, from one to sixty-seven, as if the poet did not trust the poem to chart its own trajectory. He was justified: the work reads like a rough first draft.

Lee's published work includes three odes: "Sibelius Park," in *Civil Elegies and Other Poems*; "Not Abstract Harmonies But," in *The Gods*; and the title poem of the latter collection. All are irregular, but, particularly in "The Gods," one can hear behind the free-verse cadence the longer lines, from pentameter to sonorous heptameter. All are organized by parallel and contrast, but it is applied differently in the three. "Sibelius Park" is in two parts: the first describes in the third person a tired walk home after a day working with authors and manuscripts at Anansi, memories of his misfired schoolboy evangelical fervour, and an epiphany at Sibelius Park; the second, analytical and in the first person, reflects that reality must be sought, not in any of the given periods or moments of his existence, but in the tensions among them. The final, apparently reassuring line, "There is nothing to be afraid of" (p. 25), carries a menacing undertone for nothingness is the final fear. "Not Abstract Harmonies But," also in two parts, is more serene, hortatory. Each part contains eleven sentences, but the second is much longer, having 72 of the poem's 111 lines. The first locates the poet's here and now, as against his more youthful search "with geriatric haste" (p. 18) for a transcendental ideology; the second gives a Heideggerian analysis and celebration (the German theologian brackets the two) of fullness of Being. The difficulties Lee found with Heidegger's philosophic language in the sonnets have disappeared, for here it is fused with the language of music to give a passage of extraordinary vibrancy. He has even reproduced the effect of Heidegger's prose on the reader — of trembling on the verge of meaning and judging the quest worthwhile.

Difficulties remain, which can usefully be examined by the Arnoldian method of juxtaposition. First, the closing lines of Margaret Avison's "New Year's Poem":

> Gentle and just pleasure
> It is, being human, to have won from space
> This unchill, habitable interior
> Which mirrors quietly the light
> Of the snow, and the new year.[45]

Now compare this to a verse-paragraph from Lee:

> So each real thing endures,
>   rife with the itch to pick up
>   currents that do not mesh and
>   live their concert — *each* thing, which makes a
>   welter of harmonies until the
>   jagged cadenzas of meaning
> ripple like simultaneous fields of light.
>   And if a man could stay
> clear enough, stay near and distanced enough,
> resonance by resonance it would ease down into itself, each
>   thing its own yet held in criss-cross harmonies, each
> harmony at home yet flexing into phase
>   with every flexing other, coherences
>   cohering till almost he senses
>   the world as jubilee: I mean
>   the hymn of the fullness of being—
> the ripple of luminous cosmoi, up/down &
> across the scales of orchestration in
>   ceaseless, many-
> dimensional play, here good now bad but
> telling the grace of daily infinite coherence.
>
> (p. 21)

Leaving aside for the moment Lee's conditional "if a man could," both poets are speaking about the attainment of harmony between man and his setting. For Lee the path is willed intellectual struggle, for Avison a received intuition, and the poetic forms reflect these differences in means. But, whereas Avison gives one a modest participation in the end in quiet lines that continue to reverberate within, one takes from Lee a sense of intellectual excitement in the quest. And when the excitement fades, the blackboard is left clean: his poetry contains a few felicitous phrases, but none of those poetic images which, like Lucretius' atoms, hook into the cells of the mind.

"The Gods" is Lee's closest approach to the classical ode in form. It is in three parts. The first strophe, in nine sentences, records the loss in the modern world of the numinous and jests about the gods with flippant contemporary cynicism. The nine sentences of the antistrophe, in rather dithyrambic mode, record an encounter with holy otherness in the Heideggerian clearing. The epode is made up of only two sentences: "I do say gods" (p. 32), followed by a splendidly tangled sentence of 196 words in 26 lines, the purport of which is that the poet will be faithful in his fashion.

As "The Gods" is, to my mind, Lee's most interesting ode, I want to discuss it in more detail. It was first published as a Kanchenjunga Press chapbook (as were "Not Abstract Harmonies But" and "The Death of Harold Ladoo") but was extensively revised. As first published in 1978, "The Gods" was a straightforward meditation on a topic Lee had written about in a letter to the editor of *Saturday Night* (Sept. 1972) in response to Robin Mathews' criticism of his July article on the poetry of Al Purdy:

> Canadian literature has long included an experience which the theologians call *mysterium tremendum*—the encounter with holy otherness, most commonly approached here through encounter with the land—to which an appropriate response is awe and terror. It is a very different thing from alienation.[46]

Here are the original opening lines of the poem:

   I do say
gods

                      old ripples of presence
              archaic eddies of being, a space ago

>   their strokes and carnal voltage, as
> *pineforce   potence-of-bearswipe   voicing-the-thunder.*
> In the middle of one more day, in a clearing maybe say, birches[47]

And here is the revised opening:

>   Who, now, can speak of gods —
> their strokes and carnal voltage,
> old ripples of presence   a space ago
>   archaic eddies of being?
>
>   (p. 29)

The strophe now opens with a question, and the subsequent 31 lines describing modern life when deprived of the divine dimension have been added. The three terms, line 6 of the original, which look as if they were copied from a book of Indian legends, have been excised; and the line introducing the numinous in its two aspects of terror and beauty now opens the antistrophe. About the only loss is the disappearance of the birches, which changes the clearing from a location to a concept. Perhaps in some subsequent version Lee will practise reforestation.

Poets before Lee have treated the theme of the numinous — one thinks of Duncan Campbell Scott in such poems as "The Height of Land" or "Powassan's Drum." The closing line of the penultimate stanza of "At Gull Lake: August 1810," "After the beauty of terror the beauty of peace,"[48] names the responses to the sublime and the beautiful. What gives Lee's work its distinctive tone is its urgency: the experience Scott and others could record is, Lee feels, in danger of being excluded from diminished modern consciousness. Modern society's pride in manipulative technology is in danger of destroying society's sense of community with all that is. As always, pride is reinforced by fear, for the natural world includes that most terrifying irrational, the death of each individual, to which the response has always been defiance, evasion, and retreat. Technology has merely sharpened the fangs of that oldest of all temptations, to be as gods, knowing not death. This hubris has brought Western society to a state of crisis for it has isolated itself from the natural creation it fears and despises just when technology has given it the power to ruin its planetary mite. Earth repressed festers and turns malignant: whom the gods would destroy they first make mad. In the individual, madness takes the form of banal isolation, as the ego retreats more and more to the attic of consciousness. Lee records his sense of banal cynical isolation in the strophe, and his sense of contact with the numinous lighting up the terrain in the antistrophe. In the epode, Lee attempts to present his resolution. This is not easy. Meaning has leaked away from the terminology Paul used to name the unknown god in Athens, so modern humanity must speak in silence. Yet speak it must, or lose a saving dimension of Being. In such a position, all the poet can do is commend an attitude of receptivity, to refuse to surrender and to stand the night watch.

I want to add a personal reflection. There was a time, not too remote, when for most the existence of God was a presupposition, and faith / doubt was exercised on His role in human affairs. More recently, His bare existence became a subject of willed faith, and doubters postulated a future freed from His presence. For those who have grown up in the atomic age, the idea of a future has itself become problematic, a matter of faith amid the fallout of doubt. Heidegger's identification of that which exists with the Divine is thus reassuring for those who, at the level doubt now works, know that time has run out for all creatures who on earth do dwell. The tongues of flame from Hiroshima and Nagasaki have announced that to the children of light as clearly as Nietzsche announced in his generation that God is dead. Standing in semifaithfulness may be fine, like youth breaking gravestones and other markers of continuity in time valued by those who cannot yet see their hypocrisy in treasuring the past while creating an abyss between the present and the future, but in the meantime how do we live? We have the habit of living teleologically, projecting goals on the future and limping after them, and it is a difficult habit to kick. As a disciple of Heidegger and an excellent didactic poet, perhaps Lee will treat that topic in his next (it is hard to break faith in succession) works.

Having surveyed the adult poetry Lee has published to date, we can begin to formulate an appraisal. Often the subject of Lee's work is a kind of violent confrontation with self. In a review of Lee's *Savage Fields*, Jack Healy wrote:

Lee's sense that we have to develop a cosmology of savage fields to articulate a grammar of the intolerable is probably correct from where he stands. Where he stands, however, is as crucial as what he says about Ondaatje, Cohen and the strife they bear witness to.[49]

Lee stands in the midst of civil strife. The combattants may be variously labelled: in *Savage Fields*, Lee names them "world" and "earth." World is the realm of the rational, manipulative — the mind's lust for power.[50] Earth is the emotive, cyclic, the heart's hunger for home, love, Being. Other critics have used other terms: Gaston Bachelard continues in an older tradition in calling them "mind" and "soul." Scorned, earth turns vindictive, monstrous. As the modern world is one of institutionalized psychic dislocation, the monstrous will take collective forms. The English historian E. P. Thompson, in writing that the hostile superpowers, locked into a position of impotent rage by their nuclear technologies, have imposed a balance of terror which is not a stasis but a degenerative process as commandeered rage, denied military expression, turns inward, is diagnosing the same malady.[51] Lee in his poetry is offering himself as an exemplary case, a consciousness in which we can observe and identify the victor-victims in their strife and marriage. This microcosmic stance imposes difficulties when the poet wants both to illuminate the disease as patient and suggest the physician's cure. Hence his tentative, minimal resolutions, which are both irritating and stimulating.

One danger faced by a didactic poet is to be thought facile: no one takes seriously the glib guru. Lee has avoided this. His mature work reveals a strong mind under painful self-scrutiny, and there is a laboured precision of expression, with an obvious attention to the weight of each word. As a consequence, the amount published remains small, three small collections in over fifteen years. In a sense, all are fragments of a spiritual autobiography, an updated version of John Bunyan's *Grace Abounding to the Chief of Sinners*, and have Bunyan's arrogant high seriousness. Lee has written little occasional poetry, and the qualities so obvious in the children's verse, the love of names, of whimsy, and the grotesque, are rarely represented in his poetry. He has the passion for the idea of the intellectual, and his poetry at its best deals with felt thoughts. In the closing of "The Death of Harold Ladoo," his plea for "passionate awe in our lives, and a high clean style" makes clear that "style" is not simply a question of form. Only by language, he feels, can we construe reality. As one of the symptoms of modern humanity's spiritual impoverishment is the debasing of language, the poet must struggle to restore to words their capacity for illumination. If in the beginning was the word, in the word also is continuance. It is the sense of mortal wrestling with language in Lee's poetry that gives it its deep vitality.

NOTES

[1] See Louis Dudek, ed., *Dk / Some Letters of Ezra Pound* (Montreal: DC Books, 1974), especially letters 20–27, pp. 45–56.

[2] Dennis Lee, "A Warning against This Kind of Anthology: Being an Introduction which Discusses the Reader," in *T.O. Now: The Young Toronto Poets* (Toronto: House of Anansi, 1968), p. iii.

[3] *Acta Victoriana*, 85, No. 3 (Feb. 1961), 4.

[4] *Kingdom of Absence* (Toronto: House of Anansi, 1967), p. 29. All further references to this work appear in the text.

[5] *T.O. Now*, p. 6.

[6] In *The Gods* (Toronto: McClelland and Stewart, 1979), pp. 35–59. All further references to this work appear in the text.

[7] Lionel Kearns, "If There's Anything I Hate It's Poetry," rev. of *Journeyings and the Returns*, by bpNichol, *Poems New and Collected*, by A.J.M. Smith, *Kingdom of Absence*, by Dennis Lee, and *A Silent Green Sky*, by Florence McNeil, *Canadian Literature*, No. 36 (Spring 1968), p. 68.

[8] *The Tamarack Review*, No. 47 (Spring 1968), p. 85.

[9] George Bowering, "Why Poets Are Poor," rev. of *Kingdom of Absence*, by Dennis Lee, *From the Portals of Mouseholes*, by Seymour Mayne, and *Letters from the Savage Mind*, by Patrick Lane, *Canadian Dimension*, 5, No. 7 (Dec. 1968–Jan. 1969), 43.

[10] Eric Thompson, rev. of *The Circle Game*, by Margaret Atwood, and *Kingdom of Absence*, by Dennis Lee, *The Fiddlehead*, No. 75 (Spring 1968), p. 78.

[11] *University of Toronto Quarterly*, 37 (July 1968), 374.

[12] Ann Montagnes, "Seven Canadian Poets of Varying Style and Talent Offer a Non-Transistorised Service to Piece Together Our Fragmented Times," *Saturday Night*, July 1968, pp. 27–28.

[13] Mary Keyes, rev. of *T.V. Baby Poems* and *Airplane Dreams: Compositions from Journals*, by Allen Ginsberg, *Civil Elegies*, by Dennis Lee, and *Poems for All the Annettes*, by Al Purdy, *The Canadian Forum*, Nov. 1968, p. 182.

[14] Hugh MacCallum, "Letters in Canada 1968: Poetry," *University of Toronto Quarterly*, 38 (July 1969), 347.

[15] MacCallum, "Letters in Canada 1968: Poetry," p. 347.

[16] Doug Fetherling, "A Poet-Publisher with a Voice like No One Else's," rev. of *Civil Elegies and Other Poems*, *Saturday Night*, June 1972, p. 37.

[17] *Canadian Literature*, No. 55 (Winter 1973), p. 104.

[18] *Quarry*, 21, No. 3 (Summer 1972), 66–67.

[19] Gary Geddes, "Lee, Dennis," *Supplement to the Oxford Companion to Canadian History and Literature* (1973), p. 187.

[20] Frank Davey, "Dennis Lee," in *From There to Here: A Guide to English-Canadian Literature since 1960* (Erin, Ont.: Porcépic, 1974), p. 166.

[21] *The Canadian Forum*, March 1980, p. 35.

[22] Paul McNally, rev. of *The Gods*, *Queen's Quarterly*, 87 (Winter 1980), 750.

[23] Ian Pearson, rev. of *The Gods*, *Quill & Quire*, Nov. 1979, p. 34.

[24] *Arc*, No. 1 (Spring 1978), pp. 23–28.

[25] Douglas Barbour, "'Fields' with Hope," rev. of *Savage Fields*, *Brick: A Journal of Reviews*, No. 11 (Winter 1981), pp. 6–7; Peggy Dragišić, "Between the Intolerable and the Inscrutable," rev. of *Savage Fields* and *The Gods*, *Brick: A Journal of Reviews*, No. 11 (Winter 1981), pp. 8–12.

[26] *Brick: A Journal of Reviews*, No. 13 (Fall 1981), pp. 32–39.

[27] *Dalhousie Review*, 57 (Winter 1977–78), 765–74.

[28] J.M. Kertzer, "Letters in Canada 1977: Humanities," *University of Toronto Quarterly*, 47 (Summer 1978), 454–55.

[29] Doug Fetherling, "The Savage Cosmos of Dennis Lee," rev. of *Savage Fields*, *Saturday Night*, Jan.–Feb. 1978, pp. 74–75.

[30] *Essays on Ethics, Religion and Society*, ed. J.M. Robson, Vol. x of *Collected Works of John Stuart Mill* (Toronto: Univ. of Toronto Press, 1969), p. 381.

[31] *Collected Works of John Stuart Mill*, x, 385.

[32] *The University Game*, ed. Dennis Lee and Howard Adelman (Toronto: House of Anansi, 1968), pp. 92–93.

[33] An earlier version appeared in *Acta Victoriana*, 88, No. 2 (Spring 1964), 18.

[34] Lee published a translation of Rilke's first elegy in *Quarry*, 19, No. 1 (Fall 1969), 6–9.

[35] *Civil Elegies and Other Poems* (Toronto: House of Anansi, 1972), p. 34. All further references to this work appear in the text.

[36] George Grant, *Lament for a Nation: Defeat of Canadian Nationalism* (Toronto: McClelland and Stewart, 1965), p. 64.

[37] Charles Taylor, *Hegel* (Cambridge: Cambridge Univ. Press, 1975), p. 450.

[38] Taylor, p. 541.

[39] Lee discusses the "musing" voice added to the second edition of *Civil Elegies* in R. W. Stedingh, "An Interview with Dennis Lee," *The Canadian Fiction Magazine*, No. 7 (Summer 1972), pp. 42–54.

[40] Paul-Emile Borduas, "Refus Global," in *Ecrits / Writings 1942–1958*, trans. François-Marc Gagnon and Dennis Young, ed. François-Marc Gagnon (Halifax: Nova Scotia College of Art and Design, 1978), p. 49.

[41] Borduas, p. 49.

[42] Jean Le Moyne, *Convergences* (Montreal: HMH, 1961).

[43] Joe Wallace, *Poems* (Toronto: Progress Books, 1981), p. 180.

[44] In *Tasks of Passion: Dennis Lee at Mid-Career*, ed. Karen Mulhallen, Donna Bennett, and Russell Brown (Toronto: Descant Editions, 1982), pp. 201–26. This volume was published simultaneously as *Descant*, No. 39 (Winter 1982) [*Dennis Lee Special Issue*].

[45] In *Poetry of Midcentury 1940–1960*, ed. Milton Wilson, New Canadian Library Original, No. 4 (Toronto: McClelland and Stewart, 1964), p. 90.

[46] Dennis Lee, "Rejoinder," *Saturday Night*, Sept. 1972, p. 33.

[47] *The Gods*, Kanchenjunga Chapbook, No. 9 (San Francisco: Kanchenjunga, 1978), p. 5.

[48] Duncan Campbell Scott, *The Green Cloister: Later Poems* (Toronto: McClelland and Stewart, 1935), p. 58.

[49] J. J. Healy, "Lee's Provocative Prose Poem," rev. of *Savage Fields*, *The Citizen* [Ottawa], 31 Dec. 1977, p. 41.

[50] In a review article on Michael Ondaatje's *The Collected Works of Billy the Kid*, entitled "Michael Ondaatje: The Mechanization of Death," Sheila Watson noted that Ondaatje shared with Wyndham

Lewis an interest in modern man's interiorizing of mechanization and the "brutalizing of the conceptual forms which organize the perceptual flux" (*White Pelican*, 2, No. 4 [Fall 1972], 58). Lee's concept "world" may have been influenced by the same sources.

[51] E. P. Thompson, "A Letter to America," *The Nation*, 24 Jan. 1981, pp. 68–93.

SELECTED BIBLIOGRAPHY

Primary Sources

Books

Lee, Dennis, and Roberta Charlesworth, eds. *An Anthology of Verse.* Toronto: Oxford Univ. Press, 1964.

———, and Roberta Charlesworth, eds. *The Second Century Anthologies of Verse.* 2 vols., and a *Teacher's Manual.* Toronto: Oxford Univ. Press, 1967–69.

———. *Kingdom of Absence.* Toronto: House of Anansi, 1967.

———. *Civil Elegies.* Toronto: House of Anansi, 1968.

———, ed. *T.O. Now: The Young Toronto Poets.* Toronto: House of Anansi, 1968.

———, and Howard Adelman, eds. *The University Game.* Toronto: House of Anansi, 1968.

———. *Wiggle to the Laundromat.* Toronto: New, 1970.

———. *Civil Elegies and Other Poems.* Toronto: House of Anansi, 1972.

———. *Alligator Pie.* Toronto: Macmillan, 1974.

———. *Nicholas Knock and Other People.* Toronto: Macmillan, 1974.

———. *Not Abstract Harmonies But.* Kanchenjunga Chapbook, No. 1. San Francisco: Kanchenjunga, 1974.

———. *The Death of Harold Ladoo.* Kanchenjunga Chapbook, No. 6. San Francisco: Kanchenjunga, 1976.

———. *Garbarge Delight.* Toronto: Macmillan, 1977.

———. *Savage Fields: An Essay in Literature and Cosmology.* Toronto: House of Anansi, 1977.

———. *The Gods.* 1st ed. Kanchenjunga Chapbook, No. 9. San Francisco: Kanchenjunga, 1978.

———. *The Gods.* rev. ed. Toronto: McClelland and Steward, 1979.

———. *Elégies civiles et autres poèmes.* Ed. bilingue. Traduit par Marc Lebel. Montréal: L'Hexagone, 1980.

———. *Jelly Belly.* Toronto: Macmillan, 1983.

Contributions to Periodicals and Books

Lee, Dennis. "Getting to Rochdale." In *The University Game*. Ed. Dennis Lee and Howard Adelman. Toronto: House of Anansi, 1968, pp. 69–94.

———. "Running and Dwelling: Homage to Al Purdy." *Saturday Night*, July 1972, pp. 14, 16.

———. "Rejoinder." *Saturday Night*, Sept. 1972, pp. 32–33.

———. "Cadence, Country, Silence." *Liberté*, 14, No. 6 (1972), 65–88. Rev. ("Cadence, Country, Silence: Writing in a Colonial Space") in *Open Letter*, 2nd ser., No. 6 (Fall 1973), pp. 34–53.

———. "Modern Poetry." In *Read Canadian: A Book about Canadian Books*. Ed. Robert Fulford, Dave Godfrey, and Abraham Rotstein. Toronto: James Lewis & Samuel, 1972, pp. 228–36.

———. "Reading *Savage Fields*." *Canadian Journal of Political and Social Theory*, 3 (Spring–Summer 1979), 161–83. Rpt. (revised) in *Brick: A Journal of Reviews*, No. 13 (Fall 1981), pp. 32–39.

———. "Polyphony, Enacting a Meditation." In *Tasks of Passion: Dennis Lee at Mid-Career*. Ed. Karen Mulhallen, Donna Bennett, and Russell Brown. Toronto: Descant Editions, 1982, pp. 82–99.

———. "Riffs." In *Tasks of Passion: Dennis Lee at Mid-Career*. Ed. Karen Mulhallen, Donna Bennett, and Russell Brown. Toronto: Descant Editions, 1982, pp. 201–26.

Secondary Sources

Atwood, Margaret. *Selected Poems*. Toronto: Oxford Univ. Press, 1976.

Barbour, Douglas. "'Fields' with Hope." Rev. of *Savage Fields*. *Brick: A Journal of Reviews*, No. 11 (Winter 1981), pp. 6–7.

Bilan, R. P. "Canadian Poet-Critics." Rev. of *Another Time*, by Eli Mandel, and *Savage Fields*, by Dennis Lee. *Dalhousie Review*, 57 (Winter 1977–78), 765–74.

Blodgett, Ted. "Authenticity and Absence: Reflections on the Prose of Dennis Lee." In *Tasks of Passion: Dennis Lee at Mid-Career*. Ed. Karen Mulhallen, Donna Bennett, and Russell Brown. Toronto: Descant Editions, 1982, pp. 103–17.

Borduas, Paul-Emile. "Refus Global." In *Ecrits/Writings 1942–1958*.

Trans. François-Marc Gagnon and Dennis Young. Ed. François-Marc Gagnon. Halifax: Nova Scotia College of Art and Design, 1978, pp. 45–54.

Bowering, George. "Why Poets Are Poor." Rev. of *Kingdom of Absence*, by Dennis Lee, *From the Portals of Mouseholes*, by Seymour Mayne, and *Letters from the Savage Mind*, by Patrick Lane. *Canadian Dimension*, 5, No. 7 (Dec. 1968–Jan. 1969), 43–44.

Bradshaw, Leah. "A Second Look at *Savage Fields*." *Canadian Journal of Political and Social Theory*, 3 (Spring–Summer 1979), 139–51.

Bringhurst, Robert. "At Home in the Difficult World." In *Tasks of Passion: Dennis Lee at Mid-Career*. Ed. Karen Mulhallen, Donna Bennett, and Russell Brown. Toronto: Descant Editions, 1982, pp. 57–81.

Cohen, Leonard. *Beautiful Losers*. Toronto: McClelland and Stewart, 1966.

Cooley, Dennis. "Loss and Confusion." Rev. of *The Gods*. *The Canadian Forum*, March 1980, pp. 34–36.

Davey, Frank. "Dennis Lee." In *From There to Here: A Guide to English-Canadian Literature since 1960*. Erin, Ont.: Porcépic, 1974, pp. 165–67.

Dragišić, Peggy. "Between the Intolerable and the Inscrutable." Rev. of *Savage Fields* and *The Gods*. *Brick: A Journal of Reviews*, No. 11 (Winter 1981), pp. 8–12.

Dragland, Stan. "On *Civil Elegies*." In *Tasks of Passion: Dennis Lee at Mid-Career*. Ed. Karen Mulhallen, Donna Bennett, and Russell Brown. Toronto: Descant Editions, 1982, pp. 170–88.

Duffy, Dennis. *Gardens, Covenants, Exiles: Loyalism in the Literature of Upper Canada/Ontario*. Toronto: Univ. of Toronto Press, 1982.

Fetherling, Doug. "A Poet-Publisher with a Voice like No One Else's." Rev. of *Civil Elegies and Other Poems*. *Saturday Night*, June 1972, p. 37.

———. "The Savage Cosmos of Dennis Lee." Rev. of *Savage Fields*. *Saturday Night*, Jan.–Feb. 1978, pp. 74–75.

Garneau, Hector de Saint-Denys-. *Oeuvres*. Annoté et présenté par Jacques Brault et Benoît Lacroix. Montréal: Les Presses de l'Université de Montréal, 1971.

Geddes, Gary. "Lee, Dennis." *Supplement to the Oxford Companion to Canadian History and Literature* (1973).

Godfrey, Dave. "On *Savage Fields* and the Act of Criticism." *Canadian Journal of Political and Social Theory*, 3 (Spring–Summer 1979), 152–59.

Grant, George. *Philosophy in the Mass Age.* Toronto: Copp Clark, 1959.
———. *Lament for a Nation: The Defeat of Canadian Nationalism.* Toronto: McClelland and Stewart, 1965.
———. *Technology and Empire: Perspectives on North America.* Toronto: House of Anansi, 1969.
———. *Time as History.* Massey Lectures, 9th ser. Toronto: Canadian Broadcasting Corporation, 1969.
———. *English-Speaking Justice.* Sackville, N.B.: Mount Allison Univ., 1974.
Healy, J.J. "Lee's Provocative Prose Poem." Rev. of *Savage Fields. The Citizen* [Ottawa], 31 Dec. 1977, p. 41.
Heidegger, Martin. *Being and Time.* Trans. John Macquarrie and Edward Robinson. London: SCM, 1962.
———. *Poetry, Language, Thought.* Trans. Albert Hofstadter. New York: Harper and Row, 1971.
———. *The Question Concerning Technology and Other Essays.* Trans. William Lovitt. New York: Harper and Row, 1977.
Helwig, David. Rev. of *Civil Elegies and Other Poems. Quarry,* 21, No. 3 (Summer 1972), 66–67.
Hutchings, Patrick. "Realism, Surrealism and Celebration: The Paintings of Alex Colville in the Collection of the National Gallery of Canada." *The National Gallery of Canada Bulletin,* 4, No. 2 (1966), 16–28.
Jones, D.G. "In Search of Canada: Dennis Lee's Ironic Vision." *Arc,* No. 1 (Spring 1978), pp. 23–28.
Kane, Sean. "The Poet as Shepherd of Being." In *Tasks of Passion: Dennis Lee at Mid-Career.* Ed. Karen Mulhallen, Donna Bennett, and Russell Brown. Toronto: Descant Editions, 1982, pp. 121–42.
Kearns, Lionel. "If There's Anything I Hate It's Poetry." Rev. of *Journeyings and the Returns,* by bpNichol, *Poems New and Collected,* by A.J.M. Smith, *Kingdom of Absence,* by Dennis Lee, and *A Silent Green Sky,* by Florence McNeil. *Canadian Literature,* No. 36 (Spring 1968), pp. 67–70.
Kertzer, J.M. Rev. of *Savage Fields.* In "Letters in Canada 1977: Humanities." *University of Toronto Quarterly,* 47 (Summer 1978), 454–55.
Keyes, Mary. Rev. of *T.V. Baby Poems* and *Airplane Dreams: Compositions from Journals,* by Allen Ginsberg, *Civil Elegies,* by Dennis Lee, and *Poems for All the Annettes,* by Al Purdy. *The Canadian Forum,* Nov. 1968, pp. 182–83.

Le Moyne, Jean. *Convergences*. Montréal: HMH, 1961.
MacCallum, Hugh. Rev. of *Kingdom of Absence*. In "Letters in Canada 1967: Poetry." *University of Toronto Quarterly*, 37 (July 1968), 374.
——. Rev. of *Civil Elegies*. In "Letters in Canada 1968: Poetry." *University of Toronto Quarterly*, 38 (July 1969), 347.
McNally, Paul. Rev. of *The Gods*. *Queen's Quarterly*, 87 (Winter 1980), 749–51.
Mill, John Stuart. "Nature." In *Essays on Ethics, Religion and Society*. Ed. J. M. Robson. Vol. x of *Collected Works of John Stuart Mill*. Toronto: Univ. of Toronto Press, 1969, pp. 373–402.
Montagnes, Ann. "Seven Canadian Poets of Varying Style and Talent Offer a Non-Transistorised Service to Piece Together Our Fragmented Times." Rev. of *Civil Elegies*, and six other books. *Saturday Night*, July 1968, pp. 27–28.
Mulhallen, Karen, Donna Bennett, and Russell Brown, eds. *Tasks of Passion: Dennis Lee at Mid-Career*. Toronto: Descant Editions, 1982.
Munton, Ann. "Simultaneity in the Writings of Dennis Lee." In *Tasks of Passion: Dennis Lee at Mid-Career*. Ed. Karen Mulhallen, Donna Bennett, and Russell Brown. Toronto: Descant Editions, 1982, pp. 143–69.
Ondaatje, Michael. *The Collected Works of Billy the Kid: Left Handed Poems*. Toronto: House of Anansi, 1970.
Pearson, Ian. Rev. of *The Gods*. *Quill & Quire*, Nov. 1979, pp. 33–34.
Purdy, Al. "Aiming Low." Rev. of *Kingdom of Absence*, and eleven other books. *The Tamarack Review*, No. 47 (Spring 1968), pp. 81–89, 91–97.
Schroeder, Andreas. "Difficult Sanities." Rev. of *Civil Elegies and Other Poems*. *Canadian Literature*, No. 55 (Winter 1973), pp. 102–05.
Stedingh, R. W. "An Interview with Dennis Lee." *The Canadian Fiction Magazine*, No. 7 (Summer 1972), pp. 42–54.
Sutherland, John. *The Poetry of E. J. Pratt: A New Interpretation*. Toronto: Ryerson, 1956.
Taylor, Charles. *Hegel*. Cambridge: Cambridge Univ. Press, 1975.
Thompson, E. P. "A Letter to America." *The Nation*, 24 Jan. 1981, pp. 68–93.
Thompson, Eric. Rev. of *The Circle Game*, by Margaret Atwood, and *Kingdom of Absence*, by Dennis Lee. *The Fiddlehead*, No. 75 (Spring 1968), pp. 76–78.
Wallace, Joe. *Poems*. Toronto: Progress Books, 1981.
Watson, Sheila. "Michael Ondaatje: The Mechanization of Death." *White Pelican*, 2, No. 4 (Fall 1972), 56–64.

Gwendolyn MacEwen (1941–)

JAN BARTLEY

Gwendolyn MacEwen (1941–   )

JAN BARTLEY

Biography

GWENDOLYN MACEWEN was born on 1 September 1941, in Toronto. She attended Western Technical High School in Toronto from 1955 to 1959 but left school at the age of eighteen to write. At age seventeen, she published her first poems in *The Canadian Forum*, and she completed three novels before the appearance of *Julian the Magician*, published when she was only twenty-two. One of the first three efforts became the short story "Day of Twelve Princes." MacEwen herself says, "I can't trace where the original impulse came from, but I always wanted to write."[1]

MacEwen spent a short time in Montreal editing the little magazine *Moment* from 1960 to 1962, with Al Purdy and Milton Acorn. She later married Acorn, divorced, and in 1971 married Nikos Tsingos. Some of her poetry, and later her novels, reflect her travelling experiences in Israel in 1962, Egypt in 1966, and Greece in 1971 and 1976. Although she enjoys a personal friendship with Margaret Atwood and has recently become involved in the Toronto theatre scene, MacEwen is not formally aligned with any particular group of poets. In fact, her own view of literature and experience seems to be stamped by a very personal sensibility:

> In my poetry I am concerned with finding the relationships between what we call the "real" world and that other world which consists of dream, fantasy and myth. I've never felt that these "two worlds" are as separate as one might think, and in fact my poetry as well as my life seems to occupy a place—you might call it a kind of no-man's land—between the two. Very often experiences or observations which are immediate take on grand or universal significance for me,

because they seem to capsulize and give new force to the age-old wonders, mysteries and fears which have always delighted and bewildered mankind. In my attempt to describe a world which is for me both miraculous and terrible, I make abundant use of myth, metaphor and symbol; these are as much a part of my language as the alphabet I use.[2]

The shaping of MacEwen's myth has sustained a prolific career: two pamphlets of poetry, *The Drunken Clock* (1961) and *Selah* (1961); and six collections of poetry, *The Rising Fire* (1963), *A Breakfast for Barbarians* (1966), *The Shadow-Maker* (1969), *The Armies of the Moon* (1972), *The Fire-Eaters* (1976), and *The T. E. Lawrence Poems* (1982). Her selected poems appear in *Magic Animals* (1974), together with a cycle of new poems, "Part Two: Magic Animals, 1972–1974." *Earth-Light* (1982) contains selected poems from 1963 to 1982. In addition, she has published two novels, *Julian the Magician* (1963) and *King of Egypt, King of Dreams* (1971), a collection of short stories, *Noman* (1972), and two children's books, *The Chocolate Moose* (1979) and *The Honey Drum* (1983). *Mermaids and Ikons: A Greek Summer* (1978) is a whimsical travel book, which MacEwen says she wrote more for fun than with any serious literary intent.[3] She has written several radio plays and documentary programs. One verse play, "Terror and Erebus," was published in *The Tamarack Review* (1974). More recently, she published an adaptation of Euripides' *The Trojan Women* (1979 and 1981), which was performed at the Saint Lawrence Centre in Toronto in 1978. She has received several Canada Council awards, including senior arts grants. In 1965 she was the winner of the CBC New Canadian Writing Contest. In 1969 she was the recipient of the Governor General's Award for poetry for *The Shadow-Maker*; and in 1973, recipient of the A. J. M. Smith Award.

Tradition and Milieu

Perhaps the most common critical response to Gwendolyn MacEwen, especially in the early part of her career, was the belief that both in the distinctiveness of her vision and in her use of language she stood outside, or on the periphery, of the mainstream of Canadian literature. An early statement by MacEwen, "I want to construct a myth,"[4] is much quoted and probably much misunderstood when attempting to define her place in the Canadian literary tradition. Emerging as she did from the 1960s together with such nationalistic writers as Margaret Atwood, Dennis Lee, and Alden Nowlan, the MacEwen myth was, uncomfortably, not in the least recognizable as Canadian in any obvious political or cultural sense. MacEwen does not write about new Canadian pioneers or old national ghosts; she does not urge "citizenship" in Lee's sense of the word in *Civil Elegies*; and her settings are just as frequently the face of the moon as Toronto's Yonge Street. The closest she comes to a thematic statement of Canadian identity, which is the narrow definition of "myth," lies in her voice as explorer in several poems in *The Shadow-Maker*, notably "The Discovery," "The Portage," and "Night on Gull Lake," although, even here, MacEwen warns that the most obvious interpretations of the poems are probably the most inadequate ones:

(burn your maps, that is not what I mean),
I mean the moment when it seems most plain
is the moment when you must begin again.[5]

MacEwen's myth was also interpreted as a literary device by the anthologist Gary Geddes: "MacEwen's poetry might well be discussed in terms of the peculiar ground it inhabits between the 'realists' and the 'myth-makers' in Canadian poetry. From the beginning she has repudiated the actual world for one that is ancient and mythic...."[6] The first statement by Geddes is helpful in that it leads to a consideration of MacEwen's position in the Canadian tradition as one that links the mythopoeic poets, such as James Reaney and Jay Macpherson, and the more experimental poets of the 1960s, such as George Bowering and Michael Ondaatje. However, the second statement by Geddes, that MacEwen "has repudiated the actual world for one that is ancient and mythic," reveals the most persistent misunderstanding of her use of myth and does much to explain why MacEwen has been considered to inhabit "peculiar ground."

The language of MacEwen's myth, an exotic mixture of the

traditionally poetic and the modern colloquial, serves to emphasize her distinctiveness. Of her first major publication in poetry, *The Rising Fire* (1963), Bowering states flatly: "It stands outside the mainstream of current Canadian poetry, which seems generally to belong to the post-Williams age. That is, Miss MacEwen's language is opposite to the language of (our purest example) Raymond Souster."[7] The language of the myth was seen to be the language of dream, esoteric and metaphoric, egocentric and often impenetrable.

The publication of *A Breakfast for Barbarians* (1966) marks a significant point of development in MacEwen's career and the beginnings of a wider acceptance within, rather than apart from, the Canadian literary tradition. The use of concrete imagery in *A Breakfast for Barbarians* and the development of a poetic language which insists upon paradox, inverse logic, the juxtaposition of the profound and the profane, and a mixed diction of symbolic and colloquial speech, make clear the fallacy of Geddes' interpretation of MacEwen's myth. It is not a literary device; that is, it is not the formalistic system of a modernist, but the totally involved searching of a post-modernist amid a cataclysmic environment. Of her early statement, "I want to create a myth," MacEwen says: "I used to use that phrase as a kind of quotable quote, but I'm not sure if it is quite accurate. It is not so much a matter of invention as of perception — in a way it's more a matter of saying what I see."[8] In this qualification it is important to realize that MacEwen is not repudiating the actual world; rather, she is stressing her personal involvement in a complex world in which the myth is inherent, renewed, and reinterpreted in the process of day-to-day living.

MacEwen, then, is a post-modernist, writing from within the Canadian literary tradition. Although she has never been formally aligned with any particular group of poets, she is in harmony with other Canadian poets and poetic directions. Frank Davey writes: "The post-modern particularist finds mythology innate within his environment. In the work of Gwendolyn MacEwen, Bill Bissett, Victor Coleman, Frank Davey, Robert Kroetsch, Adele Wiseman, the recent work of Eli Mandel, mythology blooms out of the mundane but effervescent realities of the everyday life."[9] Like other post-modernists, MacEwen cannot divorce herself from a fragmented age — her myth demands commitment and participation, a search for new and dynamic poetic forms, and language that will somehow embrace the outrageous incongruities of twentieth-century dragons and peanut-butter sandwiches.

MacEwen can also be seen as part of a recent movement in Canadian poetry towards the optimism of individual affirmation which comes of absorption rather than negation of what is real. For example, in the essay "Exoticism in Modern Canadian Poetry," Leon Slonim groups together MacEwen, Margaret Avison, Leonard Cohen, Earle Birney, and Michael Ondaatje in terms of their occasional, sometimes total departure from the claustrophobic bleakness in Canadian literature.[10] Further, the sense of luxury and sensuality in MacEwen's language and in her inner landscapes is not far removed from the imaginative exoticism of Robert Kroetsch's bone-strewn *Badlands* or Michael Ondaatje's invented landscapes in *The Collected Works of Billy the Kid*. In an essay called "Canadian Monsters," Margaret Atwood discusses an increasing tendency in Canadian literature to explore the supernatural, the unspeakable that lurks beneath an apparently barren and snow-covered surface.[11] MacEwen, in both her poetry and prose, can be compared to novelists such as Howard O'Hagan in *Tay John*, Sheila Watson in *The Double Hook*, and Robertson Davies in the Deptford trilogy: all suggest that the dull surface of Canada is an illusion, that there are more subtle and startling landscapes to explore underneath and inside.

In terms of the tone of her poetry, MacEwen's chants of optimistic possibility even in the midst of terror form a significant part of D.G. Jones's discussion of "the courage to be" in *Butterfly on Rock*.[12] While Jones speaks generally of this courage in relation to John Newlove, Alden Nowlan, Leonard Cohen, Raymond Souster, and Al Purdy, to name only a few, his clearest definition of the term comes from MacEwen's introduction to *A Breakfast for Barbarians*, where she speaks specifically of the need to digest and absorb the outer world before it can be given human articulation:

It is the intake, the refusal to starve.
And we must not forget the grace.[13]

MacEwen's vision has never been limited by political or cultural boundaries. Although she considers Atwood to have been particularly influential in helping her to recognize her shift to concrete imagery, she demonstrates no obvious influence from particular individuals. MacEwen's sources are, on the one hand, esoteric and psychological — Jacob Boehme, the early Christian Gnostic texts, the kabbalah, Jung, and, most notably, alchemy — and, on the other hand, the unholy but very real mixtures of grim "Kanadian" breakfasts. More recently, MacEwen has been attracted by the novels of the South American writer Gabriel García Márquez, and, in fact, in her writing she shares with him an element of the fantastic that functions to lead the reader closer to a contemplation of reality rather than away from reality.

Has MacEwen herself influenced movements and/or other individuals? There are interesting, though only speculative, answers to this question. The muse figure central to MacEwen's poetry, in his form as the symbol of alternately grotesque and holy appetite, introduces a theme of barbaric consumerism further articulated in Margaret Atwood's *The Edible Woman* and Milton Acorn's *I've Tasted My Blood*. For women's studies, the prevalence of the male muse figure in MacEwen's poetry and prose may ultimately be a continuing source of fascination.

Critical Overview and Context

In general, the early criticism of MacEwen's poetry focuses on her fascination with mystery and myth, and on the distinctiveness of her language, which, though rich and exuberant, often fails to make her vision accessible. Clearly, the major flaw in MacEwen's poetry and prose which emerges from a survey of available criticism is that her vision is, at times, an idiosyncratic one. When language, emotion, and experience combine, her poems are startling — convincing almost in the manner of a personal revelation. When she slips into excessive theorizing or overenthusiastic diction, her poems are either too obvious or too hazy, like whispered secrets one cannot quite hear. Thus George Bowering writes in his review of *The Rising Fire*:

> One is aware of something like poetic diction, not the rhythmic arrangement of a prose line. In a poem like "All the Fine Young Horses," for instance, her "issues" if she claims any, are not of matter and the senses, but of a young, feminine, *personal* imagination. (p. 70)

The danger of the "personal" vision is, of course, incomprehension — a point which Bowering alludes to when he continues, "Miss MacEwen's usual unwillingness to be direct sets a distance at first. She is not an immediate poet in this time of immediacy" (p. 71). Similarly, Frank Davey in "Gwendolyn MacEwen: The Secret of Alchemy" points to poems "which...read like mysteriously excerpted dialogue from a hidden play" and rejoices in the concreteness of *A Breakfast for Barbarians*: "Gone is the inflated poetic language of the first two books [*Julian the Magician* and *The Rising Fire*] which presented MacEwen as a variation on the ecstatic dryad."[14]

Although MacEwen's failure to communicate the unspeakable, by telling rather than evoking, is largely confined to her early publications, some critics see her vision and her language as persistently extravagant and shadowy. For example, Milton Wilson speaks of a "wide-ranging, half-disciplined imagination";[15] Eli Mandel, of "atrocious puns, execrable metaphors, impossible analogies," and "a language which 'explodes, for instance.'"[16] The majority of criticism which deals with *A Breakfast for Barbarians* and subsequent works is positive, though qualified by comments which continue to point to excess in language and exclusiveness of concern.

The Shadow-Maker (1969) received mixed reactions. Frank Davey, for instance, praises individual poems, most notably "Dream Two: The Beasts," but expresses disappointment in the shift in tone between the "vigorous actuality" of *A Breakfast for Barbarians* and the more introspective and sometimes deliberately fantastic mood of the later collection (p. 15). Gail Fox, in a detailed review of *The Shadow-Maker*, praises the "gentle recklessness" of MacEwen's poetry but also regrets a "less daring, more subdued and almost conventional and commonplace" note in the imagery.[17] Fox points to figures of speech which are "embarrassing" and "futile" and ends her review on a note which is half-disappointed, half-hopeful:

> Poems I object to in *The Shadow-Maker* are ones such as "Dream Three: The Child" which ends with this line: "and I looked and I saw it was me." This genre of ending is like that of the novel whose author gets tired of the main protagonist, and has him killed off somehow on the last page. Very easy, and what a let-down!..."The beast is

taming," she writes in another disappointing poem, "The Taming of the Dragon." Perhaps the poet is also taming. But I would prefer to think this about her new poetry: "It is not lost, it is moving forward always." (p. 59)

From a comparison of Davey's and Fox's reactions to *The Shadow-Maker*, it is possible to note a major paradox which emerges in the criticism of MacEwen's poetry. On the one hand, there is uneasiness over her excessiveness in language and her failure to translate her vision into actuality through dramatic situation; on the other hand, there is a sense of loss expressed when her language and vision are tamed. It would seem that MacEwen's exuberance is, of itself, attractive, and perhaps this explains why negative criticisms of her writing begin to sound like praise or, at the very least, are balanced by a sense of admiration. Thus Bowering writes, "Gwendolyn MacEwen gives eloquent testimony to the fact that artificial imagery can still be expressed with beautifully chosen sound patterns, and this is what makes her poetry worthwhile."[18] Mandel labels her vibrant phrasing as "the very stuff of creation";[19] and Wilson speaks of her early poems as being not so much finished as a "fluent scatter of evocative phrases," poems which fail "originally."[20] Fox refers to MacEwen as a rare poet whose rhythm and sonorous patterns of speech surround one "with the feeling that a spell has been cast and that one is in the middle of this spell" (p. 57). The paradoxical view that MacEwen's flaws in expression contribute in some way to the fascination of her poetry is given its most explicit claim in this review of *The Armies of the Moon* by Joseph Sherman:

> I am not at all sure why it is that I like and admire her poetry. Perhaps because she is so magnificently obscure, and that has always invited something like admiration. She casts such a thick and strangely woven cloth over her work that it is, at the best of times, translucent. But so skillful is she in her poetic craft that the reader is attracted again and again to her work, partly because so little can be fathomed at first reading, and partly because what is, at one moment, clear, shifts in the next moment to a further extension of meaning, or even to new meaning.[21]

Insight into the more particular features of MacEwen's myth is afforded by Margaret Atwood, Frank Davey, and Ellen D. Warwick, each of whom has attempted to deal with the poet's language, imagery, and thematic concern in some detail. For Atwood, the dominant figure in MacEwen's poetry is the male muse, "author and inspirer of language and therefore of the ordered verbal cosmos, the poet's universe."[22] Atwood's interpretation of a number of poems from *The Rising Fire* and *A Breakfast for Barbarians* identifies the muse figure as the unnamed "you" of the poems whose amorphous presence makes it possible for MacEwen to translate "her myth into life, and into the poetry which is a part of it."[23] She stresses the dynamism of the muse, his infinite potential of form, and his ability to subsume all opposites.

In his article "Gwendolyn MacEwen: The Secret of Alchemy," Davey also stresses the blending of opposites and the necessity of a binary vision. MacEwen's task is to reveal that vision in her poetry, a task that is realized only when the lessons of one of her chief sources, alchemy, are self-absorbed: that is, when she seeks "the flesh of situation to give the ideas of her poetry living artistic form" (p. 26). MacEwen, in her own art, seeks to achieve the alchemical miracle of transubstantiation in which the mythic is made flesh. It is this achievement which Davey uses to distinguish between the "ornamental" and "kinetic" application of myth (p. 12). Ornamental myth involves a superimposed structure, an inflexible pattern into which characters and situations are slotted, while kinetic myth involves an opposite flow of movement in which the mythical emanates from the real — mythical patterns are relived and renewed, often unconsciously and irresistibly. Most significantly, kinetic myth must be involved with process, with the energy and creativity of disintegration and renewal.

It is this notion of process which Warwick emphasizes in "To Seek a Single Symmetry." She cites a very early poem, "Tiamut," from *The Rising Fire*, as evidence of the thematic attempt to create a mythical framework in which "all things strain toward reunion."[24] In "Tiamut," there is more straining than reunion, because only when form and content fuse is MacEwen able to grasp momentarily the wholeness she seeks. Nevertheless, the energy of the poetry, indeed its very motivation, stems from the striving for, rather than the attainment of, perfection in an imperfect world. As Warwick points out:

> In "The Aristocracies," the moment of perfection stunned the poet into silence, the need to speak vanished when integration occurred.... Once everything is caught, taken in, synthesized, the need for poetry will be gone. Thus, both poetry and life exist not as completion, but as process. (p. 34)

The myth itself, the desire "to make concrete and particular a cosmic view" (p. 4), is process — the process of perceiving and articulating "the broken edges of the air, / the flicker of forms before they occur" (*SM*, p. 6).

Ultimately, the critical view of MacEwen's poetry as process leads to one final and perhaps obvious conclusion. Her collections of poetry, particularly *A Breakfast for Barbarians*, *The Shadow-Maker*, and *The Armies of the Moon*, should be read as organic wholes and not as haphazard groupings of poems. In a perceptive and detailed review of *The Armies of the Moon*, Stan Dragland points out that the genius of the book lies in the very deliberate arrangement of the poems, the majority of which are divided into three sections, "The Sea of Crises," "The Lake of Death," and "The Lake of Dreams."[25] Each of these sections explores a particular theme or state of mind; and each represents one step in the journey towards self-knowledge. They are followed by the nine-poem verse play "The Nine Arcana of the Kings," which Dragland sees to be both ornamental and functional. Finally, the collection is framed by the beginning title poem and by the concluding poem, "Apollo Twelve." Dragland helps to identify the "finite beginning and the infinite becoming 'end'" (p. 57), which is a trademark of MacEwen's writing. Viewed as a whole, MacEwen's poetry, as my own review of *The Fire-Eaters* suggests, mirrors the destruction-creation processes of alchemy:

> The embedded patterns of renewal so striking in her [MacEwen's] poetry seem to leave the reader expectant but never satisfied. This sense of anticipation comes closest to definition in "Animal Syllables" — a poem which, like MacEwen herself, "leaves no tracks":

Dark, I built a beachfire and thought about the flames and the earth. In the darkness I constructed a fire; in the midst of the fire I began to gather another darkness.[26]

MacEwen's Works

Although the available criticism of MacEwen's poetry speaks generally of the richness of her language — her ability to cast spells with luxurious imagery and sound patterns, or alternately her inability to communicate in the strange alphabet of the language of private reverie — a close study of the corpus of her work reveals that her craftsmanship is born both of her major sources and of her desire to reveal the mythic in the mundane. The poetry of MacEwen affirms her belief in the binary structure of existence and in the necessity to combine inherent opposites into a harmonious unity. *The Rising Fire*, *A Breakfast for Barbarians*, *The Shadow-Maker*, *The Armies of the Moon*, *Magic Animals*, and *The Fire-Eaters* represent the process towards this synthesis rather than its statement. Throughout, MacEwen is a human alchemist, accepting both good and evil, light and dark, within herself. As in "House of Mercury" from *The Armies of the Moon*, she wants to be water, to recreate internally the *aqua permanens* of alchemy, the magical fount from which totality is born.

The invocation of opposites is reflected in her recurring patterns of sun-moon, light-dark, and waking-dream imagery. Her colours are the gold, blue, and silver of alchemy, the midnight black and lunar sheen of evil, and the blazing red of fire, suggestive of the mythological phoenix in *The Rising Fire* and, most often, of Jacob Boehme's dual-natured god. Her vocabulary, as it shifts from the scientific jargon of the earlier books to the more domestic and personal detail of the later, is frequently mixed and juxtaposed with words reminiscent of a more mythical time: words such as *arcane, unspeakable, elusive, magic, holy, demonic, dreamlike,* and *unknown*. Her language reflects also a recognition of the fullness of paradox, which manifests itself in the simple use of mixed diction, or blossoms outward to include entire poems which revolve around the destruction-creation, love-hate, stasis-process paradoxes of alchemy, Gnosticism, and Christianity.

The alchemical process of breaking and repairing is the keystone of MacEwen's poetry. In *A Breakfast for Barbarians*, she writes, "in this house poems are broken, / .... that image of me in you / that image of you in me / breaks, repairs itself" (*BB*, p.3). The recurrence of themes and images throughout the poetry suggests a constant reworking directed towards a moment of totality that can be conveyed in and through art. Thus, many of her poems are arranged organically in pairs or clusters: ideas grow out of earlier ideas, images build on earlier images. But always into this recurring vision, MacEwen infuses the energy of a fresh perspective, a new dramatic situation.

The informing male muse, chief symbol, creator and destroyer of language, embraces a multiplicity of forms: he may appear as pure imagination in the realm of dream and fantasy or as a creature half-divine, half-human, incarnate as king, magician, athlete, dancer, singer, or lover. Furthermore, since the muse, master of disguise and revelation, subsumes all opposites, he is reminiscent of the winged god Mercurius, who presides over the process of alchemy, a process which strives for the *coniunctio oppositorum*, the marriage of parts. The Jungian influence in MacEwen's poetry suggests yet another source for the muse — that of an animus figure who, through his various postures, may reveal something of the nature of the total self, a harmonious potential innate in the individual. Clearly, the most significant feature of the amorphous muse is his fluidity. At his most boisterous and whimsical, he is the barbarian; at his most evocative and elusive, he is the mirror to the self; at his most sinister, he lurks in "the silver milk of night,"[27] on the dark side of the moon.

The muse as barbarian, introduced in *A Breakfast for Barbarians*, is a ubiquitous symbol: the civilized barbarian, blind consumer in an age of uncontrolled consumerism; and, more significantly, the instinctive barbarian, sensitive to the rhythms of a mythical reality, whose syllables are thunder. In both roles, the muse as barbarian is aligned with the sense of appetite which informs the entire collection:

> The particular horrors of the present civilization have been painted starkly enough. The key theme of things is the alienation, the exile from our own inventions, and hence

from ourselves. Let's say No—rather enclose, absorb, and
have done. The intake....

It is the intake, the refusal to starve.
And we must not forget the grace.
(Introd., *BB*, n. pag.)

To starve is to deny the existence of a binary structure, to prevent the digestion of evil, which then erupts in alienation, in man's perverse appetite for violence and destruction. To say grace is to heed Jacob Boehme's axiom that "the opposition of all essences" is basic.[28] Only by absorbing his myths can man hope to initiate the process of healing within himself and within a shattered universe.

In the title poem of the collection, MacEwen's references to "sweet barbarians," "unspeakable appetites," a "golden breakfast," and consumed mysteries are all suggestive of the original communion in which the body of Christ entered the body of man through the symbolic act of eating. But here the essential holiness of consumption is parodied by a celebration of unholy gluttony. The religious symbolism inherent in MacEwen's source material is only hinted at: "an eye at the navel," suggesting meditation and self-exploration, "turns the appetite / round / with visions of some fabulous sandwich" (*BB*, p. 1). Much of the poetry's humour stems from the use of mixed diction in which the sacredness of the past is juxtaposed with the junk of the present: "boiled chimera," "apocalyptic tea," "arcane salad," "spiced bibles," and "tossed dictionaries."

Just as the barbarian is a double-edged symbol, the word "appetite" implies two contradictory interpretations. At its most mundane, appetite means simply the hunger for grim "Kanadian" breakfasts, for the material objects and superficial indulgences of modern man. On a mythic level, MacEwen speaks of an "unspeakable appetite," a "golden breakfast," a "second unreal hunger." The golden hunger is Boehme's "lubet": the energy of the free will, "soaring to black or white."[29] Black and white represent dark and light, the two supreme opposites of Boehme's concept of existence:

> From the primal fire or fount of generation in its fierceness are born the pair of opposites through which the Divine

energy is manifested: the "dark-world" of conflict, evil, and wrath which is Eternal Nature in itself, and the "light-world" of wisdom and love, which is Eternal Spirit in itself....

. . . .

The business alike of universal and of human life, the essence of its "salvation," is the bringing of the Light [the eternal origin of all good powers, colours, and virtues] out of its fiery origin — spiritual beauty out of the raw stuff of energetic nature.[30]

The golden hunger is the impulse to seek salvation through the union of opposites. It is golden in the spirit of the alchemists' statement: "our gold is not the vulgar gold." The mythic interpretation of appetite is the desire to pull "spiritual beauty out of the raw stuff of energetic nature," myth from the raw stuff of reality. Thus, the majority of MacEwen's appetite poems revolve around these polarities, using concrete imagery to evoke the presence of a secondary level of reality. The mythic element arises impulsively, measured by the primitive beat of the holy barbarian running through the earth; measured by chantlike beats created by repetition and end rhyme, and by the creation of a new Babel in which impossibly incongruous words and dictions collide together in vibrant images and atrocious puns: "Salome the Immortal has a lab in Argentina" (*BB*, p. 8), and "...obviously / we can stomach anything now, anything" (*BB*, p. 6).

The muse as barbarian appears also in two variant forms: the child and the magic animal, both living close to original appetite, both complete in a capacity for joy. The child is "Generation Cometh" in *The Rising Fire*, not an ornament of innocence but a dynamic life possessed of double vision:

> he grows beneath your heels
> and the city for him is easy he
> knows it from below
> old men old women you
> cannot stop him
> growing.[31]

Lack of punctuation and the careful choice of line endings give this poem a breathless quality, deliberately mirroring the energy of the child. Furthermore, that the child embraces the destructive-creative processes of alchemy, the perpetual movement towards synthesis, is made explicit in "Dream Three: The Child" from *The Shadow-Maker*. The poem is too dogmatic to be successful, but its repetition of the word "turning" introduces a key word in MacEwen's poetic process. The child "turning" is akin to images that break and repair themselves, to the process of intake and absorption central to the appetite poems.

Part II of *Magic Animals* celebrates the barbarian as beast, and the "holy congregation" of animals is both angelic and demonic, pitting the brutal simplicity of endurance against the invented complexities of the human world. The animals are alternately the passive victims of man's bestiality and the silent and superior witnesses to man's folly. At times the barbarian as beast passes comic judgement:

> But the mandrill with his mardi-gras mask
> folds his arms and examines a world
> more surreal than his rose-red ass[32]

More often the judgement is ominous, eloquent in its wordless silence:

> Watch me
> I am moving through the cages of the animals
> I am moving through the peereek of their cells
> Watch me because
> I am watching them watching you
> They are holding your immortal souls in trust
> They have watched you since Eden
> They are waiting for their time
>
> (*MA*, p. 123)

The first fourteen poems of "Part Two: Magic Animals, 1972–1974" are numbered rather than titled, and they are more effective when read as variations on a theme, rather than as individual poems. Throughout, MacEwen relies on the association of incongruous elements to create dramatic images, the most successful of which appears in the ninth poem: "The gorilla picks up his rubber tire / and holds it like an old black halo on his head" (*MA*, p. 131). Ultimately, in "The Demon of Thursday," MacEwen is compelled to reject the surrealism of man's surface world by praying to "the angelic and demonic animals / the magic animals more real than real" (*MA*, p. 150) in the measured tones and chanting rhythms that echo the naked running feet of the holy barbarian.

The chief function of the muse figure is revealed in his role as inspirator of language. Thus, the appetite poem, at its most abstract in "The Golden Hunger," reveals an appetite peculiar to the poet: the desire to pull from the fluidity of process a form which will reveal the essence of totality:

> How to address you, who have a hundred times renamed me?...behind your fluid masks there is always something that remains the same. Not a feature, but a *cast* to which the face always returns. (*AM*, p. 51)

For MacEwen, who so clearly defines the binary structure of the cosmos, a primary means of naming the "something that remains" behind the mask of forms is through absorbing knowledge and mystery: "...there is more room inside than outside" (Introd., *BB*, n. pag.), she says. Knowledge is discoverable through inverse means. Accordingly, in "The Left Hand and Hiroshima," she states, "only because my poems are lies do they earn the right to be true" (*BB*, p. 26). In "Poems in Braille," she speaks of the value of the inner eye: "I read carefully / lest I go blind in both eyes, reading with that other eye the final hieroglyph" (*BB*, pp. 4–5). The middle stanza of "The Thing Is Violent" states explicitly the importance of knowledge gained through inverse means: "I do not fear that I will go mad / but that I may not, and the shadows of my sanity / blacken out your burning..." (*BB*, p. 42). Finally, in "The Garden of Square Roots: An Autobiography," MacEwen concentrates on an interior landscape, symbolically placing herself at its centre:

> for i was the I interior
> the thing with a gold belt and delicate ears

with no knees or elbows
was working from the inside out.

and all my gardens grew backwards
and all the roots were finally square
and Ah! the flowers grew there like algebra
                                                        (*BB*, p. 2)

The imagery in this poem combines the Gnostic theory of internal emphasis with an internalized process of reverse alchemy. The persona is fluid "with no knees or elbows"; she wears a belt of gold and her gardens grow "backwards."

The elusiveness of the muse also teaches the poet to be aware of the difficulty of describing the unfamiliar landscapes of mythic reality, and/or of communicating myth. Poetry, necessarily limited by form and language, begins to fail her. Thus, in "The Face," MacEwen describes her art in terms of "backward physiognomy":

I must stop dealing with clay, with faces
I must stop dealing with poems, with stanzas
or all your features will become typography.

How could I bend to inherit you
and find your mouth a cabinet of teeth and verbs?
                                                        (*BB*, p. 9)

The danger of losing the essence of poetry — that thing which exists beyond the poem — exists in being overconscious of its structural and technical values. Accordingly, in many poems in *A Breakfast for Barbarians*, MacEwen denies the tactile evidence of her poetry. In "You Cannot Do This," she states, "...this is not art, / this is a kind of science, a kind of hobby, / a kind of personal vice like coin collecting" (*BB*, p. 10). She confesses, in "The Metallic Anatomy," that "this is not poetry, but clean greed" (*BB*, p. 14); and later, in "The Aristocracies," she warns:

Let it be understood, this is not art,
this is not poetry; the poetry is
the breathing air embracing you,

>   the poetry is not here, it is elsewhere
>   in temples, in territories of pure blue.
>
>   (*BB*, p. 53)

In a further example, "Poem," MacEwen implies that in order to convey the elusiveness of poetry, the poet must strive towards an impression of ultimate nakedness. The process of writing, related to the destruction-creation paradox in alchemy, involves, not the accumulation, but rather the subtraction, of images for "the nude truth beneath them." The act of creation becomes "the slow striptease of our concepts" (*BB*, p. 30).

Mirroring the fluidity of the muse, MacEwen views poetry as a process and language as a living form. In "The House" (*BB*, p. 3), as in alchemy, her poems are broken. In "Poems in Braille," she introduces a word-thing metaphor with bodies as alphabets: "with legs and arms I make alphabets / like those in children's books / where people bend into letters and signs" (*BB*, p. 4). When poetry is no longer viewed as a finite entity, it must be approached in an original manner. Twice MacEwen suggests that a poem should not be read, but felt instead. This is the main theme of "Poems in Braille":

>   I will not say the cast is less than the print
>   I will not say the curve is longer than the line,
>   I should read all things like braille in this season
>   with my fingers I should read them
>
>   (*BB*, p. 5)

Similarly, in "The Cyclist in Aphelion," she desires to be reached, but reaching requires feeling, a physical contact with poetic forms that flicker like flames:

>   to reach me is to burn first
>   you cannot come if you fear fire
>   I want you to teach me how to sleep
>   to brand me with the violent suns of your coming
>   to reach me in aphelion
>
>   to violate twilight, to inherit the earth
>   blind even, and backwards

>   to become a craftsman with an iron mask
>   who welds a terrible braille of poetry
>   which burns if you read it with your fingers
>
>   (BB, p. 7)

Clearly, MacEwen is most reachable when, through concrete detail and relaxed language, she transforms divine law into actual experiences with which the reader can identify. In terms of language, she invokes the inverse to reconcile opposites, to arrive at the wisdom of paradox — for only the paradox with its logical contradictions and assertions comes anywhere near to comprehending the fullness of life. A poem which achieves this goal, both in terms of form and content, is "The Left Hand and Hiroshima," in which MacEwen takes a universal situation and transforms it into a personal and viable dilemma. The final stanza of the poem illustrates her binary vision of existence; and introduces Jekyll and Hyde as a symbol of the reconciliation of man's good and evil potential. The responsibility which all men share in the horror of Hiroshima represents an ironic negative unity. Now, in the aftermath of the holocaust, MacEwen sees the opportunity of a new beginning — the possibility of a more positive harmony:

>   you have the jekyll hand and you have the hyde hand
>   my people, and you are abominable; but now I am proud
>   and
>   in uttering love I occur four-fingered and garbed
>   in a broken gardener's glove over the barbed
>   garden
>   of Hiroshima...
>   (BB, p. 26)

She does not intend that Hiroshima be forgotten; only that man, having indulged his darker side, should now progress towards a healthier balance between the impulses of destruction and creativity. Ultimately, she urges the duplication of the alchemical process, which employs destruction only as a means of gaining the supreme gold — a renewed unity of opposites, of dark and light, of Hiroshima and Eden.

In *The Shadow-Maker*, the muse retains his primary function as orderer of chaos, initiator of the process whereby surfaces are broken and repaired to reveal a mythic level of reality. However, the symbolism of the muse shifts — he is both ghost and god, demon and healer, and within the imaginary realm of "fire gardens" and "fifth earth," he is, for the first time, both external and internal. He is at once outside of, and a part of, the poet, an extension of self. As the symbolism shifts, so too does MacEwen's language. The shadow-maker, as muse figure, inhabits the most exotic of MacEwen's landscapes, an inner landscape of dream, fantasy, and distorted perception, a world accessible only through metaphor and simile. The poetry, here, can best be described as "the broken edges of the air, / the flicker of forms before they occur" (SM, p.6).

In *The Shadow-Maker*, the primary means of obtaining knowledge is through the vehicle of dream, diametric opposite of man's waking reality. The collection relies heavily upon Jungian psychology, and the connection which Jung makes between the logic of dreams and myth is, here, particularly significant. Both originate from an unconscious process which Jung explains as "non-directed thinking" — a process which is characterized by images, by fantasy rather than reality, and subjectivity rather than objectivity. Dreams and myth explore a world of marvels and limitless creativity where the realm of impossibilities takes the place of the actual. This fact alone helps to explain the haziness of *The Shadow-Maker*, which, after the vividness of *A Breakfast for Barbarians*, cannot be anything but intentional. Since it is the "deep wants," the indefinable and the unspeakable, which MacEwen wishes to explore, the definite and the concrete naturally fade in favour of the imagery and symbolism associated with "non-directed thinking."

The third section of *The Shadow-Maker*, "The Sleeper," occupies almost exclusively the realm of dream, sometimes hypnotic, sometimes revealing, sometimes hopelessly remote. Its elusiveness is best described by a line from "Dark Pines under Water": "There is something down there and you want it told" (SM, p.50). The secret which yearns to be told is reachable only through inverse means — through the suspension of time, place, and the familiar standards of objectivity. To some extent, the abandonment of a waking reality results in an effect of haziness, as if one were reading the poems with a blurred focus. It is this blurring to which critics object, but the fascination they also confess can perhaps now be better explained by an analysis of the shifting symbolism of the muse.

In "The Sleeper," MacEwen demonstrates a recognition of the function of the fantastic in literature. As she calls upon the demons of her darker self, the beasts which animate the unconscious, she calls upon the uncanny, a term defined by Freud as "that class of the frightening which leads back to what is known of old and long familiar."[33] In his discussion of the continuum of fantasy, Eric S. Rabkin states that the uncanny is always fantastic, that it only arises when it calls up something from one's own depths: Freud and Rabkin's primary example of this effect is E. T. A. Hoffmann's short story "The Sandman." In this narrative, the childhood fears of the protagonist, though rooted in a very real and threatening world, are projections of his own imagination, which, left uncontrolled and unbalanced, eventually result in his madness and suicide. Similarly, MacEwen insists that evil is internal, a projection of the shadow self, which, left unbalanced, results also in insanity and unbridled violence. The effect of "The Sleeper" poems is to turn the poet and the reader in upon themselves. As Rabkin states: "We need the uncanny in art, we need all fantastic effects in art, because...'We need mirrors'" (p. 222). Mirrors shape our perspectives and allow us to discern reality. The dream, as mirror of the conscious — and the muse, as mirror of the self — reflect a second, more accurate reality.

The unity of opposites, achieved through the inverse vehicle of the dream, is a primary concern of "The Sleeper" poems; however, closely linked to this concern is the relationship between perspective and an apprehension of reality. In two earlier poems from *The Shadow-Maker*, MacEwen undulates between two sets of perspectives which represent two differing realities. For example, in "The Thin Garden" she travels in dream to the exotic East, from one reality to another: "...I am a citizen first of all, of snow, / though the Nile floods / the deltas of my sense" (*SM*, p. 37). Here, she seeks a fuller reality than the one inherited through Western perspectives:

> No traveller comes here from innocence
> but for that myth the snow cannot provide,
> and all our histories lie outside.
> (*SM*, p. 37)

"Lie" is an ambiguous word, implying both falsehood and the exile of myth. However, freedom from perspectives shaped by cultural influences is ironically denied in "This Northern Mouth": "I sometimes journey outward / and around; yet in the east / they ask me of the dark, mysterious / west" (*SM*, p. 21). The fuller and more startling significance of these two poems is that MacEwen seems a stranger to both perspectives, both realities. Together, these poems raise the very fundamental question of exactly what is real, a question at the heart of the fantastic.

In this sense of mystery, the symbolism of the muse and MacEwen's dream poetry can be closely linked to the philosophical queries of Jorge Luis Borges and the fluid perspectives of Gabriel García Márquez. All three writers frequently employ the diametric reversal of the ground rules of a narrative, which Rabkin defines as the hallmark of fantasy; in *One Hundred Years of Solitude*, García Márquez, like MacEwen, draws heavily upon alchemy and the concept of appetite — hunger for a secondary reality. Further, MacEwen, Borges, and García Márquez see self-reflection as fundamental to human perception, and all create in their writing mirrors which make self-reflection mandatory. A fuller explanation of the effect of the diametric reversal is provided by Borges as quoted by Rabkin:

> Why does it make us uneasy to know that the map is within the map and the thousand and one nights are within the book of *A Thousand and One Nights*? Why does it disquiet us to know that Don Quixote is a reader of the *Quixote*, and Hamlet is a spectator of *Hamlet*?...those inversions suggest that if the characters in a story can be readers or spectators, then we, their readers or spectators, can be fictitious. (pp. 220–21)

In the final pages of *One Hundred Years of Solitude*, the last surviving character is decoding and reading the mysterious parchments of the alchemist Melquíades, which turn out to be the novel *One Hundred Years of Solitude*. In *Through the Looking-Glass*, a book which MacEwen quotes in *A Breakfast for Barbarians*, Alice does not know if she dreams the red king or if he dreams her. In MacEwen's poem "The Swimmer," the poet demands of her muse, "...Is this my dream / or your reality?" (*SM*, p. 52). As Rabkin points out: "Self-reflection in raising questions about the ontology of the real world, serves to keep our perspectives 'in perspective'" (p. 221). The inversions and distorted perceptions of MacEwen's dream poetry help us to overcome too much reality in the same way that a recognition of the golden hunger in *A Breakfast for Barbarians* helps us to overcome our grim "Kanadian" breakfasts.

For the poet, the primary risk of the dream is not so much its exploration as its verbalization. Accordingly, MacEwen devotes one section of *The Shadow-Maker*, "The Unspeakable," to her search for the words and forms which can decode dream and make it accessible. For this reason, the epigraph by Anatole France is particularly significant. It is taken from a larger quotation from France which is used as supportive evidence in a discussion of language by Jung in *Symbols of Transformation*. Jung claims that language, in its origin and essence, is simply a system of signs or symbols that denote real occurrences or their echo in the human soul.[34] Similarly, France's theory is that thought and language are part of an infinite cycle which begins with primitive or basic feelings and instincts, progresses to a sophisticated mode of expression of such instincts, and ultimately returns to its sensual origin. Such is MacEwen's approach to language: she attempts to strip away obscuring layers of connotation and habit which surround the usage of words in order to reveal basic sensations — in order to arrive at a more immediate mode of expression that may come closer to explaining the inexplicable.

Accordingly, in the first poem of "The Unspeakable," the poet describes her meeting with an old sailor, who teaches her a new respect for words. The dialogue of "The Compass" is marked by the well-placed use of jumbled vocabulary and by the recurring thought that "...everything's gotta go and come back home / like the tides" (*SM*, p. 18). Words, too, despite their intellectual pomposity, are subject to the patterns of nature. MacEwen offers the sailor a book of poems, ironically, "a pointless gift." Reinforcement for the irony is provided immediately by the man's spontaneous reaction:

...taking it he smiled and said,
"*I've* been doing some writing too

to get ahead in life!"
And pulled out from a suitcase old
as the crazy seas he sailed
something he handled with great respect —
a battered notebook where he'd written
in big scared lines
the first few letters of the alphabet.

(*SM*, p. 20)

The most important phrase in this closing section of "The Compass" is "in big scared lines." The fundamentals of language, the alphabet, are given a fresh perspective. One becomes conscious of a renewed awareness of the mystery and potential power of the tools of communication. "The Compass" effectively dramatizes MacEwen's wish to approach language, not in the customary way as an established system of expression, but rather in a more individual and personal way as a key to sensual experience which may help to unlock the blocked passages of the unknown. Like the sailor, MacEwen must begin with basics: she must relearn the alphabet with an attitude of awe, rather than habit.

In *The Shadow-Maker*, MacEwen takes a courageous if not wholly successful step into the unknown: many of the poems fail to communicate with the immediacy of "The Compass," or with the urgency of "Dark Pines under Water." However, the collection ends, as many of MacEwen's do, with the possibility of a more positive beginning. In "The Shadow-Maker" and "The Return," the muse is not simply mirror and creator, he is lover, as well, the sensual experience behind and beyond language. In the title poem, MacEwen does not invoke the inverse; through the eagerness of tone, she seduces it:

I have come to possess your darkness, only this.

My legs surround your black, wrestle it
As the flames of day wrestle night
And everywhere you paint the necessary shadows
On my flesh and darken the fibres of my nerve;
Without these shadows I would be
In air one wave of ruinous light

And night with many mouths would close
Around my infinite and sterile curve.

Shadow-maker create me everywhere
Dark spaces (your face is my chosen abyss),
For I said I have come to possess your darkness,
Only this.

(*SM*, p. 80)

The first line of the second stanza, reminiscent of "Black and White" in *The Rising Fire*, signifies, not only the complementary opposites necessary for totality, but also the unknown sexual quality of her lover-muse. His shadow, his dark mystery, rescues her from sterility, from the "ruinous" light of an unbalanced extreme. The excellence of the poem lies in the repetition of the opening line, which, after the middle stanza, shifts slightly in meaning. What seems a meagre and ominous possession in the beginning becomes, by the ending, a creative gift.

"The Return," as the title indicates, is animated by cyclical motion. It touches upon many of the themes MacEwen explores in *The Shadow-Maker* — the inadequacy and sensuality of language, the process of infinite change, the mirror symbolism of the muse, and the demand for harmony. The tone of the first two stanzas is one of loss — the lover-muse seems only an elusive flicker in the distance:

I gave you many names and masks
And longed for you in a hundred forms
And I was warned the masks would fall
And the forms lose their fame
And I would be left with an empty name

(For that was the way the world went,
For that was the way it had to be,
To grow, and in growing lose you utterly)

(*SM*, p. 81)

Remember that the muse is the inspirator of language: MacEwen is writing a love poem to her own poetry. What stuns her is that when the aim of poetry is achieved, the muse is internalized, a part of the self, crashing through flesh. There is silence. The "forms," the "masks," are stripped away to reveal an appalling emptiness. In the last two stanzas, however, the cycle begins to move upwards:

> But grown, I inherit you, and you
> Renew your first and final form in me,
> And though some masks have fallen
> And many names have vanished back into my pen
> Your face bears the birth-marks I recognize in time,
> You stand before me now, unchanged
>
> (For this is the way it has to be;
> To perceive you is an act of faith
> Though it is you who have inherited me)
>
> (SM, p. 81)

The paradox of the final verse is particularly effective. MacEwen is both an active and passive lover, perceived and perceiving in and by her poetry, by an "act of faith," a confession of devotion. Having disregarded the masks and names, it is the "first and final" form she comes to cherish.

MacEwen's fourth book of poems, *The Armies of the Moon*, blends the vitality of *A Breakfast for Barbarians* with the elusiveness of *The Shadow-Maker*. As a result, the intrusion of dogma and theory so common in *The Rising Fire* all but disappears — the lesson of speaking the unspeakable through indirect means, through dramatic situations in which the unspeakable is imminent, reaches maturity in the lunar and domestic imagery of *The Armies of the Moon*. As the title suggests, MacEwen invokes here the lunar celestial bodies, the lunar side of man associated with the destructive half of the alchemical cycle. Yet she invokes also the creative half of the cycle through her insistence on the value of knowledge gained through inverse means, through the consumption of evil and its subsequent balance with positive human potential. Thus the moon, like the muse figure who embodies it, is a ubiquitous symbol: impaled by the political flag of American space travel, yet still defiant in its mystery, despite the permanent footprints of man.

In the title poem (*AM*, p. 1), MacEwen visualizes an impending clash between the "unseen silver armies" and the blind earthmen. Their battleground is "the gorgeous anonymous moon," the mystery of which is unspoiled by the outrageous golf balls of the earth's explorers and untouched by the frenzied gathering of "white rocks and sand." The lunar forces, "invisible and silver as swords turned sideways," gather in "the Sea of Crises" patiently waiting for "earthrise and the coming of man." But the earthmen are unable to see the silver edges of the moon's army (silver being the colour associated with the alchemical god Mercurius, the symbol of synthesis and totality) and, accordingly, are presumed blind. The earthmen are destroyed in "the Lake of Death" by an intangible band of soldiers, since only by succumbing to their swords can they finally enter the landscape of the moon. In the last stanza, the lunar army mourns its absurdly easy victory. Their home is "the Lake of Dreams," the landscape of possibility where ineffectual man cannot hope to follow. The title poem is powerful in itself, yet its initial position in the collection serves a vital function: it provides for the reader a map of the moon. In the progressive stanzas of the poem, MacEwen defines the progressive movement of each section to follow: "a gathering of forces" in "the Sea of Crises"; "showdown" in "the Lake of Death"; and, ultimately, "quicksilver tears" in "the Lake of Dreams."

In "The Sea of Crises," the first major section, MacEwen creates and sustains a sense of having lost something valid, a sense of precariousness, and a suspicion of lurking myths and marvels that have been suppressed by dreary routine. Many of the poems revolve around the process of "gathering," meaning both the frenzied activity of the title poem and the desire for enclosure, for the consumption of the unknown central to MacEwen's appetite poems, And, as in *A Breakfast for Barbarians*, material objects, rather than mystery, are finally consumed. Man yearns for myth but cannot digest its dangerous possibilities. Thus, in a key poem, "Phobos," MacEwen writes:

> Last week lightning clove the mighty tree
> outside my house, and the leaves turned in
> surrendering their white sides; I learned
> that lightning cleaves what it most loves
> and cuts in half what it means to caress
>
> (*AM*, p.24)

This same paradox of love-death, creation-destruction, is echoed in the appetite poems "Dining at the Savarin" and "Memoirs of a Mad Cook" and, in modified form, in "The Vacuum Cleaner Dream." Engaged in an orgy of domesticity, the persona sweeps up the world "with a sickening efficiency" and discovers in the bag of her "blind machine" "the sleeping body of my love" (*AM*, p. 18).

Finally, in "The Holy Burlesque" (*AM*, pp. 16–17), the muse figure dances into secret knowledge in a performance which epitomizes the essential brilliance and horror of embracing myth. With colloquial language, MacEwen establishes a comfortable but superficial atmosphere which is soon undercut by the subtle intrusion of deeper realities. At first, the seductive wriggling of the dancer, Laki, only serves to parody the predictable grindings of "...the large mammalian thing / who keeps falling over backwards / into her seventh orange veil." But the casual laughter of the poem's first section quickly becomes a kind of protective hysteria in the last ten lines. Laki's eyes promise to reveal unspeakable secrets, the "...Oh so lovely sins / of Sodom and Athens and East Toronto" which have long since been suppressed. The bathetic irony created by the anticlimactic ordering of the three cities, together with their unlikely conjunction, signals MacEwen's change of mood. Laki's dance threatens to strip away the gaudy nightclub madness and reveal instead a naked stage of possibility—the stripping and nakedness are crucial to MacEwen's poetic process:

> if we didn't laugh for heaven's sake
> if there was one minute of silence
> in the Greek nightclub down the street
> Laki's laugh would sound so still and pure
> we'd fall over backwards
> into our *retzinas* or our seventh orange beer
> and rise, and repossess the stage
> we occupied before two thousand years.
> Our lies in a blaze of orange veils would vanish
> and the very gods might reappear.
>
> (*AM*, p. 17)

Man's masks are shattered; he falls "backwards" only to "rise" and "repossess." In a reenactment of the destruction-creation paradox, the protective crassness of the "orange veils" and their accompanying lies is crushed by the unleashed purity of the gods.

In "The Lake of Death," the central section of the collection, MacEwen exposes and internalizes the horrific aspect of the moon symbol. Those horrors which previously lurked on the periphery of the conscious are now pushed forward under the glaring spotlight of responsibility — for only by confessing evil can the fullness of double vision be achieved. Accordingly, in the fourth stanza of "The Other Underground," reminiscent of an earlier poem from *A Breakfast for Barbarians*, MacEwen assumes responsibility for Hiroshima, seeing in that act a kind of reverse alchemy:

> ...I remember that the cockpit of the plane
> was silent in Hiroshima,
> as silent as my skull, O silent
> was my skull before eyes bled from heads,
> dripped out or melted inward,
> before the man sitting in the sun somewhere
> *dissolved* and left the black atomic shadow
> of his soul upon the stairs
>
> (*AM*, p.34)

Manifestations of brutality become the *prima materia* for an alchemical process which transforms sun into shadow, light into dark. Instead of gathering opposites, evil shatters them; man dissolves rather than fulfils the potential for completeness.

In the final section of "The Other Underground," MacEwen, exploring the dark side of the moon, exposes the very core of evil — it is a private, habitual "tyranny." While its ugliness is often recognized only in spectacular eruptions, its roots grow in the most trivial. Here, too, the moon is a mirror of the self just as the muse is a mirror in *The Shadow-Maker*: "...the Enemy is where he always was — / in the bleak lunar landscapes of our mirrors" (*AM*, p.35). By indulging rather than digesting his lunar aspects, man has eclipsed his own potential for binary vision, hacked to shreds the possibility of totality.

In "The Lake of Dreams," MacEwen's task is to begin anew the coupling of opposites, to reinstate the moon with a holier beauty. Not unexpectedly, she does so by appealing to the muse / Mercurius figure in "The Golden Hunger." The moon becomes, not a symbol of crippled potential, but a benign witness to the poet's effort for achievement, specifically in terms of craft. Early in the poem, MacEwen sees the moon "yellow and terrifically full" (*AM*, p. 51), which implies that its silver sheen has mellowed, that its bladelike curve, suggestive of a weapon in "The Lake of Death," has achieved the completeness of a circle. Thus, in "Jewellery," MacEwen becomes a willing captive within a "glittering prison," for her greatest desire is to submit to the gold of the moon and the gold of alchemy:

> ...I want
> to be the prisoner of gold,
> to hear my voice break through
> the chain which holds my song
> in check....
>
> (*AM*, p. 53)

The words "voice" and "song" emphasize the "gold" to be found in poetry, an emphasis which recurs in "The Hour of the Singer." Here, the persona is freed from "the years of false singing" and defined by "the blind mouth of the singer... in the naked pause between his words" (*AM*, p. 60). In the final stanza, the poetic vision is crystallized, the final secret illuminated:

> Now you comprehend your first and final lover
> in the dark receding planets of his eyes,
> and this is the hour when you know moreover
> that the god you have loved always
> will descend and lie with you in paradise.
>
> (*AM*, p. 60)

It is important to note, here, that the muse-lover descends towards MacEwen — she has acquired, if only briefly, a moment of equality.

Clearly, MacEwen's poetry is at its most golden, its most evocative and accessible, when she submits to her craft, to the sensuality and rhythm of language and form that displace dogmatic statement. Such is the case in "The Nine Arcana of the Kings" (*AM*, pp. 63–72), a remarkable cycle of poems in which structure and substance reflect through dramatic narrative

MacEwen's fascination with the destruction-creation paradoxes of alchemy, Gnosticism, and Christianity. The nine poems unfold the story of sister-brother lovers and their father, the king, beginning with an innocent love, tracing the complications which eventually lead to death and separation, and ending with rebirth and a reunion that is all the richer for its combination of "heaven" and "hell." The connections between the prince and alchemy are frequent, but never obtrusive: his body is alternatively "a long broken necklace," or "a living syllable / in... golden script." He is both "founting water" and "Ghost of the morning." Similarly, the king is "the very lord of gold" whose blood is the "birth" of the prince's soul. In death, the prince is assailed by "silvery guards"; he comes to his lover as a reincarnated muse figure, as Zeus in mythology came to Leda: "your tired wings were songs among the leaves / and on my thighs you left your shining, unreal seed" (*AM*, p. 69). The once simple love between brother and sister grows in dimension until the circle is complete, until the lovers in symbolic union wear, like MacEwen, the "cursed" double crown, emblem of the unity of opposites. Rich with the fullness of paradox and emotion, "The Nine Arcana" are called a gift by Dragland (p. 61); the realization of the secrets of alchemy by Davey (p. 23); and by Ralph Gustafson, vibrant examples of poetry in which "the expository is obliterated."[35]

The concluding poem in *The Armies of the Moon*, "Apollo Twelve," reveals that the journey through "the breathless valley of the moon" has not ended, but rather just begun. The beginning/ending is a MacEwen trademark — the structure of the collection as a whole again reflecting the secrets of her dominant sources. MacEwen, like the astronaut in the poem, is led irresistibly "through vacuous doorways to the gasping dark beyond" (*AM*, p. 75). The new darkness is then absorbed and reshaped to emerge in new forms, in the strangely accented anthem of the beasts in *Magic Animals*, for instance, or in the "edibile" and "living flame"[36] of fire in *The Fire-Eaters*.

Magic Animals and *The Fire-Eaters* did not receive much critical attention, perhaps because the poems tend to reaffirm MacEwen's vision rather than to extend it. Yet both are interesting in terms of experiments with form: she demonstrates an increasing use of internal and end rhyme, and an increasing use of single-word and line repetition. In *Magic Animals*, Part II, she numbers rather than titles the first fourteen poems, thereby emphasizing the need to read and weigh them collectively. In *The Fire-Eaters*, she experiments with prose passages, the best of which is the series called "Animal Syllables" (*FE*, pp. 41–46). This last piece is particularly significant for it contains explicit statements about her craft and, perhaps, an implicit, even impatient desire to find new forms, new voices in her poetry. It begins, characteristically, with a warning: "Let me say right off that this is no answer, for no question has as yet been posed" (*FE*, p. 41). Yet the question which emerges and disturbingly recurs in the poem is whether there is anything left to say:

> We fold in upon ourselves like the waves, we fold under, falling in and out of the world's vision. How many languages can we know? We approach the end of utterance.... The waves insist it has all been said before. Somehow they must convince me, somehow I must believe them. The body has its own speech to be heeded now. Move swiftly in these snows, and leave no track. (*FE*, p. 46)

Has the poet lost sight of "those orderly, censured gardens" (*FE*, p. 44), the exotic gardens of her own poetry? Have her words become liquid and trickled away? Or is she merely waiting, gathering new alphabets — "great cryptic arcs across the darkness" (*FE*, p. 46)?

Six years after the publication of *The Fire-Eaters*, MacEwen answers these questions in *The T.E. Lawrence Poems*, and she answers with a kind of rekindled energy, a renewed and graceful fluidity in language and form, and the clear-sighted confidence of a mature poet. Still wedded to a vital sense of myth and paradox, she interprets Lawrence, and his life so imbued with personal and political contradictions, as the hostage of his own legend. However, it is the voice of these poems, rather than their factual detail, which is so remarkably convincing. Asked by an interviewer for *Poetry Canada Review*, "How did you get inside Lawrence?", MacEwen answers, "I think he got inside me."[37] Her statement is immediately reminiscent of a line from her short story "House of the Whale," in which the narrator, Lucas George, describes an argillite carver who shapes the figures of myth into stone. George always imagined that there was "a little man, who lived inside the argillite and worked it from the inside out."[38] In a similar fashion, it seems as if Lawrence is indeed inside MacEwen, that she is not so much the inventor as the interpreter of these poems. Throughout the collection, she scatters phrases and "turned-about versions" (*PCR*, p.8) of Lawrence's own words from *Seven Pillars of Wisdom*, and her adopted persona is a very dangerous, a very innocent, and a very human Lawrence.

The collection begins with a Foreword recounting MacEwen's memory of photographs of Lawrence seen in Israel in 1962, "photographs of blurred riders on camels riding to the left into some uncharted desert just beyond the door."[39] What MacEwen attempts, in part, is to bring the blurred riders into focus, into a recognizably human shape, but to maintain also the spirit of the uncharted desert, the mystery and the searching that is inextricably a part of the human condition. Not surprisingly, Lawrence embraces many of the qualities of MacEwen's muse figure. He is, first of all, a dreamer, and he is a consummate alchemist. In the first poem, "Water," the persona insists "... water is everything. Or rather, / Water ventures into everything and becomes everything" (*TEL*, p.3). Water, symbolically the *aqua permanens* of alchemy, is also "self-quenching" (*TEL*, p.3), promising completeness.

Later, in "The Mirage," the persona confesses,

> I have come to uncover the famous secrets
>   of earth and water, air and fire.
> I have come to explore and contain them all.
>   I am an eye.
>
>   (*TEL*, p.37)

These lines echo a familiar theme in MacEwen's writing, but here energy is renewed by the poem's delicate irony, inherent in the title and explicit in the poem's previous stanza:

> There are no easy ways of seeing, riding
>   the waves of invisible seas
> In marvellous vessels which are always
>   arriving or departing.
>
>   (*TEL*, p.37)

It is as if Lawrence has tasted defeat before he is defeated; as if he knows everything and that everything is nothing; as if all things are invisible and all imagined things real. There is self-mockery here and also a gentle warning: "I am the living center of your sight; I draw for you / this thin and dangerous horizon" (*TEL*, p.37). Mirage is, in fact, an apt description of whatever knowledge the reader might claim of Lawrence's life. He is but a horizon in the desert, a landscape where there are no landmarks, a landscape stunned by light and studded by deep wells of darkness.

In terms of form, *The T.E. Lawrence Poems* heralds a new maturity in MacEwen's writing. In MacEwen's own words: "I'd say that twenty years plus [of publishing] have taught me how to write a longer, clearer line, and to look at the world with a longer, clearer gaze. Things slow down, in a very exciting way" (*PCR*, p.8). The longer lines, experimented with in the prose passages of *The Fire-Eaters*, are, in the Lawrence poems, visual reinforcements of content: the lines stretch and shift across the page much like the horizon and the sands of a desert, and they convey, seemingly effortlessly, the philosophical stance of Lawrence.

The collection is unified largely by its tone, by the clarity of Lawrence's voice, and by open-ended last lines which urge the reader forward to new poems, and also backward to rereadings. Often two poems are juxtaposed in such a way as to invite a multilevel reading or a deeper meaning through association. Perhaps the finest example of this effect is provided by the two poems "Ghazala's Foal" and "The Death of Dahoum," which appear side by side near the end of the collection's second section. The first poem begins with a matter-of-fact, even amusing, line: "Ghazala was the second finest camel in all Arabia, and / She did not know it" (*TEL*, p.50). The Lawrence persona speaks enviously of her: "She had absolutely no mission in life / and no sense of honor or of shame; she was / almost perfect" (*TEL*, p.50). The poem proceeds with an unemotional listing of the various and numerous deaths of camels, but then shifts in tone abruptly at the death of Ghazala's foal:

> Mostly I remember Ghazala's foal, getting up and walking
>   when it was three hours old, then falling down
>   again, in a little heap of slippery limbs.

One of the men skinned it, and Ghazala cried and sniffed
   the little hide.
            Then we marched again, and often
   she stopped short, and looked around wildly,
   remembering something that was terribly important,
   then lapsing into a blank, dazed stare.
                              Only
   when the poor, tiny piece of skin was placed
   before her on the ground would she
Murmur something, nudge it, ponder a while, and walk on.
                              (*TEL*, p.50)

The compassion evoked here by the visual imagery is powerful enough, yet it flows over to the next poem, which recounts the death of Lawrence's inspiration, the beloved Dahoum, to whom Lawrence wished to give the freedom of his race:

No one was there when the world began for you, Dahoum,
   and I was not there when it ended,
   when your lungs filled up with water
   and water filled the dark well of your mouth.
Once I could have drowned in your liquid eyes, forever.

I had this gift for you — the freedom of your race. But
   you come in dreams to tell me
   it was wasted; and in those dreams
   you wear your death well, gracefully.
                              (*TEL*, p.51)

MacEwen, like the biographers Phillip Knightley and Colin Simpson, interprets Dahoum as the mysterious S.A. in Lawrence's dedication poem from *Seven Pillars of Wisdom*. His death occurred before Lawrence ever reached Damascus, and it haunted him until his own death years later. Most significantly, it cast a tragic shadow over Lawrence's glorious deeds, already dissolving in a quicksilver of ambiguous motivations, promises, and lies. Thus a rereading of "Ghazala's Foal" now reveals a symbolic level of meaning: Lawrence, like the camel, dazed by loss and pitifully trudging behind the hide of a dream.

"Departures," the last poem in the collection, is much more a gentle slipping away than a final note: "The air / Is silk with locusts; / then the drawn sword breaks the silk / And the sky heaves open. / Night comes and the stars are out. Salaam" (*TEL*, p. 70). The spell is broken again momentarily, and those readers who know MacEwen only for her poetry may well have to be patient before another is cast. She confesses to the need for involvement in "a novel or some larger work,"[40] and she is currently writing a play. As MacEwen says, "I don't regard myself as a poet only, but as a writer."[41] And she is, undoubtedly, one of Canada's most gifted.

NOTES

[1] Interview with Gwendolyn MacEwen, 1 May 1979.

[2] *Rhymes and Reasons: Nine Canadian Poets Discuss Their Work*, ed. John Robert Colombo (Toronto: Holt, Rinehart and Winston, 1971), p. 65.

[3] Interview, 1 May 1979.

[4] Gary Geddes and Phyllis Bruce, eds., *15 Canadian Poets* (Toronto: Oxford Univ. Press, 1970), p. 280.

[5] "The Discovery," in *The Shadow-Maker* (Toronto: Macmillan, 1969), p. 30. All further references to this work (*SM*) appear in the text.

[6] Geddes and Bruce, eds., p. 280.

[7] George Bowering, "A Complex Music," rev. of *The Rising Fire*, *Canadian Literature*, No. 21 (Summer 1964), p. 70. All further references to this work appear in the text.

[8] Interview, 1 May 1979.

[9] *From There to Here: A Guide to English-Canadian Literature since 1960* (Erin, Ont: Porcépic, 1974), p. 22.

[10] *Essays on Canadian Writing*, No. 1 (Winter 1974), p. 21.

[11] In *The Canadian Imagination: Dimensions of a Literary Culture*, ed. David Staines (Cambridge: Harvard Univ. Press, 1977), p. 100.

[12] *Butterfly on Rock: A Study of Themes and Images in Canadian Literature* (Toronto: Univ. of Toronto Press, 1970), pp. 181–82.

[13] Introd., *A Breakfast for Barbarians* (Toronto: Ryerson, 1966), n. pag. All further references to this work (*BB*) appear in the text.

[14] Frank Davey, "Gwendolyn MacEwen: The Secret of Alchemy," *Open Letter*, 2nd ser., No. 4 (Spring 1973), pp. 17, 19. All further references to this work appear in the text.

[15] Milton Wilson, rev. of *Selah*, and *The Drunken Clock*, in "Letters in Canada 1961: Poetry," *University of Toronto Quarterly*, 31 (July 1962), 448.

[16] Eli Mandel, "Seedtime in a Dark May," rev. of *Poems*, by David Donnell, *Double Persephone*, by Margaret Atwood, and *The Drunken Clock*, by Gwendolyn MacEwen, *Alphabet*, 1, No. 4 (June 1962), 70.

[17] Gail Fox, rev. of *The Shadow-Maker*, *Quarry*, 19, No. 2 (Winter 1970), 57–58. All further references to this work appear in the text.

[18] George Bowering, "The Canadian Poetry Underground," rev. of *Than Any Star*, by Pádraig Ó Broin, *D-Day and After*, by Frank Davey, *The Drunken Clock*, by Gwendolyn MacEwen, and *Poems*, by David Donnell, *Canadian Literature*, No. 13 (Summer 1962), p. 66.

[19] Mandel, p. 70.

[20] Wilson, p. 448.

[21] *The Fiddlehead*, No. 94 (Summer 1972), p. 119.

[22] Margaret Atwood, "MacEwen's Muse," *Canadian Literature*, No. 45 (Summer 1970), p. 31.

[23] Atwood, p. 31.

[24] Ellen D. Warwick, "To Seek a Single Symmetry," *Canadian Literature*, No. 71 (Winter 1976), p. 21. All further references to this work appear in the text.

[25] Stan Dragland, rev. of *The Armies of the Moon*, *Quarry*, 21, No. 4 (Autumn 1972), 57. All further references to this work appear in the text.

[26] Jan Bartley, "Into the Fire," rev. of *The Fire-Eaters*, *Open Letter*, 3rd ser., No. 5 (Summer 1976), p. 87.

[27] "Two Aspects of the Moon," in *The Armies of the Moon* (Toronto: Macmillan, 1972), p. 29. All further references to this work (*AM*) appear in the text.

[28] Jacob Boehme, *Six Theosophic Points*, trans. John Rolleston Earle (Ann Arbor: Univ. of Michigan Press, 1958), p. 150.

[29] Gwendolyn MacEwen, *Julian the Magician* (Toronto: Macmillan, 1963), p. 35.

[30] Evelyn Underhill, Introd., *The Confessions of Jacob Boehme*, comp. and ed. W. Scott Palmer, 2nd ed. (London: Methuen, 1954), pp. xxvii, xxix.

[31] *The Rising Fire* (Toronto: Contact, 1963), p. 80.

[32] *Magic Animals: Selected Poems Old and New* (Toronto: Macmillan, 1974), p. 131. All further references to this work (*MA*) appear in the text.

[33] As quoted by Eric S. Rabkin in *The Fantastic in Literature* (Princeton: Princeton Univ. Press, 1976), p. 222. All further references to this work appear in the text.

[34] Carl G. Jung, *Symbols of Transformation: An Analysis of the Prelude to a Case of Schizophrenia*, trans. R. F. C. Hull, Bollingen Series, No. 20, Vol. v of *The Collected Works of C. G. Jung* (New York: Pantheon, 1956), p. 12.

[35] Ralph Gustafson, "Circumventing Dragons," rev. of *Intense Pleasure*, by David McFadden, *A Few Myths*, by Peter Stevens, *The Chains of Lilliput*, by Fred Cogswell, and *The Armies of the Moon*, by Gwendolyn MacEwen, *Canadian Literature*, No. 55 (Winter 1973), p. 108.

[36] "Second-degree Burns," in *The Fire-Eaters* (Ottawa: Oberon, 1976), p. 59. All further references to this work (*FE*) appear in the text.

[37] "Interview with Gwendolyn MacEwen," *Poetry Canada Review*, 4, No. 3 (Spring 1983), 8. All further references to this work (*PCR*) appear in the text.

[38] Gwendolyn MacEwen, *Noman* (Ottawa: Oberon, 1972), p. 7.

[39] *The T. E. Lawrence Poems* (Oakville, Ont.: Mosaic / Valley, 1982), n. pag. All further references to this work (*TEL*) appear in the text.

[40] Patricia Keeney Smith, "Interview with Gwendolyn MacEwen," *Cross-Canada Writers' Quarterly*, 5, No. 1 (1983), 15.

[41] Smith, p. 14.

SELECTED BIBLIOGRAPHY

Primary Sources

MacEwen, Gwendolyn. *The Drunken Clock*. n.p.: Aleph [privately published], 1961.
———. *Selah*. n.p.: Aleph [privately published], 1961.
———. *Julian the Magician*. Toronto: Macmillan, 1963.
———. *The Rising Fire*. Toronto: Contact, 1963.
———. *A Breakfast for Barbarians*. Toronto: Ryerson, 1966.
———. *The Shadow-Maker*. Toronto: Macmillan, 1969.
———. *King of Egypt, King of Dreams*. Toronto: Macmillan, 1971.
———. *The Armies of the Moon*. Toronto: Macmillan, 1972.
———. *Noman*. Ottawa: Oberon, 1972.
———. *Magic Animals: Selected Poems Old and New*. Toronto: Macmillan, 1974.
———. "Terror and Erebus: A Verse Play for Radio." *The Tamarack Review*, No. 63 (Oct. 1974), pp. 5–22.
———. *The Fire-Eaters*. Ottawa: Oberon, 1976.
———. *Mermaids and Ikons: A Greek Summer*. Toronto: House of Anansi, 1978.
———. *The Chocolate Moose*. Toronto: NC, 1979.
———. *The Trojan Women*. Toronto: Playwrights Co-op, 1979.
———, and Nikos Tsingos, trans. *Trojan Women*: The Trojan Women *by Euripides and* Helen *and* Orestes *by Ritsos*. Toronto: Exile, 1981.
———. *Earth-Light: Selected Poetry of Gwendolyn MacEwen, 1963–1982*. Toronto: General, 1982.
———. *The T. E. Lawrence Poems*. Oakville, Ont.: Mosaic / Valley, 1982.
———. *The Honey Drum*. Oakville, Ont.: Mosaic, 1983.

Secondary Sources

Atwood, Margaret. "MacEwen's Muse." *Canadian Literature*, No. 45 (Summer 1970), pp. 23–32.

———. "Canadian Monsters." In *The Canadian Imagination: Dimensions of a Literary Culture*. Ed. David Staines. Cambridge: Harvard Univ. Press, 1977, pp. 97–122.

Bartley, Jan. "Into the Fire." Rev. of *The Fire-Eaters*. *Open Letter*, 3rd ser., No. 5 (Summer 1976), pp. 85–87.

Boehme, Jacob. *The Confessions of Jacob Boehme*. Comp. and ed. W. Scott Palmer. Introd. Evelyn Underhill. 2nd ed. London: Methuen, 1954.

———. *Six Theosophic Points*. Trans. John Rolleston Earle. Ann Arbor: Univ. of Michigan Press, 1958.

Bowering, George. "The Canadian Poetry Underground." Rev. of *Than Any Star*, by Pádraig Ó Broin, *D-Day and After*, by Frank Davey, *The Drunken Clock*, by Gwendolyn MacEwen, and *Poems*, by David Donnell. *Canadian Literature*, No. 13 (Summer 1962), pp. 66–67.

———. "A Complex Music." Rev. of *The Rising Fire*. *Canadian Literature*, No. 21 (Summer 1964), pp. 70–71.

Colombo, John Robert, ed. *Rhymes and Reasons: Nine Canadian Poets Discuss Their Work*. Toronto: Holt, Rinehart and Winston, 1971, pp. 65–71.

Davey, Frank. "Gwendolyn MacEwen: The Secret of Alchemy." *Open Letter*, 2nd. ser., No. 4 (Spring 1973), pp. 5–23.

———. *From There to Here: A Guide to English-Canadian Literature since 1960*. Erin, Ont.: Porcépic, 1974, pp. 177–81.

Dragland, Stan. Rev. of *The Armies of the Moon*. *Quarry*, 21, No. 4 (Autumn 1972), 57–62.

Fox, Gail. Rev. of *The Shadow-Maker*. *Quarry*, 19, No. 2 (Winter 1970), 57–59.

Geddes, Gary, and Phyllis Bruce, eds. *15 Canadian Poets*. Toronto: Oxford Univ. Press, 1970, pp. 279–81.

Gustafson, Ralph. "Circumventing Dragons." Rev. of *Intense Pleasure*, by David McFadden, *A Few Myths*, by Peter Stevens, *The Chains of Lilliput*, by Fred Cogswell, and *The Armies of the Moon*, by Gwendolyn MacEwen. *Canadian Literature*, No. 55 (Winter 1973), pp. 105–08.

"Interview with Gwendolyn MacEwen." *Poetry Canada Review*, 4, No. 3 (Spring 1983), 8.

Jones, D. G. *Butterfly on Rock: A Study of Themes and Images in Canadian Literature*. Toronto: Univ. of Toronto Press, 1970, pp. 180–84.

Jung, Carl G. *Symbols of Transformation: An Analysis of the Prelude to a Case of Schizophrenia*. Trans. R. F. C. Hull. Bollingen Series, No. 20. Vol. v of *The Collected Works of C. G. Jung*. New York: Pantheon, 1956.

Mandel, Eli. "Seedtime in a Dark May." Rev. of *Poems*, by David Donnell, *Double Persephone*, by Margaret Atwood, and *The Drunken Clock*, by Gwendolyn MacEwen. *Alphabet*, 1, No. 4 (June 1962), 70.

Rabkin, Eric. S. *The Fantastic in Literature*. Princeton: Princeton Univ. Press, 1976, pp. 220–27.

Sherman, Joseph. Rev. of *The Armies of the Moon*. *The Fiddlehead*, No. 94 (Summer 1972), pp. 118–20.

Slonim, Leon. "Exoticism in Modern Canadian Poetry." *Essays on Canadian Writing*, No. 1 (Winter 1974), pp. 21–26.

Smith, Patricia Keeney. "Interview with Gwendolyn MacEwen." *Cross-Canada Writers' Quarterly*, 5, No. 1 (1983), 14–17.

Warwick, Ellen D. "To Seek a Single Symmetry." *Canadian Literature*, No. 71 (Winter 1976), pp. 21–34.

Wilson, Milton. Rev. of *Selah*, and *The Drunken Clock*. In "Letters in Canada 1961: Poetry." *University of Toronto Quarterly*, 31 (July 1962), 448.

INDEX

Absinthe Drinker, The (Degas) 140
"Absinthe Drinker, The" (Lane) 140
"Accessions" 203, 222n. 33
"Acid Sibyl, The" 31
Acorn, Milton 2, 135, 137, 138, 139, 231, 236
"Acrobat, The" 203
Acta Victoriana 2, 189, 192, 222n. 33
"Act of the Apostles" 151
Acton, Lord quoted 3
"Adonais" 205
"After Jaynes" 57, 63
"After the Flood, We" 33-34
"Afterwards" 66, 77 n. 67
A. J. M. Smith Award 232
Albino Pheasants 143-44, 167
"All Bread" 56-57
Allen, Carolyn 73 n. 50, quoted 70 n. 23
Alligator Pie 10, 191
"All the Fine Young Horses" 236
Alphabet 135
Amabile, George 144
Amprimoz, Alexandre L. quoted 145
Anatomy of Criticism 191
"Anima" 192
Animals in That Country, The 22, 30, 36-40

"Animal Syllables" 240-41, 262
"Annex Elegiac" 202
Another Time 197
Anthology of Verse, An 189
"Antibes: Variations on a Theme" 107
"Apollo Twelve" 240, 261
"Apple Jelly" 56
"April, Radio, Planting, Easter" 55
"Archaeopteryx" 177
Archer, The 207, 208
"Aristocracies, The" 240, 247-48
Aristotle 198, 206
"Armies of the Moon, The" 240, 256-57
Armies of the Moon, The 232, 238, 240, 241, 256-61
Arnold, Matthew 9, 195, 204, 205, 208, 215
As for Me and My House 1
"At Gull Lake: August 1810" 217
"At the Edge of the Jungle" 165-66
"At the Window: Late November" 102
Atwood, Margaret 1, 2, 5-8, 13, 137, 139, 166, 167, 174, 189, 192, 197, 201, 208, 231, 233, 235, 236, 239, quoted 5, 11, 239

Aubert, Rosemary 147, quoted 147
Auden, W. H. 8, 20, 21, 88
Avison, Margaret 9, 19-20, 88, 193, 215-16, 235, quoted 215

Bachelard, Gaston 219
"Backdrop Addresses Cowboy" 40, 73 n. 48
Badlands 235
Barbour, Douglas 91, 197, quoted 87, 142, 143
Barnes, William 166
Bartley, Jan quoted 10, 11, 240-41
Baudelaire, Charles 8, 140, 212, quoted 105
Beardsley, Doug quoted 146
"Beating the Bushes: Christmas 1963" 120
Beautiful Losers 190
"Beauty" 85
Beckett, Samuel 192, 193
Beckwith, John 189, 209
Belford, Ken 140
Bennett, Donna 196
"Bermudas, The" 53
Bess Hopkins Prize 68 n. 1
Beware the Months of Fire 2, 135, 141, 142-43, 157, 163, 165-67
"Beyond the Photograph" 112
Bible 96, 97, 98, 210
Bilan, R. P. 197
"Birches at RMC" 101
"Bird, The" 161-62
Birney, Earle 97, 135, 137, 138, 140, 201, 235
bissett, bill 20, 135, 137, 140, 234

"Black and White" 255
"Black Colt, The" 160, 165
"Black Filly, The" 160
Black Mountain poets 87, 137, 139
Blake, William 191, 192
Blavatsky, Madame 10
Blew Ointment 135
Blodgett, E. D. 3, 92, 93, 200, quoted 3, 4, 92
"Blue Valley Night" 172
Bly, Robert 20
Boatman, The 191
Boehme, Jacob 236, 241, 243, quoted 243
"Book of Ancestors" 54
Book of Canadian Poetry, The 19
Book of Hours 108, 109
Books in Canada 133, 136, 143, 147, 197
Borduas, Paul-Emile quoted 209, 210
Borges, Jorge Luis 252, quoted 252
Bowering, George 88, 93-94, 97, 99, 112, 116, 124 n. 11, 137-38, 194, 233, quoted 11, 29, 90, 93, 94, 115-16, 194, 234, 236, 237, 238
Bowering, Marilyn 144, quoted 144
"Boy in the Lamont Poetry Room, Harvard" 110
Bradshaw, Leah 197, 199
"Breakfast for Barbarians, A" 243
Breakfast for Barbarians, A 232, 234, 235, 237, 239, 240, 241, 242-43, 246, 247, 250, 253, 256, 257, 259

INDEX

Brett, Brian quoted 143
Brick: A Journal of Reviews
  191, 197
Bringhurst, Robert 200
Brown, Russell 27, 196
Bruce, Phyllis quoted 93
"Brunswick Avenue" 213-14
"Buffalo Stones" 175
Bunyan, John 219
"Bushed" 201
Butterfly on Rock: A Study of Themes and Images in Canadian Literature 3, 4, 86, 94-98, 99, 103, 235

"Cadence, Country, Silence: Writing in a Colonial Space" 190, 191, 196, 205
"Calgary City Jail" 152, 153
"Camera" 34-35
Canada Council awards 136, 232
Canadian Author & Bookman 145
Canadian Broadcasting Corporation 136
Canadian Dimension 194
Canadian Forum, The 135, 146, 190, 194, 196, 197, 231
Canadian Journal of Political and Social Theory 191, 197
Canadian Literature 136, 142, 143, 145, 146, 194, 195, 197
Cantos 2, 85, 175
Capra, Fritjof 127 n. 50
"Carnival Man, The" 148
Carrier, Roch 211
CBC *Anthology* 136
CBC New Canadian Writing Contest 232

Céline, Louis-Ferdinand 12, 13, 141, 157, 158, quoted 141
Centennial Commission Prize 68 n. 1
Cézanne, Paul 89
Chagall, Marc 89, 110
Charlesworth, Roberta 189
Chicago Review, The 136
"Chicken Poems, The" 176-77, 178
Chinada: Memoirs of the Gang of Seven 177
"China Poems" 177-78
"Chinook" 171
Chocolate Moose, The 232
"Circe/Mud Poems" 6, 26-27, 30, 40, 48-50, 70 n. 23
"Circle Game, The" 34, 53
Circle Game, The 18, 19, 24-25, 28, 31, 33-36, 52, 55, 64, 68 n. 1, 77 n. 68
"Cities of the Mind Interred" 202
"City Girl, The" 20
City of Toronto Book Award 68
Civil Elegies (1968) 190, 194-95, 201, 205
Civil Elegies and Other Poems (1972), 9, 190, 195-96, 201, 204, 205, 207-10, 213, 214, 222 n. 39, 233
CIV/n 2, 86
Clare, John 166
"Clotheslines" 119
Cogswell, Fred 195
Cohen, Leonard 190, 219, 235
"Cold Eye and Optic Heart: Marshall McLuhan and Some Canadian Poets" 99
Coleman, Victor 234

Coleridge, Samuel Taylor 54, quoted 210
Collected Works of Billy the Kid, The 190, 199, 222 n. 50, 235
Colville, Alex 4, 89, 119, 213
"Coming Home" 171-72
"Compass, The" 253-54
Confederation poets 3, 92, 97
Conrad, Joseph 97
Contact 2, 86, 87
"Conversation of Prayer, The" 76 n. 64
"Conversation with Margaret Atwood, A" 19-20
Cook, John 92, quoted 88, 92
Cooley, Dennis quoted 196
"Corpse Song" 48
Crashaw, Richard 8
"Creatures of the Zodiac, The" 42
Creeley, Robert 87
Creighton, Donald 205
"Crow Song" 48
Cruikshank, John 147, quoted 147
CV/II 144
"Cyclist in Aphelion, The" 248-49

Dabrowski, Kazimierz 126 n. 45
Dainty Monsters, The 91
Dale, Stephen 133, 134, 136
Dalhousie Review 197
"Damside" 67
"Dance, The" 175
"Dance for One Leg" 117
"Dancing Practice" 44, 53, 60, 73 n. 52
"Dark Pines under Water" 250, 254

Darwin, Charles 94, 198
Davey, Frank 26, 27, 86, 92-93, 137, 195, 234, 237, 238, 239, 261, quoted 26, 93, 195, 234, 237, 239
Davies, Robertson 235
Daybook poems 55, 62
"Day of Twelve Princes" 231
"Death by Water" 75 n. 54
"Death of a Hornet" 105, 107
"Death of a Young Son by Drowning" 69 n. 15
"Death of Dahoum, The" 264, 265
"Death of Harold Ladoo, The" 193, 196, 211-13, 216, 220
Decadent poets 140
Degas, Edgar 140
"Delayed Message" 43
de Man, Paul quoted 118
"Demon of Thursday, The" 246
"Departures" 265-66
Deptford trilogy 235
Descartes, René 202, 205
"Descent through the Carpet, A" 33
"Development" 112
"D. G. Jones: An Interview, February, 1978" 89-90, 100
"Diamond Sutra, The" 122
Diefenbaker, John 191, 192
"Digging" 47
"Dining at the Savarin" 258
"Dinner" 60
"Dirge at a Wake" 192
"Discovery, The" 233
"Disintegration in a Dream of Love" 107
Djwa, Sandra 28
"Dog, The" 160-61

Donne, John 8, 21, 117
Don Quixote 252
Dostoevsky, Feodor Mikhailovich 8
Double Hook, The 235
"Double Persephone" 29
Double Persephone 18-19, 20, 29-30, 31, 68 n. 1
Douglas, Charles 193
"Dover Beach" 63-64, 208
Dragišić, Peggy 197
Dragland, Stan 200, 201, 240, 261, quoted 142-44, 240
"Dream Three: The Child" 237, 245
"Dream Two: The Beasts" 237
Drunken Clock, The 232
Dryden, John 8-9
Dudek, Louis 2, 13, 86, 87, 94-95, 145, 193, 195, quoted 94, 95, 145
Duffy, Dennis 195-96
Duino Elegies 205, 222 n. 34

"Earth" 64
Earth-Light: Selected Poetry of Gwendolyn MacEwen 12, 232
"East Coker" 74 n. 52
Edel, Leon 1
"Eden Is a Zoo" 41
Edible Woman, The 29, 68 n. 1, 236
Edmonton Journal 142
E. J. Pratt Medal 68 n. 1
"Elegy for the Giant Tortoises" 38
"Elegy Written in a Country Churchyard" 205
"Elephants" 152, 153-55

"11/9/75" 120
El Greco 198
Eliot, T. S. 8, 20, 36, 44, 46, 73 n. 52, 75 n. 55, 87, 192, 198, 205, quoted 74 n. 52
ellipse 86
Euripides 232
"Evening Trainstation before Departure" 66

"Face, The" 247
"Faculty Party" 87, 103
"Fall and All" 31
"Fall and All: A Sequence" 20, 31
Fetherling, Doug 195, 197, quoted 142
Fiddlehead, The 135, 194
15 Canadian Poets 233
Findley, Timothy 174
"Fire-Crackers" 103
Fire-Eaters, The 232, 240, 241, 261-62
"Fire of Eros, The" 192
"Fireweed Seeds" 161
"Fishing for Eel Totems" 27-28
"Five Poems for Dolls" 54
"Five Poems for Grandmothers" 56
"Flute Notes from a Reedy Pond" 66, 75 n. 57
"Footnote to the Amnesty Report on Torture" 59
"For Eve" 114
"For Françoise Adnet" 109
"Formal Garden" 29-30
"For Rita — in Asylum" 152, 153
"Fortification, A" 37-38
"Foundling, A" 37
"Four Auguries" 50

"Four Evasions" 50
Four Quartets 73 n. 52, 205
"Four Small Elegies" 56
Fox, Gail 238, quoted 237-38
France, Anatole 253
Frankenstein 71 n. 46
Frazer, Sir James 11, 192
"Free-Fall Lovers" 193
Freud, Sigmund 94, 251, quoted 251
Frost, Robert 88
Frost on the Sun 1, 2, 86, 89, 92, 99, 100-04, 105, 107, 109, 115, 116, 119, 121
Frye, Helen 191
Frye, Northrop 2, 4, 86, 90, 94, 116, 139, 191, 193, 197, quoted 1
Fulford, Robert 190

"Game after Supper" 41
Garbage Delight 191
Garcia Marquez, Gabriel 236, 252
"Garden, The" 53
"Garden of Square Roots, The: An Autobiography" 246-47
"Garland of Milne, A" 116, 117
Garneau, Hector de Saint-Denys- 207, 209, 210
Garnet, Eldon 193
Gasparini, Len quoted 143
Geddes, Gary 142, 177, 233, 234, quoted 9, 10, 93, 142, 195, 233
"Generation Cometh" 244-45
"Gerald" 163
"Getting to Rochdale" 201
"Ghazala's Foal" 264-65
Gibbs, Jean quoted 26
Gibson, Graeme 17, 68 n. 1

"Girl and Horse, 1928" 41-42
Godfrey, Dave 189, 190, 191, 197
"Gods, The" 214, 216-18
Gods, The 191, 193, 196, 201, 211, 213, 214
"Gods Avoid Revealing Themselves, The" 38
"God Who Is Goshawk, The" 161
Golden Bough, The 192
"Golden Hunger, The" 246, 259-60
Golding, William 192
"Gothic Letter on a Hot Night" 46-47
Governor General's Award 24, 68 n. 1, 86, 135, 136, 190, 195, 232
Grace Abounding to the Chief of Sinners 219
Grant, George 9, 192, 195, 198, 204, 205, 207
Grant, Peter 189
Gray, Thomas 205
"Green Man, The: For the Boston Strangler" 37
"Grounds for Translation" 99
Guerre, Yes Sir!, La 211
Gustafson, Ralph quoted 261

Hamilton, Mary 89, 100
Hamlet 252
Hardy, Thomas 20, 66, quoted 77 n. 67
"Head against White" 50-51
Healy, Jack quoted 219
Hébert, Anne 20, 104, 106, 110
Hegel, Georg Wilhelm Friedrich 206

INDEX

Heidegger, Martin 193, 198, 200, 201, 203, 204, 208, 214, 216, 218
"Height of Land, The" 217
Helwig, David 195
Herbert, George 8
"Highest Altitude" 67
"High Park, by Grenadier Pond" 213-14
Hitler, Adolf 94, 198, 209, 212
Hiway 401 Rhapsody 162
Hoffman, E. T. A. 251
Hokusai 89
Hölderlin, Friedrich 200, quoted 212
Hollingshead, Greg 193
"Holy Burlesque, The" 258-59
Honey Drum, The 232
Hopkins, Gerard Manley 21, 175, 192
"Hotel" 59-60
"Hour of the Singer, The" 260
"House, The" 21, 248
House of Anansi 2, 17, 68 n. 1, 166, 189, 190, 211, 212, 214
"House of Mercury" 241
"House of the Whale" 262-63
"Houses" 20-21
Hutcheon, Linda quoted 95

"I Am Tired of Your Politics" 13, 138, 158-59, 172
"Ice Storm" 161
"Iconic Landscape" 29
"If" 157
"If I Travel Alone" 148-49
"I Fled the Night" 106, 107
Imagist poets 3, 88
"Indian Tent Rings" 175-76
In Memoriam 205

Innis, Harold 198
"In Search of America" 99
"In Search of Canada: Dennis Lee's Ironic Vision" 98, 99
"Interview with a Tourist" 42
"Interview with Dennis Lee, An" 222 n. 39
Interview with Gwendolyn MacEwen (Bartley) 231, 234
"Interview with Gwendolyn MacEwen" (*Poetry Canada Review*) 262, 263, 264
"Interview with Gwendolyn MacEwen" (Smith) 11, 266
"Interview with Margaret Atwood, An" (Hammond) 20
"Interview with Margaret Atwood, An" (Struthers) 19
"Interview" with Patrick Lane 133, 134, 136-37
Introduction to *The Terror of the Snows* 123
Irvine, Lorna 29
I've Tasted My Blood 236

Jaynes, Julian 57
Jean, Duc de Berry 89, 108
Jelly Belly 191
"Jewellery" 260
"John Donne" 103
"John Marin" 92, 100, 101, 109, 122
Johnson, Samuel quoted 9
Johnston, Gordon 27
Jones, D. G. 1, 2-5, 9, 12, 20, 196-97, 235, quoted 1, 4-5
Jong, Erica 20, 22
Journals of Susanna Moodie, The 40-41, 69 n. 15, 73 n. 49, 73 n. 50

Joyce, James 193
Julian the Magician 231, 232, 237, 243
"July" 165-66
"June" 165-66
Jung, Carl Gustav 11, 94, 96, 97, 198, 236, 242, 250, 253

Kane, Sean 200
Kearns, Lionel 194
Keats, John 20, 53, 75 n. 56, 192, quoted 111
Kennedy, Leo 192
Kertzer, J. M. 197
Keyes, Mary 194, quoted 194
"Keynote" 103
"Kingdom of Absence" 190, 202
Kingdom of Absence 189, 193, 194, 201-04
King of Egypt, King of Dreams 232
Klee, Paul 89
Klein, A. M. 19, 204
Knightley, Philip 265
Koestler, Arthur 199
Kroetsch, Robert 175, 234, 235

Ladoo, Harold 211-12
"Lady" 203
"Lady Lazarus" 72 n. 47
"Lake of Death, The" 240, 259, 260
"Lake of Dreams, The" 240, 259-60
Lampman, Archibald 3, 88, 92
"Lampman Poems, The" 86, 117-18, 121
Lane, Patrick 1, 2, 11, 12-13, quoted 12, 13

Lane, Red 133, 135, 137, 148
Lanthier, Philip quoted 146
Lapointe, Paul-Marie 85-86, 123
"Last Day" 65-66, 75 n. 57
"Last Poem" 63-64, 65, 67
"Late August" 53-54, 75 n. 56, 75 n. 57
"Late Night" 59
"Later in Belleville: Career" 69 n. 15
Laurence, Margaret 88
Lawrence, D. H. 165, 197
Lawrence, T. E. 12, 262, 263, 264, 265
Layton, Irving 19, 85, 87, 91, 97, 138, 139, 147
Leacock, Stephen 120
League of Canadian Poets 2
Lee, Dennis 1, 2, 8-10, 12, 17, 20, 98, 233
"Left Hand and Hiroshima, The" 246, 249
"Legacies" 151
Le Moyne, Jean 210
Le Pan, Douglas 20
Letter, D. G. Jones to E. D. Blodgett, 13 June 1982 85, 88
Letter, Patrick Lane to George Woodcock, n.d. 133
"Letter on Poetry and Belief, A" 97, 123
"Letters" 55
Letters from the Savage Mind 135, 142, 147, 148-53, 161, 166
Lewis, Wyndham 9, 222 n. 50
Liberté 190
Linder, Norma West quoted 145, 146
"Little Night Journey" 107, 114

INDEX

Livesay, Dorothy 91, 93, 137, 138, quoted 91
"Loading Boxcars" 161
Locke, John 205-06
London Free Press, The 142
"Loving She Stood Apart" 152
Lowry, Malcolm 193
Lowther, Pat 140
Lucretius 216
"Lycidas" 205

MacCallum, Hugh 194, quoted 24-25, 194-95
"Macchu Picchu" 164-65
Macdonald, Sir John A. 205
MacEwen, Gwendolyn 1, 2, 10-12, 13, 20, quoted 10-11
"MacEwen's Muse" 11, 239
Mackenzie, William Lyon 205, 207
Macpherson, Jay 17, 19, 20, 69 n. 8, 191, 193, 233
"Mad Mother, The" 31-32, 35
Magic Animals: Selected Poems Old and New 12, 232, 241, 245, 261-62
Malahat Review, The 136, 144
Mallinson, Jean 6-7, 8, 69 n. 8, 71 n. 43, 144, 145, quoted 5, 6, 7, 143
Mandel, Eli 20, 28, 87, 92, 197, 234, quoted 92, 237, 238
Manitoba Arts Council awards 136
"Man with a Hole in His Throat, The" 57
Marin, John 89, 100, 116
"Marrying the Hangman" 57
"Marsh, Hawk" 57-58
Marty, Sid 140, 175

Marvell, Andrew 53
Mathews, Robin 216
Matisse, Henri 89
Matrix 146
Maugham, W. Somerset 203
Mayne, Seymour 135, 137, 140
McCombs, Judith 28, 73 n. 50, 74 n. 53
McGill Fortnightly Review, The 1
McNally, Paul quoted 196
"Measure, The" 174
Measure, The 138, 146-47, 170-72, 174
"Medusa" 72 n. 47
Melnyk, George quoted 142
"Memoirs of a Mad Cook" 258
Mermaids and Ikons: A Greek Summer 232
"Metallic Anatomy, The" 247
Metaphysical poets 192
Middlebro', T. G. 9, quoted 9
Mill, John Stuart quoted 198-99
Miller, Henry 141
Milne, David 4, 89, 116-17
Milton, John 205
"Mirage, The" 263-64
"Mr. Wilson, the World" 112
"Modern Poetry" 190
Moers, Ellen 22, 71 n. 46
Moment 231
"Monarch IV" 176-77
"Monarch II" 176
Montagnes, Ann 194
Moodie, Susanna 88
Moore, Henry 207, 208
Morris, William 8
"Mountain Oysters" 160, 165
Mountain Oysters 156, 159-61, 167

Mulhallen, Karen 196
Munton, Ann 200-01
"Mushrooms" 65, 67-68
"Muskoka Elegiac" 201-02
"Myth, Frye and Canadian
  Writers" 106

"Nature" 198-99
Neruda, Pablo 141
New, W.H. quoted 94
*New: American and Canadian
  Poetry* 134
Newfeld, Frank 191
Newlove, John 2, 20, 137, 139,
  140, 175, 235
Newton, Sir Isaac 202
"New Year's Poem" 215
*Nicholas Knock and Other
  People* 191
Nietzsche, Friedrich Wilhelm
  13, 134, 155, 218
"Night on Gull Lake" 233
"Nine Arcana of the Kings,
  The" 240, 260-61
Ni Tsan 89, 90
"Ni Tsan" 89-90
No Longer Two People 136,
  169-70
Noman 232
No Pain like This Body 211
"Northern Water Thrush" 102
"Not Abstract Harmonies But"
  214-16
"Notes from Various Pasts" 36
"Notes toward a Poem That
  Can Never Be Written"
  62-63
Nowlan, Alden 139, 233, 235

"Ode to Autumn" 53

"Odysseus" 107
Odyssey 48
"Of Eros, in Shiny Degree"
  213-14
O'Hagan, Howard 235
Old Mother 135, 146, 163-64,
  173, 174-78
Olson, Charles 87
"On a Picture of Your House"
  112
Ondaatje, Michael 25, 91, 190,
  219, 222 n. 50, 233, 235,
  quoted 25
One Hundred Years of Solitude
  252
"One More Garden" 59
Onley, Gloria 28-29, 74 n. 53
Ontario Arts Council awards
  136
"On the 24th of May" 101-02,
  121
Open Letter 190
Orwell, George 158
"Other Underground, The" 259
"Over the Slow Rivers" 178
"Owl Song" 48

Pachter, Charles 17, 68 n. 1
Page, P.K. 19, 20
"Paper Bag, A" 54
"Part Two: Magic Animals,
  1972–1974" 232, 245-46
Pascal, Blaise 203, 210
Passing into Storm 162
"Pastoral" 30
Paul, Saint 218
Pearson, Ian quoted 196
Penfield, Dr. Wilder 199
"Perishing Bird, The" 110
"Phobos" 257

INDEX

"Phrases from Orpheus" 93, 111, 112-15
Phrases from Orpheus 4, 86, 87, 91, 93, 103, 110-15, 116, 120
Picasso, Pablo 89, quoted 170
"Pictures by Colville" 115, 119
"Pig-Girl" 30-31, 38, 47
"Pig Song" 47-48
"Place, A: Fragments" 36
"Place for 'P,' A" 110
Place of Meeting 189, 209
"Places of Memory" 111
Plath, Sylvia 21, 22, 40, 44, 66, 72 n. 47, 75 n. 57, quoted 72 n. 47, 75 n. 57
Plumly, Stanley 76 n. 59, quoted 75 n. 56
Poe, Edgar Allan 19
"Poem" 248
"Poems in Braille" 246, 248
Poems New and Selected (Lane) 135, 145-46, 157, 166-68, 169
Poésie/Poetry 64 20, 21, 31
Poetry [Chicago] 68 n. 1
Poetry Canada Review 262
Poets '56 86
"Polyphony, Enacting a Meditation" 191
"Portage, The" 233
"Portrait of Anne Hébert" 104-05, 110, 117
"Postcard" 59
Pound, Ezra 2-3, 20, 85, 87, 88, 91, 93, 175, 189
"Powassan's Drum" 217
Power Politics 5, 7, 22, 30, 40, 44-46, 48-49, 55, 60, 61, 62, 74 n. 53, 74 n. 54, 76 n. 57
"Prairie Poems" 176
Prato, Edward 145

Pratt, E. J. 19, 88, 97, 190, 191, 192, 201, 202
President's Medal (Univ. of Western Ontario) 86
Prism International 136
"Problem of Space, A" 89, 100, 115
Procedures for Underground 26, 30, 41-44, 69 n. 15
"Progressive Insanities of a Pioneer" 40, 73 n. 48, 208
"Prospector" 152, 153
"Puppet of the Wolf, The" 58
Purdy, Al 2, 20, 91, 134, 137, 138, 139, 140, 175, 190, 194, 231, 235, quoted 142, 194
"Putting on the Storms" 114

Quarry 135, 195
Queen's Quarterly 196
"Quiet Normal Life, A" 69 n. 3
Quill & Quire 143, 147 196

Rabkin, Eric S. 251, 252, quoted 251, 253
Radcliffe Medal 68 n. 1
Rader, Ralph 73 n. 49
"Rain" 66-67
"Rat Song" 48
Read, Herbert 8
Read, Robert 193
Read Canadian: A Book about Canadian Books 190
"Reading *Savage Fields*" 191, 197
Reaney, James 19, 20, 22, 91, 135, 193, 201, 233, quoted 87, 91
"Red Shirt, A" 55, 58
Reed, Henry 21

"Rejoinder" 216
"Remember, Woman" 213-14
"Request" 104
"Return, The" 254, 255-56
"Revenant, The" 62
Rhymes and Reasons: Nine Canadian Poets Discuss Their Work 10-11, 231-32
Rich, Adrienne 20, 21, 22, 69 n. 12
Richards, I. A. 75 n. 55
"Riffs" 214
"Right Hand Fights the Left, The" 57
Rilke, Rainer Maria 200, 201, 205, 207, 222 n. 34
Rising Fire, The 232, 234, 236, 237, 239, 241, 244, 255, 256
"River, The: North of Guelph" 1, 4-5, 105-06, 110
Roberts, Charles G. D. 9, 88, 205
"Robin" 101
Romantic poets 54
"Roominghouse, Winter" 39
Ross, Gary 25, quoted 25
Ross, Sinclair 1
Rotstein, Abraham 190
Royal Society of Canada 86
"Running and Dwelling: Homage to Al Purdy" 190
Ruskin, John 207

Salinger, J. D. 192
"Sandman, The" 251
Saraha 207
Sartre, Jean-Paul 192
Saturday Night 190, 194, 195, 197, 216

Savage Fields: An Essay in Literature and Cosmology 190-91, 197-200, 209, 218-19, 222 n. 50
Schroeder, Andreas quoted 195
Scott, Duncan Campbell 3, 88, 217, quoted 217
Scott, F. R. 1, 3, 19, 88, 105, 116
"Sea of Crises, The" 240, 257-59
Second Century Anthologies of Verse, The 189
"Second-degree Burns" 261
Selah 232
Selected Poems (Atwood) 77 n. 68
Separations 136, 142, 152-56, 167
Seven Pillars of Wisdom 263, 265
Sexton, Anne 22, 44
"Shadow-Maker, The" 254-55
Shadow-Maker, The 232, 233, 237-38, 240, 241, 245, 249-56, 259
"Shadow Voice, The" 36-37
"She Considers Evading Him" 71 n. 39
Shelley, Mary 71 n. 46
Shelley, Percy Bysshe 8, 19, 205
Sherman, Joseph quoted 238
Shrouding, The 192
"Sibelius Park" 214
"Sibyl, A" 35-36, 52-53, 71 n. 43
"Silk Factory" 177-78
Sillers, Pat 70 n. 27
Simpson, Colin 265
"Siren Song" 48
Skelton, Robin 26, 27-28, 70 n. 27, quoted 27

"Sleeper, The" 250-51
"Sleep Is the Silence Darkness Takes" 163
"Slideshow, The" 20, 31
Slonim, Leon 235
"Small Poems for the Winter Solstice" 60, 67
Smith, A. J. M. 1, 3, 19, 88, 97, 194
"Snow Buntings" 109-10, 111
"Soliloquy to Absent Friends" 106, 107-09, 110
"Solstice Poem" 55
"Something Other than Our Own" 172
"Song" 213-14
"Song: Lay Down" 193
"Song of Seasons" 192
"Song of the Fox" 48
"Song of the Hen's Head" 48
"Song of the Worms" 48
"Songs of the Transformed" 26, 30, 40, 47, 63, 69 n. 8
"Soul, Geologically, A" 42-43
Souster, Raymond 2, 86, 87, 91, 121, 234, 235
Sowton, Ian 146, quoted 146-47
"Speeches for Dr. Frankenstein" 22, 39-40, 72 n. 47
Spender, Stephen 8
Spettigue, D. O. 94, quoted 94
"Spring in the Igloo" 35
"Spring Poem" 47, 76 n. 65
Stalin, Joseph 94
"Stars over Evil Houses" 103
Stevens, Peter 91, quoted 25, 91
Stevens, Wallace 20, 69 n. 3, 76 n. 62, 87, 99, 102, quoted 18, 59
"Still Hunting" 167-68

Suknaski, Andrew 140, 145, 175
Sullivan, Rosemary 146, quoted 8, 146
"Summer Song" 213-14
Sun Has Begun to Eat the Mountain, The 162
Sun Is Axeman, The 86, 87, 91, 93, 99, 103, 104-10, 112, 114, 116
Surfacing 29
Sutherland, John 86, 190
Swift, Jonathan 13, 60, 158
"Swimmer, The" 252-53
Symbolist poets 140
Symbols of Transformation 253

Talon 135, 137
Tamarack Review, The 136, 194, 232
"Taming of the Dragon, The" 237-38
"Tantramar Revisited" 205
Tasks of Passion: Dennis Lee at Mid-Career 191, 196-97, 200-01
Tay John 235
Taylor, Charles quoted 206
T. E. Lawrence Poems, The 12, 232, 262-66
"Ten Miles In from Horsefly" 152, 153
Tennyson, Alfred, Lord 205
"Terror and Erebus: A Verse Play for Radio" 232
"There Is Only One of Everything" 51, 52-53
"Thin Garden, The" 251-52
"Thing Is Violent, The" 246
"Thirty Below" 162

"Thirty Miles In from the Coast" 162
"This Is a Photograph of Me" 25, 33, 37, 55, 57, 66, 76 n.57
This Magazine 68 n.1
"This Northern Mouth" 252
Thomas, Dylan 20, 21, 76 n.64, 193
Thompson, E.P. 219
Thompson, Eric 25, 194, quoted 25, 194
Thomson, Tom 208, 209
Thomson, Virgil 69 n.12
Thousand and One Nights, A 252
"Three Cast with the I Ching" 119
"Three Days after Crisis in Cuba" 149-50
Through the Looking-Glass 252
"Thyrsis" 205
"Tiamut" 239
"Tigerlily" 192
"Time of the Fictitious 'I,' The" 102
Times Literary Supplement, The 136
Tish 137
"Titanic" 192
"Today" 55-56
"To Eve in Bitterness" 114
T.O. Now: The Young Toronto Poets 190, 193
Toronto Globe and Mail, The 142, 145
Toronto Star, The 142
"Totems, The" 38
"To the Outlaw" 12, 134, 136, 138-39, 141, 155
Toye, William 166

Traill, Catharine Parr 88
"Trainride, Vienna-Bonn" 62
"Treaty-Trip from Shulus Reservation" 150-51
Très riches heures 89
Trojan Women, The (1979) 232
Trojan Women: The Trojan Women *by Euripides and* Helen *and* Orestes *by Ritsos* (1981) 232
"True Romances" 60-62
True Stories 59-68, 75 n.57
Turner, Frederick Jackson 94
"28/10/76" 121
"Two Aspects of the Moon" 242
Two-Headed Poems 29, 30, 54-58, 59
"Two Miles Away" 56
"Two Versions of Sweaters" 43

Uher, Lorna 136, 169, quoted 169
Ulysses 175
"Unborn Things" 165-66
Unborn Things: South American Poems 135, 136, 143, 163, 164-66, 167
Underhill, Evelyn quoted 243-44
Under the Thunder the Flowers Light Up the Earth 4, 86, 88, 89, 90, 92, 109, 111, 115-22, 123
Union League Civic and Arts Foundation Prize 68 n.1
University Game, The 201
University of Toronto Quarterly 194, 197
"Unspeakable, The" 253
"Use" 64

"Vacuum Cleaner Dream, The" 258
Vancouver Province 143
Vancouver Sun, The 143
van Gogh, Vincent 202
"Variations on the Word *Love*" 64
"Variations on the Word *Sleep*" 64-65, 76 n. 64
Vaughan, Henry 203
Vendler, Helen 59, 75 n. 55, 76 n. 62, quoted 38, 75 n. 55
Vergil 113
Victoria Times-Colonist 146
Vision, A 198
Voyage au bout de la nuit 141
"Vultures" 63

Wagner, Linda 69 n. 15, quoted 69 n. 15
Wallace, Joe quoted 213
Warwick, Ellen D. 239, quoted 239, 240
Waste Land, The 34, 36, 46, 47, 74 n. 54, 75 n. 55
"Water" 263
"Water-Truck, The" 152, 153
Watson, Sheila 193, 235, quoted 222 n. 50
Watson, Wilfred 20
Waves 145
Webb, Phyllis 20, 87, 91, quoted 3, 87, 88, 91
"We Don't Like Reminders" 42
"Weed Seeds near a Beaver Pond" 75 n. 57
"Weight, The" 174-75
Weir, Lorraine 73 n. 50
West Coast Review 135, 145
Whalley, George 85

"What Happened" 38-39
"When It Is Over" 213-14
"When I Went Up to Rosedale" 196
White, Howard 144
Whiteman, Bruce 92, quoted 92
Whiteman, Neil 144, 145, quoted 144
White Pelican 193
Wiggle to the Laundromat 10, 191
Wijngaard, Juan 191
"Wild Birds" 168
"Wild Dogs" 156-57, 160
"Wild Horses" 152, 153, 155-56, 157
Wilkinson, Anne 20
Williams, William Carlos 20, 87, 92, 102, 108, 124 n. 11, 234
Wilson, Milton quoted 237, 238
"Wings" 177
Winter Sun 20
Wiseman, Adele 234
"Witnesses, The" 163
"Woman Skating" 43
"Women's Issue, A" 62
Wood, Gayle 69 n. 15, quoted 69 n. 15
Woodcock, George 7, 94, quoted 3, 4, 7-8, 87, 94, 95, 143, 144
Wordsworth, William 54, 159, 171, 201
Writers Union of Canada 2, 17, 68 n. 1

Yeats, William Butler 20, 31, 124 n. 11, 159, 192, 198
Yesterdays 211

York University Poet's Award
136
You Are Happy 5, 26, 30, 31,
46-54, 69 n. 8
"You Begin" 58
"You Can Climb Down Now"
213-14
"You Cannot Do This" 247
Young, Ian 193

Zieroth, Dale 140
Zonailo, Carolyn 144